Watershed Politics and Climate Change in Peru

'This superb ethnography invites us to "slow down" the assumption that water is either a resource or a vital force and attend to how its multiplicity implies a politics of entangled worldings. This book will change how you think about the politics of water!'

—Mario Blaser, Associate Professor of Archaeology, Memorial University, Canada

'Though many recent researchers have examined water through a climate change lens, this highly original book is distinctive in examining climate change through a water lens.'

—Ben Orlove, anthropologist and Professor of International and Public Affairs, Columbia University, New York

'This book expresses the power of ethnography. Using her kaleidoscopic notions, Astrid Stensrud presents an analysis of a politics of water that empirically emerging from multiple worlds to transform political ecology and political economy into pluriversal analytics.'

—Marisol de la Caden, Professor of Anthropology, UC-Davis, California and author of *Earth Beings: Ecologies of Practice Across Andean Worlds*

'An exemplary ethnographic analysis that, focusing on "waterworlds" in Peru, illuminates the many and diverse ways that people conceptualise and value water, engage with water, and compose human and non-human relationships through water.'

—Veronica Strang, Executive Director, Institute of Advanced Study, University of Durham and author of *Water, Culture and Nature*

Anthropology, Culture and Society

Series Editors:
Jamie Cross, University of Edinburgh,
Christina Garsten, Stockholm University
and
Joshua O. Reno, Binghamton University

Recent titles:

The Limits to Citizen Power: Participatory Democracy and the Entanglements of the State
Victor Albert

The Heritage Machine: Fetishism and Domination in Maragateria, Spain
Pablo Alonso González

Becoming Arab in London: Performativity and the Undoing of Identity
Ramy M. K. Aly

Vicious Games: Capitalism and Gambling
Rebecca Cassidy

Anthropologies of Value
Edited by Luis Fernando Angosto-Ferrandez and Geir Henning Presterudstuen

Ethnicity and Nationalism: Anthropological Perspectives Third Edition
Thomas Hylland Eriksen

Fredrik Barth: An Intellectual Biography
Thomas Hylland Eriksen

Small Places, Large Issues: An Introduction to Social and Cultural Anthropology Fourth Edition
Thomas Hylland Eriksen

What is Anthropology? Second Edition
Thomas Hylland Eriksen

Deepening Divides: How Territorial Borders and Social Boundaries Delineate Our World
Edited by Didier Fassin

At the Heart of the State: The Moral World of Institutions
Didier Fassin, et al.

Anthropology and Development: Challenges for the Twenty-first Century
Katy Gardner and David Lewis

Children of the Welfare State: Civilising Practices in Schools, Childcare and Families
Laura Gilliam and Eva Gulløv

Faith and Charity: Religion and Humanitarian Assistance in West Africa
Edited by Marie Nathalie LeBlanc and Louis Audet Gosselin

Private Oceans: The Enclosure and Marketisation of the Seas
Fiona McCormack

Grassroots Economies: Living with Austerity in Southern Europe
Edited by Susana Narotzky

The Rise of Nerd Politics: Digital Activism and Political Change
John Postill

Base Encounters: The US Armed Forces in South Korea
Elisabeth Schober

Ground Down by Growth: Tribe, Caste, Class and Inequality in Twenty-First-Century India
Alpa Shah, Jens Lerche, et al

When Protest Becomes Crime: Politics and Law in Liberal Democracies
Carolijn Terwindt

Race and Ethnicity in Latin America Second Edition
Peter Wade

Watershed Politics and Climate Change in Peru

Astrid B. Stensrud

PLUTO PRESS

First published 2021 by Pluto Press
345 Archway Road, London N6 5AA

www.plutobooks.com

British Library Cataloguing in Publication Data
A catalogue record for this book is available from the British Library

ISBN 978 0 7453 4020 3 Hardback
ISBN 978 1 78680 747 2 PDF
ISBN 978 1 78680 757 1 EPUB
ISBN 978 1 78680 758 8 Kindle

This book is printed on paper suitable for recycling and made from fully managed and sustained forest sources. Logging, pulping and manufacturing processes are expected to conform to the environmental standards of the country of origin.

Typeset by Stanford DTP Services, Northampton, England

Simultaneously printed in the United Kingdom and United States of America

Contents

Maps and Figures

Maps

Figures

List of Acronyms and Abbreviations

AAA: Autoridad Administrativa del Agua (Administrative Water Authority)

ALA: Administración Local del Agua (Local Water Administration)

ANA: Autoridad Nacional del Agua (National Water Authority)

ATDR: Administración Técnica de Distrito de Riego (Technical Administration of the Irrigation District)

Autodema: Autoridad Autónoma de Majes (Autonomous Authority of Majes)

CASS: Comité de Administración de Servicios de Saneamiento (Administrative Committee of Sanitary Services)

Desco: an NGO working in Caylloma Province

IWRM: integrated water resources management

JASS: Junta de Administración de Servicios de Saneamiento (Administrative Board of Sanitary Services)

JUPM: Junta de Usuarios Pampa de Majes (Board of Water Users in Pampa of Majes)

JUVC: Junta de Usuarios Valle del Colca (Board of Water Users in Colca Valley)

lps: litres per second

MACON: Majes Consorcio (Consortium Majes)

Majes-Siguas II: the second phase of the irrigation project

MIP: Majes Irrigation Project (Proyecto Irrigación Majes)

MMC: million cubic metres (*millon metros cúbicos*)

Profodua: Programa de Formalización de Derecho de Uso de Agua

PSI: Programa Subsectorial de Irrigaciones (Subsectoral Irrigation Programme)

Sedapar: Servicio de Agua Potable y Alcantarillado de Arequipa S.A. (Public Company of Potable Water and Wastewater Service of Arequipa)

WRL: Water Resources Law (Ley de recursos hídricos)

List of Words in Quechua and Spanish

apu: 'lord', mountain-being
ayllu: community; kinship-based collective of humans and non-humans
ayni: reciprocal exchange of labour and help
bofedal: cushion bogs in the headwaters, pasture for llamas and alpacas
campesinos: peasants, often associated with indigeneity and the highlands
ch'alla: form of libation; sharing drink with the earth-beings
chicha: fermented maize drink
comadre: co-mother
compadre: co-father
cuenca: watershed/river basin
faena: collective/communal work party
iranta: offering (like *pago*)
k'intu: bouquet of three coca leaves
libreta: control book for members of water users commissions
madrina: godmother, 'sponsor'
minka: form of collective work based on reciprocity
Pachamama: the earth mother
padrino: godfather, 'sponsor'
pago: offering made to the earth, springs and mountains
paqu: ritual expert (also called *curandero*, which means 'healer')
puna: high-altitude areas
samay: breath, life-force
sierra: highlands
sol: Peruvian Nuevo Sol (PEN), currency in Peru. In 2013 and 2014, 1 PEN = US $0.35.
t'inka: form of libation, sprinkling of alcohol to earth-beings
tirakuna: 'earths', or 'earth-beings'
untu: llama fat
Yakumama: the water mother

Series Preface

As people around the world confront the inequality and injustice of new forms of oppression, as well as the impacts of human life on planetary ecosystems, this book series asks what anthropology can contribute to the crises and challenges of the twenty-first century. Our goal is to establish a distinctive anthropological contribution to debates and discussions that are often dominated by politics and economics. What is sorely lacking, and what anthropological methods can provide, is an appreciation of the human condition.

We publish works that draw inspiration from traditions of ethnographic research and anthropological analysis to address power and social change while keeping the struggles and stories of human beings' centre stage. We welcome books that set out to make anthropology matter, bringing classic anthropological concerns with exchange, difference, belief, kinship and the material world into engagement with contemporary environmental change, capitalist economy and forms of inequality. We publish work from all traditions of anthropology, combining theoretical debate with empirical evidence to demonstrate the unique contribution anthropology can make to understanding the contemporary world.

Jamie Cross, Christina Garsten and Joshua O. Reno

Acknowledgements

Growing up in Norway, I took water for granted. Except for the dry summers when restrictions on watering the lawns were implemented to ensure enough water for the agricultural fields, we never experienced any shortage of water and there was always abundant water for domestic purposes. We learned in school that the hydrological cycle constantly renewed itself and thus the water supply seemed infinite. Consequently, there was no reason to question the sources of water and even less to question the ontology of water. The purpose of this book, however, is to challenge hegemonic understandings of water, watersheds and water sources. I show how watersheds are not stable and entirely 'natural' entities and that we cannot take for granted what water '*is*'. This insight did not come easily, and the book is a result of many years of thinking and pondering together with a multitude of people – friends, interlocutors, colleagues, family, scholars and thinkers, who have in different ways accompanied me, taught me and contributed to the process of learning and thinking about water in its various forms. Naturally, however, I take full responsibility for the content of the book.

As I'm writing these words, ten years have already passed since I first went to Colca Valley to learn about how people's relationships with water are affected by climate change. First of all, I want to thank my friends, *compadres* and neighbours in Colca and Majes; I am forever grateful for the way you included me in your work and family lives. *Mil gracias a* Martha and Martin Taco, Clever, Gina, and Eber, as well as the rest of the extended Taco family, and my *amigas* Florencia, Rutsana and Juanita for their kindness and the many conversations and invitations. I am extremely grateful to all the people working with irrigation, water management and public affairs in the Majes-Colca watershed – the farmers who regularly irrigate their fields, the *comisiones*, *la Junta*, ALA, AAA, Autodema, PSI, Sedapar, JASS, the Health Ministry, and the employees and elected representatives of the municipalities of different districts – who took the time to talk to me, show me, teach me and invited me to accompany them in different activities, meetings and field trips. I thank all the water users in Colca Valley and Majes who talked to me about the water worlds they lived and worked in, either in formal interviews or informal conversations, and all the engineers and technicians and secretaries working in different water institutions, organisations and programmes. *Muchas gracias*, especially to: Álvaro Cáceres Llica, Jesus Mamani, Isidro Huanca, Jesus Prado, Mirian Herrera, Noemi Castro, Edmundo Paco, Abdul Huamani, Pablo Tejada, Florencia Cabana, Nicolas Taco, Aldo Huamantinco (RIP), Carlos Ramos, Andrés Noa (RIP), Daniel Ortega, Henry Chaca, Alberto Osorio, Napoleon Ocsa, Luís Ccasa, Lardy Chalco, José Montenegro, Helen Vera Lopez, Miguel Lima, Brenda Legua, Aurora, and Monica. In 2011, Emily Cutipa worked for me in Chivay, assisting with a household survey and transcribing interviews, and I am tremendously happy with her work. In 2014, another field assistant helped me with logistics and interviews in Majes, and I am forever grateful to him and his wife for their help and kindness.

I have been associated with the PUCP (Pontifical Catholic University of Peru) in Lima (formally for a year), and was very glad to use their library and discuss research interests with academics there. I have especially benefited a lot from conversations with water scholar and sociologist Teresa Oré over the years. I have presented papers about my research in Colca at PUCP events, first in 2011 in a forum about climate change and water, and later in 2019 in an event on climate change organised by the Insitute of Human Rights (IDEHPUCP), where I was grateful for comments given by Dr Patricia Urteaga and Dr Deborah Delgado.

Although I had been engaged with Peru for many years – following people and ideas through ethnographic research, I did not know that I wanted to study water in Colca Valley until I was invited to the University of Copenhagen by Professor Karsten Paerregaard to participate in his project 'From Ice to Stone' in 2010. I am grateful to Karsten for giving me the opportunity to spend two years as a post.doc and do fieldwork in Chivay in 2011, for sharing his extensive and long-term ethnographic knowledge of Colca Valley, and for making it a fun experience to collaborate both in the field and at the University of Copenhagen. 'From Ice to Stone' was funded by the Danish Research Council. As part of this project, Astrid O. Andersen became a close friend and co-worker in fieldwork, in Copenhagen and beyond. She offered me a home in Arequipa city when I was visiting from Chivay, and the opportunity to compare what we had learned about water, and I cherish our shared experiences in Arequipa and Colca. I am also very grateful to Professor Kirsten Hastrup for including me in the Waterworlds research group at the Department of Anthropology in Copenhagen, where I was greatly inspired by anthropological discussions about water and climate change. A big thanks to all the members of the Waterworlds group who commented on the earliest papers from this research: Frida Hastrup, Mattias B. Rasmussen, Christian Vium, Mette Fog Olwig, Maria-Louise Bønnelykke, Jonas Østergaard Nielsen, Frank Sejersen, Cecilie Rubow and others.

In 2012, I had the chance to continue my research on water and climate change in Peru thanks to funding for a post.doc. from the FRISAM programme of the Research Council of Norway (project number 222783), and, in addition, funding from the project 'Overheating: the three crises of globalization', financed by the European Research Council (ERC), under the European Union's Seventh Framework Programme (FP7/2007–2013) / ERC Grant Agreement (number 295843). The project was led by Professor Thomas Hylland Eriksen and located at the Department of Social Anthropology (SAI), University of Oslo. I am grateful to Thomas for hiring me as a post.doc in the Overheating project, which gave me the opportunity to do further fieldwork in Colca and Majes, and also to participate in and organise seminars, conferences and workshops both in Oslo and internationally. I benefited greatly from taking part in these activities and am thankful for all the interesting and inspiring conversations and discussions with Thomas and the rest of the research group: Elisabeth Schober, Lena Gross, Robert Pijpers, Henrik Sinding-Larsen, Wim van Daele and Catherine Thorleifsson. I'm thankful for the opportunity to present, and receive comments on, the first drafts of my book proposal and chapters from this group and other scholars at the department. A special thank you to Penny Harvey, Professor II at SAI, for many insightful comments, and María Guzman-Gallegos, fellow post.doc at the time, who commented on various drafts, always making me strive to be more precise and dig into the troubling complexities. A warm hug of gratitude to Professor Marisol de la Cadena, who encouraged me to think about water through concepts – and *not only*. Participating in the Indigenous Cosmopolitics seminar series at University of California Davis in 2012–13 was foundational in forming my thinking around water practices. I also treasure our conversations during later meetings in Copenhagen and Oslo, and I often revisit my notes on the comments and ideas that emerged from our discussions.

A big thank you to those who have read and commented on the latest chapter drafts in 2019 and 2020: Aase Kvanneid, I really appreciated our regular book meetings with strict deadlines and encouraging discussions. Thanks to my current colleagues at the Department of Global Development and Planning (IGUS), University of Agder, for encouragement and discussions when I presented my paper at the research seminar. I owe a special thanks to 'decolonial seminar group' that started at SAI in 2017 and whom I continue to meet regularly on Skype. *Gracias a* María Guzman-Gallegos, Mónica Amador, Cecilia Salinas and Mario Blaser for reading and discussing the Introduction and chapter 5; your insightful and thought-provoking comments inspired me and helped me to sharpen my arguments. I would also like to thank my editor at Pluto Press, David Castle, for his immense support and patience throughout the process. I also want to thank the anonymous reviewers for their helpful comments on the manuscript.

Finally, I want to thank all members of my family for all the help with childcare and moving and other kinds of practical and moral support. I deeply appreciate your help and encouragements: Gunn, Jan Harald, Anne-Bente, Sigrid, Ingvar, Jasmina, and mamma Inger.

Last, but dearest, thank you to Halvar, for coming to Peru in 2011 and 2013/14, accompanying me to the mountain tops in Colca, and in the fiesta of Virgen Asunta in Chivay, for embracing the role as *padrino*, drinking with your *compadres* and being only amusingly annoyed when awakened by a brass band in the backyard at 5 a.m. next morning. Seeing how you related to life and friends in Peru convinced me that you were the right one for me. Thank you for always challenging my ideas and arguments, and for being supportive and loving in so many ways through the bumpy ride of the last years, combining two people's research, making a family and moving to new places at the same time. *Takk* to Ingunn Andrea, who unknowingly accompanied me to Chivay and Majes in 2013–14 and as she grew and made me grow, changed how the surroundings perceived me and how I perceived the world. Since you were born in July 2014, my life and everything I did was filled with new meanings. And to Hannah Sofie, who has filled our lives with joy and love since 2017. Although (or because) you forced me to postpone many deadlines – you have made it clear that there are some things in life that are more important.

Introduction: Water and Watershed Politics

The United Nations (UN) World Water Day, which was declared at the UN Conference on Environment and Development in 1992, is marked on 22 March every year in cities and villages all over Peru. In 2014, World Water Day was celebrated throughout the whole month of March in different locations along the Majes-Colca watershed in southern Peru, where I was doing ethnographic research on climate change and water management at the time. In a collaboration of the public water administration, the water users associations,[1] the municipality and non-government organisations (NGOs), different events were organised: workshops, seminars, and a procession where farmers and school children marched with banners on the public plaza in Chivay, the main town in Colca Valley. The banners had messages like: 'Water is a treasure like your life – don't waste it'; 'Water is life for Chivay – take care of the water', and 'The water should not be sold – The water should be defended!' The farmers – or water users as they are called in the Water Resources Law – carrying the banners were worried because there had been three months of drought since December, in what was supposed to be the rainy season. In the semi-arid Colca Valley, water has been a matter of concern since people started cultivating the land thousands of years ago. In the past two decades, however, new concerns have emerged as many farmers have noted changes in the weather, the landscape and the water supply: irregular rain, springs that disappear and dry pastures. In the same period, international NGOs and national public agencies have introduced the narratives of global warming and climate change, through talks, workshops and pamphlets, which resonate, confirm and give new meanings to the observations that many farmers make in their everyday life. In March 2014, the crops were suffering, and the farmers had to carefully distribute the water that was available for irrigation.

At the same time, water born in the headwaters in the Colca highlands was sent through a 100-km-long canal down to the Majes Irrigation Project (MIP) in the desert flatlands in the lower parts of the watershed. This large-scale irrigation project was constructed in the 1970s in order to create export-oriented agribusiness and economic development for the region. However, the project has also generated tensions and conflicts with the Quechua-speaking peasants in the highlands, as well as frustrations and problems in Majes, where the urban centre soon became a business hub and the surrounding desert was populated by squatters. Since the Majes canal started to bring water from the Colca highlands to the arid pampa of Majes in 1983, both the economy and the population increased at an accelerated speed. While the booming agro-export economy has made it a prosperous place, its vulnerability is also becoming increasingly obvious, since life in Majes is totally dependent on continuous water supply from Colca (Stensrud 2016a).

On Friday 7 March 2014, a ritual offering ceremony (*pago*) for the earth-mother Pachamama and the water-mother Yakumama was performed on the public plaza of Chivay. A ritual expert (*paqu*) was in charge of preparing and assembling the *pago* on a table, and among those closest to the *paqu* were the representatives from the state water administration (ALA – Administración Local del Agua, Local Water Administration), the representatives of the water users associations, as well as the vice-mayor and a couple of aldermen from the municipal council. Everyone was welcome to watch and participate, even tourists, who often spend a day in Chivay after hiking in Colca Canyon. The participants received coca leaves to make small bouquets (*k'intus*) and pieces of llama fat (*untu*) to roll in their hands and were instructed to blow their vital breath (*samay*) into the balls of fat and coca bouquets. The *paqu* invoked the names of the local mountain-beings, with special attention to Cotallaulli who overlooks the town, and he placed a starfish from the sea into the main fountain as a way to attract water. Afterwards, the *pago* was burnt on the plaza. The stones on the ground cracked and broke with a lot of noise, something which startled some of the onlookers and was interpreted by others as a positive sign. A couple of hours later, when the ceremony was finished, the rain started pouring down. Was it a result of the *pago*? Did it work? It was the topic of conversation around town the whole afternoon. Some farmers commented later, however, that the rain had been too strong, and it had come with lightening, thunder and hail. It was also too short and didn't help the plants. Likewise, my friend and interlocutor Sara, who was a daughter of farmers and working as an accountant at the *Junta* office, told me that she was worried about her family's beans because the hail ruins the plants. The farmers I talked to concluded that the *pago* had not been well prepared. They didn't question the general functions of *pagos*, which are usually made as an integral part of agricultural work and community life. But some criticised this particular *pago*, which had been part of a public spectacle.

The story of the World Water Day in Chivay in 2014, illustrates one of the main points in this book: that watersheds are constituted by a plurality of water practices and relations, including relations to other-than-human beings. All these practices produce diverse versions of water and different yet entangled water worlds. However, the explicit aim of the World Water Day celebrations was to create awareness about the importance of creating a 'new water culture', which seeks to teach people that they should be more efficient in their water use. This focus on efficiency comes from an understanding of water as primarily an economic resource, and is part of the project to produce measurable and standardised water, which in the end can be commodified: this is what I call the 'singularisation' of water. This process is never complete, however, and water constantly continues to multiply. I propose that water is always made in practices, relationships and encounters, and this book will explore the multiplicities of water that come out of different practices and how they are negotiated in various encounters.

Water often flows in watersheds, also called river basins, or *cuencas* in Spanish. The water in this book flows through a *cuenca* that is officially called Cuenca Camaná-Majes-Colca by the National Water Authority in Peru. However, this and other *cuencas* do not exist a priori in nature or in state administrations; they are made by different policies, practices and encounters. Water flows are also manipulated by infrastructure, by which humans attempt to direct and control water according to their predominant needs. Since demands tend to be contested, infrastructures are frequently made into objects of contestation and sites of politics (Barry 2001). As emergent and experimental systems, which hold the potential capacity to make new forms of sociality, remake landscapes, define novel forms of politics, reorient agency, and reconfigure subjects and objects, they also generate unplanned and unforeseen effects (Jensen and Morita 2017). By discussing how different parts of the landscape, infrastructure, water users, and different water practices are negotiated and put together, the book will demonstrate how the watershed – *la cuenca* – has emerged as a socio-material assemblage that is being shaped and consolidated as a singular unit of management. In this process, a diversity of existing water practices and beings are being excluded, yet they continue to exist, emerging from multiple practices and encounters. I will in this book take a closer look at the multiplicity of water and the politics of singularisation in the Majes-Colca watershed: How are watersheds made into functional and manageable units? How are different parts of a watershed gathered and joined into a whole, and in this process how are diverse practices, meanings and values negotiated? This work of gathering together and unifying requires careful attention to different water ecologies, and the negotiations of the needs and demands of different water users, sources and regulating entities, both human and non-human.

I will explore a set of questions related to how water is valued, engaged with, regulated and managed by different actors and in different kinds of relations. I will particularly scrutinise how water is part of state policies of singularisation, while simultaneously emerging as multiple waters, disrupting the often taken-for-granted dichotomies of nature–culture, subject–object, active–inert, living–non-living and human–non-human. In order to think beyond these dichotomies, I suggest that there is a need to 'slow down' reasoning and to provoke the kind of thinking that would allow a *cosmopolitics*, which in Stengers' use, is understood as a space for hesitation in the construction of a common world (Stengers 2005b).

The way water flows are guided and shaped by and in human–non-human interactions, and simultaneously are shaping and changing landscapes and socio-ecological relations, allows us to see how water practices are constantly making worlds emerge. Anna Tsing (2015) has explored the worlds emerging from the multiple encounters and practices (picking, exporting, consuming) taking place in the supply chain of the matsutake mushroom, and she argues that following these practices shows us the 'possibilities of coexistence within environmental disturbance' (2015: 4). Tsing suggests that world-making projects emerge from practical activities of making lives; in the process these projects alter our planet. Peasant and indigenous livelihoods and water-related activies that are not part of the hegemonic idea of 'progress' make worlds too, and they 'show us how to look around rather than ahead' (Tsing 2015: 22). Worlds are made through encounters that Zhan (2009) calls translocal. Zhan forcefully argues that what is known as 'Chinese medicine' is not an unchanging body of knowledge, but an emerging 'worlding' made in translocal movements and multiple, often contradictory, practices. This focus is also a critique of dominant dichotomies such as traditional–modern, local–global and cultural–scientific. Worlds in the making are open-ended and can 'serve as a constant reminder that the worlds we inhabit are by no means finite' (Zhan 2009: 24). This also implies that when multiple worlds coexist, they are neither completely separate nor completely equivalent, but what Marilyn Strathern has called 'partially connected' because they are 'neither singular nor plural, neither one nor many' (Strathern 2004 [1991]: 54), but always overlapping in different degrees.

Acknowledging that other worlds are possible, also requires us to rethink the concept of politics. Thinking with Rancière (2010: 37), who defines politics as 'the manifestation of dissensus as the presence of two worlds in one', I suggest that the encounters of different – and partially connected – water practices, can be seen as everyday politics of world-making in the Majes-Colca watershed. Here, I am inspired by de la Cadena (2015), who, building on Stengers, Rancière, Haraway, Strathern and others, argues that practices that enact earth-beings and humans as inherently related to each other, are continuously making worlds in the Andes. Rather than focusing on 'cosmologies', and following Tsing's take on assemblages as open-ended gatherings that make worlds and lifeways, Zhan's point about the translocal, and de la Cadena's analysis of emerging worlds in the Andes, I aim to describe water-related worlds as open-ended and emerging through practices and encounters. Different practices enact different worlds;

Figure 1 A view of Colca Valley from the 'left side' looking over to the 'right side'. We see the village of Lari, the agricultural terraces in a semi-arid landscape, and the snow topped mountain Suriwiri in the background.

these worlds are fragmented, overlapping and changing, and they can all co-exist as part of each other through negotiation. The negotiations and the tensions involved in making the watershed, is what I call 'watershed politics.' Hence, when I argue that water is a highly political issue, I refer not only to the politics of distributing water-as-resource to different uses and among different groups of humans (rural and urban communities, extractive industries), but also to the politics of what water is: who has the power to represent what water is, what it can be and should be?

Water as a matter of concern in the Andes

Water as a limited resource that needs to be properly managed has gained increased attention all over the world in the past few years. Population growth, urbanisation, extractive industries, inequality and climate change are factors that contribute to dwindling water supplies and conflicting demands all over the world. The Intergovernmental Panel on Climate Change (IPCC) states that freshwater-related issues play a pivotal role among the key regional vulnerabilities in Latin America (Bates et al. 2008). Climatological and hydrological measurements indicate that the near-surface air temperature in the tropical Andes has significantly increased over the last 70 years, and most station records in southern Peru indicate a precipitation decrease after 1950 (Vuille et al. 2008). This means that rain-fed agriculture has become more difficult and, at the same time, the glaciers – which are natural containers of freshwater – have been shrinking rapidly during past decades. Peru contains 70 per cent of the world's tropical mountain glaciers, which are the most visible indicators of climate change due to their sensitivity to increased temperatures (Vuille et al. 2008). Glacier scientists have been monitoring the retreat and melting of these glaciers since the 1970s (Carey 2008, 2010), and calculations indicate that all glaciers below the altitude of 5,500 metres will disappear by 2025 (Oré et al. 2009). Glacier retreat is a particularly serious concern in the semi-arid southern tropical Andes, because of the long dry season that usually lasts from April until September (Vuille et al. 2018). Peru is vulnerable to these climate changes primarily because of the unequal distribution of resources, money, people and water, in a country where poverty-induced migration to cities in the coastal desert has been going on since the 1970s (Altamirano 1983; Paerregaard 1997; Ødegaard 2010). When peasant farmers lack the economic means to improve their production under declining environmental conditions, they tend to migrate to the urbanised and industrial coast, where they live in poor neighbourhoods in the desert. In Peru, 65 per cent of the country's 31 million people live along the arid Pacific coastline yet have access to only 1.8 per cent of the total water resources in the country (Defensoría del Pueblo 2015: 12). This makes water management a crucial and highly political issue. The number of environmental conflicts in Peru has escalated since the 1990s, a decade that was characterised by radical neoliberal reforms and a mining boom. Between 2011 and 2014, a total of 539 social conflicts were registered, and 153 of these (28.36 per cent) were linked to water (Defensoría del Pueblo 2015: 35). In 2017 it was reported that approximately half of all social conflicts in the last decade were related to water (*Perú 21* 2017): cases of water grabbing and pollution by mines, cases of enclosures by dams for hydropower and export agribusiness, and conflicts related to legal pluralities and contested rights to water (Guevara 2008). More than issues of distribution and access, however, these conflicts are also often about something more profound: how we understand and relate to land and water (Paredes and Li 2019). As described in the ethnographic vignette above, there were different entities that intervened in the celebration of World Water Day in Chivay in March 2014: not only the international and national institutions, but also the mountains, the earth-mother (Pachamama), and the water-mother (Yakumama) were addressed and their response was interpreted and discussed among people. People I came to know in Colca Valley often interacted with sentient and responsive water-beings, like springs, lakes and ponds, who responded to human action.

Anthropological studies of water since the 1970s have observed the central importance of water in the political life and symbolic worlds of peasant communities: how water has played a central role in origin stories, cosmologies and rituals since precolonial times (Earls and Silverblatt 1978; Sherbondy 1982; Allen 1988; Valderrama and Escalante 1988; Gose 1994; Salomon 1998; Sherbondy 1998; Gelles 2000; Hogue and Rau 2008). Jeanette Sherbondy, who has done research on water and canal systems in the Andes since the 1970s, describes water as 'the dynamic principle that explains movement, circulation and the forces for change. Water is considered the essence of life itself' (Sherbondy 1998: 212). These studies have focused on the culturally embedded practices of irrigation in the Peruvian Andes, where irrigation technologies that include agricultural terraces and canals, have been used since at least 2400 BC (Denevan 2001). Much of this scholarship has focused on the uses and distribution of water in terms of power, control, and kinship structures

(Paerregaard 1994; Sherbondy 1994; Gelles 2000; Trawick 2003). Several scholars have analysed different phases of state intervention in local water governance as a matter of opposition and conflict (Boelens 2009, 2015; Guillet 1992; Guillet and Mitchell 1994; Vera Delgado 2011; Paerregaard 2013) and in terms of hegemony and citizenship (Paerregaard et al. 2016). More recent scholarship has scrutinised processes of marketisation and commodification (Hogue and Rau 2008; Boelens et al. 2014; Paerregaard and Andersen 2019), and several scholars have shown how changes in glaciers and water supply are entangled in socio-economic structures and neoliberal policies (Oré et al. 2009; Carey 2010; Lynch 2012; Rasmussen 2015; Boelens 2009). Most studies of the social life of water and irrigation in the Andes have focused on indigenous peasants, while the state is often presented as an impersonal force. María Teresa Oré and Edwin Rap (2009; Rap and Oré 2017) are an exception, with their research on the practices and social networks of hydraulic engineers, who since the 1970s have formed an epistemic community and a hydraulic bureaucracy with huge influence on Peruvian water policies. However, recent studies of water and infrastructure in other parts of the world indicate that hydraulic engineers and bureaucrats are often not detached from water users, but rather engage and negotiate with them in networks of reciprocity (Barnes 2014; Anand 2017).[2] Everyday relations, connections and practices tend to be complex, and as noted by David Mosse (2005), we need to look at institutional practices ethnographically. By discussing the everyday work of engineers, managers and administrators, I will in this book not only look at how the state intervenes in local forms of governance, but also analyse encounters that are socially embedded and where power and values are negotiated.

There has been a commendable shift towards a focus on water flows, rather than uses and distribution, allowing a more dynamic approach to understand ongoing struggles for water and life in rural highlands (Rasmussen 2015), as well as the urban ecologies of water (Swyngedouw 2004; Andersen 2014) and hydropower development (Hommes and Boelens 2018). These studies, founded in the political economy and political ecology of water (Swyngedouw 2009), have contributed to the understanding of different 'hydrosocial cycles' – a term that captures 'the deepening entanglement of water flows and power relations' (Budds et al. 2014: 167) – and have asserted the inequality and injustice of water distribution and access. Although I am inspired by this shift towards more dynamic analysis, I intend with this book to take a step further and include the non-human to show how hydrosocial relations are part of the mutually constitutive relationships in which people, land, mountains, water and other beings co-constitute each other (Kohn 2013; de la Cadena 2015). By looking at socio-material practices and what they enact, this book aims to go beyond the onto-epistemic limits of political economy, political ecology and cultural/symbolic representation of water. With their focus on the distribution of water resources and different perspectives on water, these fields of research imply a fundamental discontinuity of nature–culture and human–non-human. Inspired by the term 'political ontology', as 'an imaginary for a politics of reality' (Blaser and de la Cadena 2018: 5), I will rather look into how different water practices and water worlds are enacted, and how they coexist and are deeply entangled. Through which practices is water being produced as an 'economic resource', and in which encounters does water as multiplicity emerge?

Water extractivism

> 'Resource' originally implied life. Its root is the Latin verb surgere, which evoked the image of a spring that continually rises from the ground. Like a spring, a 're-source' rises again and again, even if it has repeatedly been used and consumed. (Shiva 2010: 228)

In her chapter on 'resources' in the *Development Dictionary*, Vandana Shiva (2010) shows how the connotations of the concept of resources changed with the advent of industrialism and colonialism, when nature was transformed into resources for production and trade. The treatment of nature as resource for economic growth – as a container for raw materials waiting to be exploited and transformed into inputs for industrial production of commodities – has been central to the project of development, and has resulted in the desacralisation of nature and the destruction of the commons through enclosures and privatisation (Shiva 2010). In his analysis of how water became 'modern', Jamie Linton (2010) argues that modern water is an understanding of water as simply a resource: 'stripped of any cultural, or even political and ethical connotations'. Water-as-resource is a precondition for 'water management', a term that 'implies a particular kind of water, stripped of its complex social relationships such that it may be managed by experts who are not necessarily directly involved in these relationships' (Linton 2010: 58). Jeremy J. Schmidt (2017) discusses how a philosophy of water management that developed in the United States at the beginning of the 20th century, is today forming the basis for what is called 'global water governance'. In the United States water was not categorised as a 'resource' until 1909, yet today this classification is so common that it appears natural. Analysing how this particular approach to water management became the consensus, Schmidt defines this common thinking 'normal water'. It was 'by gathering different kinds of social, technical, geological contingency into a common way of imagining the health of societies and the Earth that a particular philosophy of water management became normal' (Schmidt 2017: 6–7).

The turn towards neoliberalisation in the global economy, understood as a political project to minimise state intervention and enhance the conditions for capital accumulation (Harvey 2005), was accompanied by a neoliberalisation of nature, characterised by a rapid increase in the involvement of private corporations in resource ownership and the provision of ecosystem services (Bakker 2015). The neoliberal turn also affected international agreements of water: in the 1992 Dublin Statement on Water and Sustainable Environment, it was declared that water has economic value and should be recognised as an economic good (Franco et al. 2013).[3] Since the rapid and radical neoliberal restructuring of the Peruvian economy under President Alberto Fujimori in the 1990s, development policies have been based on deregulating markets, encouraging private investment and corporate extractivism. Extensive concessions have been granted to foreign corporations that extract value from nature, and these extractive practices have created socio-environmental conflicts across the country. In addition to the well-known conflicts related to oil, minerals and logging, another form of extractivism that is growing in importance is the extraction of economic value from water in megaprojects for hydropower and export-oriented agribusiness.

What I call *water extractivism* is the practice of singularising and standardising water into the category of 'resource' in order to master it and extract as much economic value from it as possible. This practice of resourcification is concomitant with the rise of capitalist markets and the modern state, or what James C. Scott (1998) calls 'high modernism'. Scott argues that state control requires a narrowing of vision of complex and unwieldy realities and a simplification of nature. This simplification makes the phenomenon at the centre of the field of vision – in this case water – more legible and more susceptible to measurement and calculation, thus making possible a high degree of schematic knowledge, control and manipulation (Scott 1998). Hence, in order to extract value, water must be standardised and singularised into a universal resource that can be measured, quantified, registered and licensed, and thus controlled and commodified (see Bakker 2010; Swyngedouw 2015; Strang 2016). The Peruvian state's project of modernisation and development is based on an extractivist logic, where every drop counts; the goal is to not waste any of the water flowing downriver from the Andean highlands into the Pacific Ocean. Every drop should be put into production and used to create value, whether in electricity, mining, agriculture, business or to sustain a growing population. As a project initiated by the Peruvian state in its quest for modernity, the MIP aims to conquer water and nature in order to extract value and create progress. The planned second phase of the irrigation project – Majes-Siguas II – is a hydraulic megaproject that will be constructed in a public–private partnership, implying a 'temporary commodification' (Ullberg 2019). The 2009 Peruvian Water Resources Law acknowledges water as public property yet emphasises its economic value and encourages private investment. Hence, the law allows and enables a kind of indirect privatisation and commodification process.

In the Water Resources Law, water is explicitly valued as an economic good but at the same time valued as a basic human right to be equitably distributed, a principle that is not consonant with its market value (Orlove and Caton 2010: 409). On the one hand, the law recognises the fundamental right of humans to consume water as well as the right of native and peasant communities to use the water that flows through their land. On the other hand, it emphasises the economic value of water and the importance of efficient use of the resource.[4] This law is inspired by and integrated in the water resources management (IWRM) approach, which, since the early 1990s, has become the hegemonic paradigm for legitimising and implementing water management policies all over the world (Orlove and Caton 2010).[5] According to the UN (2014), the IWRM approach that has now been accepted internationally 'as the way forward for efficient, equitable and sustainable development and management of the world's limited water resources and for coping with conflicting demands'. As Orlove and Caton (2010: 410) point out, however, IWRM hardly questions what is meant by a basic right or a commodity and does not venture into the complex political question of how its principles will be struggled over in concrete settings.

Although IWRM aims for a holistic approach based on the three principles of social equity, economic efficiency and ecological sustainability, it does not acknowledge the conflicts between these three principles, and the value of water as an economic resource is often given priority. IWRM is implemented by promoting 'new water cultures' in populations, creating new water legislation that privileges economic efficiency, and consolidating administrations based on watersheds (or basins) as units of management. As a result, people all over the world are thinking about watersheds as units of management, which implies a 'watershed logic' of efficiency. The goal is to achieve efficient water cycles where flows and uses are regulated and where the extraction of value is maximised.

As the most used water resources term worldwide, IWRM has been likened to a mantra more than professional tool (Delli Priscoli 2013), and it has been criticised for not being sensitive to power and inequality (Mehta et al. 2016). Instead of policy transfer, which assumes perfect rationality of actors, stability of governance and the immutability of policy ideas in different places or contexts, Mukhtarov (2014) suggests policy translation as an approach to study how policy ideas travel. As the IWRM travels around the world, it is translated and implemented in particular socio-material environments. In Peru, the first watershed council (*consejo de cuenca*) was created in *la cuenca* Quilca-Chili, which is the neighbouring watershed to Majes-Colca (Arequipa). The rationale was to include the different actors and water users (agriculture, industry, municipalities) in the governance of the watershed/basin, and the first phase of planning and implementation was characterised by tensions originating from huge differences in power and influence (Andersen 2014).

One of the reasons for organising management in watersheds is to see water use as integrated across the political borders of the administrative units such as districts, provinces and departments. However, watersheds are not necessarily entirely and unproblematically present as units in nature: they vary in scale, may contain smaller sub-watersheds and connections with groundwater and may be modified by infrastructure that transfers water between watersheds (Strang 2004; Orlove and Caton 2010). To create a united watershed as a functioning unit of management necessitates a lot of work bringing people and institutions together, and careful attention to different water ecologies and water users' needs. However, according to Phillips and Roberts (2019), there is – even within the technocratic realm of modern water management – an increasing recognition of the need to consider and incorporate multiple perspectives; both human and wider ecological interactions with water.

Water multiplicity

Among social scientists doing research on water, it is widely recognised that water and social relations co-constitute each other (Linton 2010; Budds and Hinojosa 2012; Wagner 2013; Hastrup and Hastrup 2016). Seeing social realms as being built, at least partially, in and through engagements with water, one could argue that water is multiple; not only in its meanings, but in its very materiality (Barnes and Alatout 2012). I suggest that to fully understand the dynamics and tensions that are produced by water extractivism, scholars should not take for granted what water is but acknowledge that it can have many natures (Bonelli et al. 2016; Stensrud 2016b). Socio-environmental conflicts concerning mining activities in the Andes have shown that ontological multiplicity can lead to contestations about whether water is always the same and negotiations of the 'equivalence' of water; for example, whether dammed water can replace lagoon water (Li 2013; Paredes and Li 2019).

In the Majes-Colca watershed, water does not flow by itself; different practices are employed to guide, domesticate, channel the water, and these practices involve investment in different kinds of relationships with multiple entities: offering gifts in relations of reciprocity, constructing and maintaining infrastructure, organising distribution, regulating access and sharing food and drink with humans and other-than-human beings (Stensrud 2016b). I suggest that the different water-practices enact multiple versions of what water is and can be. Furthermore, I propose that, in Colca Valley, water and its users are also part of a mutual composition of place, as in the concept of being 'in-*ayllu*', which describes how 'humans and other-than-humans are inherently connected' (de la Cadena 2015: 101) and their relationship is also part of them (2015: 102). In other words, hydrosocial relations exist within the practices and relationships in which people, land and water co-constitute each other. Put differently, people's ontological design of land- and waterscapes – as heterogeneous assemblages of life – enact non-dualist, relational worlds (Escobar 2018: 66). The practice of a world of many worlds is what Escobar (2018) and Blaser and de la Cadena (2018) call a pluriverse: 'heterogeneous worldings coming together as a political ecology of practices, negotiating their difficult being together in heterogeneity' (Blaser and de la Cadena 2018: 4).

Finding ways to grasp the complex relationships between humans and the environment in terms of singularity and multiplicities, I am inspired by various scholars and concepts that destabilise previous 'common-sense' categories like 'nature', 'human' and 'reality'. Arguing against the assumption that reality is a determinate set of discoverable entities and processes – a singular reality or 'one-world world' – John Law (2004) suggests that particular realities are constructed by particular practices and that ethnography lets us see the relative messiness of practice. Inspired by Annemarie Mol's (2002) study of how the practices of doctors, patients and laboratory scientists in a Dutch hospital enact multiple, but overlapping, versions of a body and of the illness arthrosclerosis, I decided to look ethnographically at how particular water-practices enacted different versions of water and water bodies in the Majes-Colca watershed. However, multiple realities do not mean that there are different and possibly flawed perspectives on the same object. Different realities are being created and mutually adjusted so they can be related, and realities depend upon their continued crafting and enactment – in a combination of people, things, techniques and natural phenomena. The absence of singularity does not imply that we live in a world composed of an indefinite number of disconnected water bodies, water management institutions and political decisions. It does not imply that reality is fragmented, but that the different realities overlap and interfere with one another, and that their relations, partially coordinated, are complex and messy (Mol 2002; Law 2004: 45–69). Hence, the water in this book is not one singular kind of water; there are many different waters, yet these are not separated, but partially connected: more than one and less than many (Mol 2002; Law 2004). This approach implies considering how particular practices impinge upon and relate to other practices that simultaneously exist. The philosopher Isabelle Stengers (2005a) calls this an *ecology of practices*, which does not have any ambition to describe practices 'as they are' – water management as we know it, for instance – but as they may become and how they may connect. This mode of thinking requires a 'radical openness', which means to risk one's own categories of recognition (Blaser 2019: 77). Said differently, to maintain an openness towards other worlds, other histories and other futures, one must resist the temptation to recognise or predict and keep a sense of ethnographic amazement or 'wonder' (Ballestero 2019b). As Ballestero points out, engaging the future of water does not necessitate having an image of how that future looks; on the contrary, by tapping into the non-imaginable dimension of the future, we can see that a future history of water is unpredictable and uncertain and the 'result of an awareness of the interminable practices, material processes, imaginaries, and mere coincidences that ultimately shape the yet-to-come' (Ballestero 2019b: 26). Water is a key concern in the Andes, both because it enables fertility and life, but also because of the danger it presents in the form of floods and landslides. The earth- and water-beings in Colca are not inherently good or evil, but capricious and unpredictable, just as the weather in the mountains is unstable (and with climate change, increasingly so), and just as markets, development projects and state presence are also often perceived as volatile and random. Hence I suggest that we follow Stengers' (2005b: 994) proposal to 'slow down reasoning' to arouse a different awareness of the problems mobilising us. Slowing down the analysis of practices will allow us not only to see what is being done in different situations, but also to explore what emerges in the practices. The question of who and what might compose the common world (Latour 2004; Blaser 2016) necessitates taking into account questions of political ontology, understood as the power-laden practices, negotiations and conflicts involved in the interrelations and interactions among worlds (Blaser 2009; Blaser and de la Cadena 2018).

In this book, I give special attention to the people I met who negotiated different worlds on a daily basis in their work and everyday life. Many of these people worked in water institutions: the public water administration, local and regional water user associations, the regional authority in charge of the Majes canal, and district and provincial municipalities in Majes and Colca. I observed how they pragmatically combined diverging world-making practices and worlds, like Christianity, earth-beings and secular modernity, science and technology, for example by relating to water both as a technically manageable resource and as a living being. As we will see throughout the book, very often different waters and water worlds, exist together pragmatically and unproblematically. Nevertheless, many of my interlocutors insisted on making distinctions between categories that were mixed in everyday practice. These distinctions can be seen as forms of bifurcations, understood as ongoing attempts that are never fully finalised (Ballestero 2019b: 6). In her work, Ballestero looks at how regulators and activists continuously perform distinctions between water as human right versus water as commodity; this requires a lot of work, in a never-ending process of bifurcation (Ballestero 2019b). In Majes and Colca, the separations made between water-as-living and water-as-resource would make new complexities arise and, with them, the need to always make new distinctions. In this way, multiplicity is always produced as part of our lives, not separately from what is represented as the 'modern' world, but as inherently a part of world-making practices across the taken-for-granted separations of modern/indigenous worlds. Thus, a key question to discuss is, in which situations/contexts/relationships is the distinction between water-as-living and water-as-resource relevant/important (and for whom)? When are other/multiple/'indigenous' practices deemed irrelevant, or unreasonable (Blaser 2016)? And when is the distinction between singular water and multiple water important? When are these distinctions made relevant, and by whom and why? The moments of making visible the entities and beings that are usually relegated to a status of irrelevance and illegible 'noise' opens up the politics of water worlds. Here, I am inspired by Rancière's understanding of politics as the meeting of two heterogeneous processes; one process establishing uniformity (called 'the police process') and the other establishing multiplicity, which Rancière calls 'the process of equality', understood as 'equality between any and every speaking being' (Rancière 1999: 30). However, as I hope to contribute to an 'anthropology beyond the human' (Kohn 2013), speech does not exclusively refer to human language and representation, but the material semiotics of non-humans and other-than-human beings. In Colca Valley, I learned that rain can think, springs can feel thirsty, mountains can be hungry, and water can respond to human actions. One aim in this book, then, is to elicit those situations in which multiplicity becomes contentious and political in the making of the Majes-Colca watershed.

The Majes-Colca watershed

The highlands of Caylloma province, in the region of Arequipa, are part of the headwaters for two watersheds: the Camaná-Majes-Colca watershed, where the water is channelled to the export agriculture in the pampa of Majes,[6] and the Quilca-Chili watershed, where the water is used for hydropower and mining, as well as urban consumption in the city of Arequipa. These water connections raise questions about responsibility: who is responsible for the maintenance of the headwaters – the local herders and farmers, the local or regional authorities, the government, the farmers in the pampa, the hydroelectric plant, or the mining companies? In a vertical landscape, where the lower parts depend on the actions in the higher parts, water management necessitates cooperation, and this requires a lot of translation and mediation work. In this way, connections in the watershed are made not only by flows of water, but also movement of money, people and ideas.

Parts of the watershed are modified by infrastructure. Since 1954 water has been transferred from the Camaná-Majes-Colca watershed to the neighbouring Quilca-Chili watershed, which provides water to the large city of Arequipa, as well as a hydroelectric power plant and the large Cerro Verde copper mine. Moreover, water from the Condoroma dam in Callalli district is taken from the Colca River and led through the large Majes canal to the pampa of Majes, where 15,000 hectares of former desert have been made fertile and now produce agriculture products for export and grass for large-scale milk production. Since the Majes Irrigation Project started in the 1980s, people from the highlands have been migrating there to seek new opportunities, and during the past 30 years, a new city – Villa El Pedregal – has grown up. The office of the local water administration (ALA Colca-Siguas-Chivay) is located in Villa El Pedregal, a location that reflects the economic priorities of the government. However, the export economy in Majes depends totally on the water from Callalli and the surrounding highland districts, which are the most poverty-stricken areas of the province.

The economy of Colca Valley is mainly based on small-scale farming and the rearing of animals, in addition to commerce and tourism. Thousands of tourists come each year to admire the stunning landscapes and the impressive flight of the condors in the Colca Canyon, and the fiestas and Wititi dance where men and women whirl around in colourful dresses. Most farmers in Colca are bilingual in Quechua and Spanish and identify with the Collagua-Cabana culture. However, they do not explicitly identify as 'indigenous', which in Peru is a stigmatised category, but as peasants (*campesinos*) or farmers (*agricultores*). Approximately 10,000 families of peasant farmers (called 'water users' by the 2009 Water Resources Law) cultivate fields of potatoes, beans, barley, quinoa and maize on a total of 12,000 hectares of land. Since Colca Valley is semi-arid and the rain patterns have become increasingly irregular in the past few years, the farmers are highly dependent on irrigation, which they organise in water users commissions (*comisiones de usuarios*). Upriver in the highlands the majority of people are pastoralists: there are approximately 3,500 families who are solely dedicated to the small-scale rearing of some 400,000 alpacas and 50,000 llamas in Caylloma province (*Correo*, 9 July 2013).[7] This area is the headwaters of the Camaná-Majes-Colca basin that runs down the western slope of the Andes, and where the water is born: it comes from rain, springs, and melting glaciers and snowfields between 4,000 and 6,000 metres above sea level. Water flows into streams that become the Colca River, which is dammed in the Condoroma reservoir. Downstream the water is conducted into the Majes canal by the water intake (*bocatoma*) in Tuti, before it brings the water down to the irrigation project in the desert. The rest of the water flows through the river valleys of Colca and Majes before it reaches the Pacific Ocean in the coastal province of Camaná (Map 1).

The MIP is founded on the idea of using water and land to produce, export and create economic value, and it is thus presented as being in the centre of the Peruvian government's vision of development. In addition to the Condoroma dam in Callalli district, the Tuti water intake and the 100 km long Majes canal, the plans for the second phase of the project include two hydropower plants in Lluta and Llucta, and an extensive network of irrigation infrastructure covering more than 50,000 hectares in the desert flatlands of Majes. As of 2017, 15,800 hectares have been irrigated, while the upcoming second phase – in which the remaining 38,500 hectares

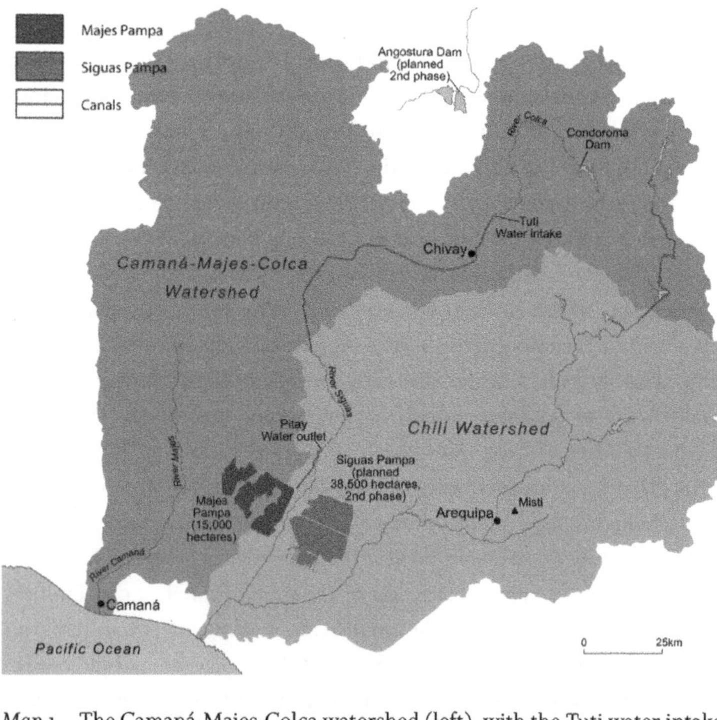

Map 1 The Camaná-Majes-Colca watershed (left), with the Tuti water intake, Chivay and the irrigated pampa of Majes. The map also shows Majes-Siguas II project: the planned Angostura dam and the planned irrigation of Siguas (to the right of Majes). (Source: Autodema)

will be irrigated – has been delayed for various reasons such as changing governments, economic crisis and protests. In 2009, farmers in Espinar province, in the neighbouring region of Cusco, started to protest against the new Angostura dam contending that it will leave them without water. In 2011, the constitutional court halted the project and ordered a new environmental impact assessment and water balance report. In 2013, after the new report concluded that there is enough water for both regions, the court allowed the US $550 million project to proceed as planned (see Map 1).

Fieldwork in a watershed

When I first arrived in Chivay by bus from Arequipa in the beginning of March 2011, I expected to spend some time tuning into life before starting to search for information about water. I soon realised, however, that water was on the surface of everyday conversations among people all over Chivay. While farmers were mostly concerned with the supply of irrigation water and the rain, other villagers had concerns about the quality and the price of the service of domestic potable water. On one of my first days there, I visited the office of the water users board of Colca Valley, which in Spanish is called la Junta de Usuarios Valle del Colca (JUVC) and in everyday speech just '*la Junta*'. Their office had a central location in an old wooden two-storey building by the main plaza, beside the office of the Ministry of Agriculture. Standing in the plaza, looking at the building, I had the Catholic church on the left, the town hall on the right, and the bank and the marketplace behind. Inside the office, I was welcomed by Miguel, the daily manager, who showed great interest in the project and enthusiastically told me about how the *Junta* worked and explained in detail the intricacies of the regulations and tariffs, and the changes brought by the 2009 water law. With time, he would become one of my main interlocutors and friends in Chivay, as I would accompany him and other members of the *Junta* on water inspections and meetings. Generous with his time and knowledge, he shared his experience of working with water management in Colca for many years. After talking to the elected president of the *Junta*, I presented a formal letter, accompanied by documentation from my home university, and received the *Junta*'s approval – materialised in an official document with stamps and signatures – to do research on water management among the water users commissions in Colca Valley. I found a room in the house of a family who rented out rooms to visitors and tourists, and although I initially thought of it as temporary, I ended up staying in that room for almost eight months. During that time, I got to know the family well, and when my partner visited in August, we were included in the family as godparents (*padrinos*) for the youngest son. The family, who became my *compadres*, did not own land, since the now deceased grandfather had sold his fields many years earlier. The family had been one of the first to rent out a room with a bed to tourists when they started to come in the 1980s, and they had slowly expanded by adding more rooms to their house surrounding the backyard. When I first came, they had six rooms, and before my second visit in 2013, they had built a couple more rooms and a new kitchen and dining room. They also invested a lot in bathrooms and showers with hot water, which tourists appreciate. My first direct experience with water in Chivay, was what I learned in this household: learning how to use the gas heater, observing how they used water for cooking and cleaning, and listening to their stories while washing my laundry together with my *comadre* and her children in the backyard. They used to sit on the fountain which my *compadre* had built many years ago. Earlier, it was filled with running water, but after the public company Sedapar (Servicio de Agua Potable y Alcantarillado de Arequipa SA) took over the water administration and started measuring and charging money for potable water in Chivay, it has been dry. The water used in households and businesses in Chivay comes from a spring called Mamaccocha, from which water flows through a variety of pipes, canals, ponds and filters, towards fields as irrigation water and the town as potable water. When Sedapar started to produce chlorinated drinking water, they also installed meters and sent out bills, which provoked protests among the population and demands for water administration to be returned to the municipality. Since my *compadres* ran a small hostel, they had two water meters: one for household use and one for the hotel business, which is more expensive. Tourists are known to use much water, and my *compadre* was constantly watching the meter and trying to save money by reducing water use whenever he could, without reducing the service to the guests. This included, for example, watering the plants in the backyard with used washing water.

My *comadre* came from Puno originally, but had lived in Chivay for many years, and she proudly wore Colca-style *polleras* (long embroidered skirts) in the fiestas. Only a few days after my arrival, it was time for the carnival festivities in Chivay, and my *comadre* and her daughter dragged me along, dressed me up in a Colca *pollera*, and taught me how to dance the typical Colca Wititi dance in circles around the plaza for hours on end. With this intense introduction to sociality in Chivay, I not only came to know people, but people came to know me as the dancing anthropologist who was interested in water and who showed up at every water-related activity in the area.

I did not have to look hard to find water-related activities and events. On the contrary, I often had to choose between various invitations and activities on the same day. This also meant that if one activity was cancelled or postponed (as sometimes happened), I could often go to another meeting or activity. The manager of the *Junta* was a busy man and, as I slowly came to know more people working in the water administration, in the agricultural ministry, in NGOs and in the water users commissions, I also got busy juggling the different activities I could observe or participate in. Much of the fieldwork took place on the road, as I travelled a lot by bus and car together with engineers and water users from Chivay to districts in the highlands, like Tuti and Callalli, and villages in the lower parts of Colca Valley, like Pinchollo and Cabanaconde, and to Majes (see Map 2). Some of the journeys continued to smaller villages by mule and on foot. A few journeys also took me to the city of Arequipa, where the main offices of the regional government and water administration are located. I found that people in Colca Valley tend to travel quite often to Majes and Arequipa for various reasons: work, business, bureaucratic paperwork, and to visit family.

In addition to accompanying Miguel or others on inspections and meetings around the valley, I also travelled alone by bus to 16 different villages where I interviewed the presidents of the water users commissions and others.[8] The differences between the 'left' and the 'right' bank of Colca River (*margen izquierda y derecha*) soon became clear. Standing in Chivay and looking downriver, the left side had access to water from the Majes canal and income opportunities from the thousands of tourists who came to admire the beautiful scenery of Colca Canyon and the flight of the majestic condors, as well as the folkloric dances of people in colourful dresses. The condors ascended every morning with the sunlight to a place by the road outside Cabanaconde called 'Cruz del Condor', where, at around 8 a.m., they would fly over the heads of groups of tourists with cameras, before continuing the journey downriver. Women in Cabana-style *polleras* and hats were also there every morning to sell embroidered blankets, purses and other souvenirs. It was easier to travel to the villages on the left bank since it was more tourist-friendly and there were many bus companies driving this route. To get to the villages on the right bank, where the bus service was limited, I made a deal with a taxi driver who could take me if I needed to go to a meeting or an interview. Since farmers spend most of the day in their fields, the office hours and the meetings of the water users commissions were usually very early in the morning, at 5 or 6 a.m., or late at night, after 7 or 8 p.m. In Chivay, I spent a lot of time in the *Junta*'s office, where water users from all over the valley came to ask for advice. I participated in meetings and communal work and fiestas of the water users commissions, and I visited people in their homes, shared meals and participated in harvests. Building trust and friendships takes time; it requires personal investments and participation in relations of reciprocity. After some months, I was very honoured when I was asked to be *madrina* for the inauguration of the roof of the new communal building of the *comisión de usuarios* in Chivay Urinsaya (the lower part of Chivay).

With a few exceptions, like the secretary and the accountant in the *Junta* office, one leader of a water users commission, and one engineer at the Autonomous Authority of Majes (Autodema) office in Arequipa, all the people who worked in water institutions and users organisations were male. Being a female researcher in a male-dominated domain required some negotiations of boundaries, although I was always met with respect and friendly invitations to observe, participate and learn. What I found most difficult was the lack of control I had over others' perceptions of my person and role in water management in Chivay. For example, it was hard to gain trust and confidence from peasants when I arrived at a place together with the water engineers, since I was from the start associated with institutions of power. With time, I also got to know many women, both the wives and relatives of the men I met in water organisations, and women living in the neighbourhood, and women working in shops and at the market. I often spent hours on end sitting with my female friends at the marketplace. Some of them combined selling vegetables or crafts with farming, while others dedicated themselves full-time to embroidery and/or market vending, in addition to taking care of their families. Sitting in their stalls, chatting, drinking tea and eating biscuits, I learned a lot about life in Chivay, the history of the place, the webs of relationships, the rules of conduct, what is and is not appropriate, and how these women reflected upon and discussed different topics from the news, politics and their own lives. These female friends became especially important during my second period of fieldwork, which started in the beginning of November 2013. A week before, I discovered that I was pregnant, which meant that I had to change some of my fieldwork plans. I decided to not stay in Callalli, above 4,500 metres, and I went back to Norway in April 2014, which was earlier than planned. During these months, my friends took care of me by offering me chairs to rest on and sharing experiences and advice about pregnancy and motherhood. Carrying a new life, and thinking about the baby growing in water in my womb – the water that would eventually 'break' – while researching water gave rise to a whole range of thoughts and concerns about water quality, and made me worry about the potential dangers in eating uncooked food or drinking unboiled ('raw') and potentially polluted water. My attentiveness to women's knowledge about what could affect pregnant women and babies inevitably became more personal. Although the 'rules' of what to do and not to do were quite different than in Norway – and premised on other relationships of body-mind-surroundings and the human–non-human as mutually constitutive, where my surroundings could influence the being that grew inside my body in ways I had never imagined before – I felt remarkably safe among my friends in Chivay who cared for and protected me.

From January to March 2014, I stayed in Villa El Pedregal in order to learn more about life in the irrigation project of Majes. Being a busy place of trade, business and transit for many people, I found it harder to find friends there than in Chivay. People were always on the move; many travelled back and forth from Arequipa and those who lived there permanently were busy working and making money. I made some friends among women working in the market and in small shops, where I could sit and talk and help with minor tasks without interfering with their business. I also knew quite a few of the employees in the ALA and also got to know some of their families, among them José and his wife Melissa, who lived in a small house with their two children. Little by little, I got to know their parents and siblings, aunts, uncles, cousins, *compadres* and friends. José had an extensive network of friendships and colleagues from the places he had worked earlier. As he was between jobs for a while during my fieldwork, he helped me to find my way around and introduced me to people that I could interview: farmers, workers, business owners, municipal employees, politicians, leaders of associations and organisations. These weeks were the most intense in terms of work, and somehow reflected the tempo of the life in Villa El Pedregal. After long days of interviews, driving, walking, waiting, asking questions and making notes, José and Melissa would often invite me to dinner and some rest in their house, where we could also more calmly and slowly talk through things and events.

I sometimes took the opportunity to travel with the ALA engineers when they were going on field trips to the highlands, and it was not only because I missed the crisp air, peaceful atmosphere and friendly sociality of Colca Valley, although that was also true. It was by accompanying engineers and water users in their travels up and down the watershed, that I learned about the different ways the places were interconnected. Often, I met people in different places, sometimes unexpectedly. Engineers travelled from Majes to Colca and Condoroma and the surrounding headwater communities to assist with water claims and conflicts, and water users travelled from the highlands and valley to Chivay (the administrative centre and capital of Caylloma province), the city of Arequipa and Villa El Pedregal (the urban centre of the MIP, where the ALA office is located), to do business and paperwork, attend meetings, knock on the doors of public offices and NGOs, and visit friends and family. Most people travelled by public transport (bus or the smaller combi), while some of the engineers had access to cars. Sometimes the cars broke down, however, or they had to go to places not accessible by car. During my fieldwork, I travelled by bus, combi, car, motorbike, mule and/or on foot.

This book is based on what I learned about water during 13 months (in 2011, 2013 and 2014) of participant observation in the Colca Valley and the pampa of Majes. The interviews that complemented my participant observations in everyday work and family life, often mixed personal memories, shared experiences, unconfirmed gossip and political opinions, 'shaken together into a cocktail of meanings' (Mayer 2009: xviii), just as

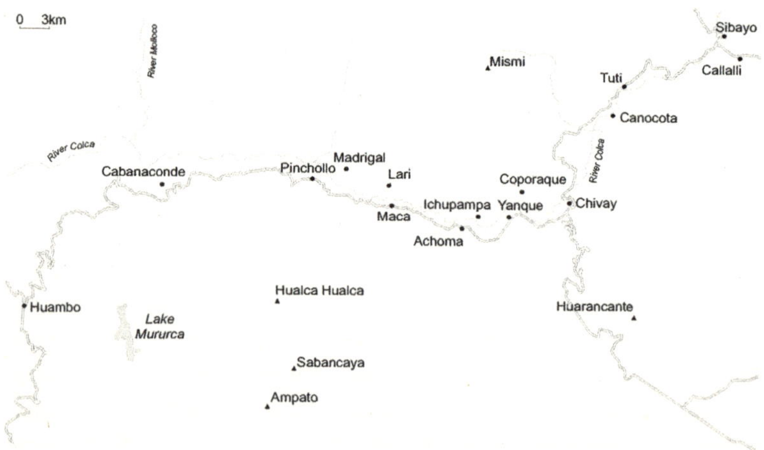

Map 2 Villages and mountains in Colca Valley. (Source: Google Maps)

my interpretations of fieldnotes and transcribed interviews are mixed with embodied experiences of 'being there' and vivid memories evoked by pictures and videos from fieldwork.

The chapters

In chapter 1, 'Engineering Water Flows', I discuss the regulatory work of hydraulic engineers and the effects of hydraulic infrastructure in the watershed. The chapter demonstrates how the Majes canal not only transformed the environment in Colca Valley, but it also altered social and economic relations, and influenced farmers' relationships to the state. By showing how hydraulic engineers travel up and down the watershed, I suggest that the work of engineers is embedded in social relationships. Chapter 2, 'Colonising the Desert', discusses how the Majes desert was (and still is) colonised using water from the watershed, modern technology and the hard work of settlers and engineers. The chapter shows how the population has increased due to a dynamic and growing economy, yet new inequalities and uncertainties are also produced, mainly due to free market policies. I argue that the role of Majes in the watershed is ambivalent: privileged and powerful, yet dependent and vulnerable at the same time. In chapter 3, 'Water Payments', I discuss different relationships to nature by contrasting different ways of paying for water. The chapter demonstrates the implementation of state legislation and water tariffs on the one hand and the daily work of farmers and water users commissions on the other. I argue that the practices of paying money to institutions and giving food to sentient mountain-beings reveal fundamentally different ways of engaging with the environment, yet at the same time, these practices are entangled and partially connected in everyday life of farmers. Chapter 4, 'Water Uncertainties and Disasters', examines how changes in the environment and weather in the watershed are discussed in terms of global climate change. I show how climate change and neoliberal policies create and exacerbate uncertainties in everyday life, and I suggest that the perception of climate change contributes to generating new meanings in collective rituals performed in the public.

The remaining three chapters explore how the watershed is constituted by responses to water uncertainties, like measuring, registering, formalising, and introducing new technologies, which are all modes of controlling uncertainty, creating predictability and singularising water. Chapter 5, 'Water Efficiency', discusses the idea of efficiency as part of the modernisation project, the introduction of modern irrigation technology, and how non-efficient practices disrupt the idea of 'the modern'. I furthermore discuss the tensions generated by enclosures of water and different understandings of leakage, which I analyse as 'efficient use' versus 'good use': different practices that are also entangled in the everyday work of water organisations. Chapter 6, 'Legible and Illegible Water', focuses on the state's project of making water legible. I discuss how water for population use was included in the management of the watershed, and the negotiations and tensions caused by the new requirements for formalising the right to use water. The chapter also shows how the growing population in the desert around the project creates challenges for the municipality regarding the provision of water and infrastructure. In chapter 7, 'Owning Water', I discuss forms of ownership that go beyond the usual dichotomies of public vs. private or commons vs. commodity. I show that the water law's emphasis on the economic value of water creates new political and economic demands. The chapter focuses particularly on a land claim in Majes, based on notions of ownership that emerged from particular ontological relations of water, mountains and the earth in the headwaters. The book concludes by showing how a focus on flows and connectivity, rather than sites and locations, allows us to see the different processes and practices that enable or hinder the flows of water, and to see water in its multiple forms and modes that connect places, beings and entities in the world.

1
Engineering Water Flows

> [T]he Special Project Majes-Siguas, an ingenious hydraulic work of high engineering, constructed in 11 years (1971–1982) [...] served to direct the water from Colca River to the desert Pampas of Majes. This work involved an ambitious colonizing effort on land with no register of previous human action, but thanks to this titanic work, the expansion of the agricultural frontier has been accomplished, making it the fourth greatest valley of Peru.
>
> (Zamalloa 2013: 2)

This quote is taken from the introduction of a book on the history of the MIP, a book that I bought in the author's seed shop in Villa El Pedregal in 2014.[1] Edgar Zamalloa is an engineer by profession and came to Majes to work on the construction of the irrigation project in 1985. A self-taught historian, he wrote a book about how the MIP came into being: the construction of the Condoroma dam, the Tuti water intake, the Majes canal and the irrigation of the pampa of Majes. Presenting the MIP largely as a success story, the book emphasises the vision and ingenuity of the politicians and engineers who designed and constructed the infrastructure, which is intrinsically associated with the condition of modernity (Edwards 2003). Zamalloa's descriptions of the engineering and infrastructure are infused with an 'enthusiasm of the imagination' (Mrázek 2002) and 'deep affectual commitments' (Larkin 2013). By focusing on the achievements in the unpopulated desert, however, the public story of MIP overlooks the damages and problems that people struggle with in Colca Valley.

It is easy to be enchanted by large-scale infrastructure because of the promise of emancipatory modernity it retains, even though it often fails to deliver, as Harvey and Knox (2012) have shown in their work on roads in Peru. In the process of planning and construction, dams and canals might – like roads – hold divergent expectations together. People in the highlands might, for example, hope to get work and be integrated in the national project of modernity and progress. However, unlike roads, large-scale dams and irrigation systems only promise connectivity, integration, freedom and prosperity to those at the receiving end of the canal, while those living by the dam or alongside the canal soon realise that they have been left out of the circuit of value and prosperity. Infrastructure often appears to be paradoxical – constructive and destructive; solid and durable, yet doomed to be ruined and exceeded (Howe et al. 2016). More than paradoxical, however, the Majes canal is political; it is involved in negotiations and struggles over the flow and distribution of water. The Majes canal soon became an object of contestation (Barry 2001), where the construction through mountains and fields, and the access to water and work were contested and negotiated. During the planning and construction of the MIP, the possible consequences for the farmers in Colca Valley were not taken into consideration. Yet, the impact was huge; the MIP transformed the ecological and social composition of the watershed, and opened spaces for economic and political demands and struggles. The possibilities for extending areas of cultivation improved greatly for some, while others were left with water scarcity. The canal altered relations between those who were able to tap into the water flow and those who did not (cf. Barnes 2012). Like the Colorado River in Richard White's (1995) analysis, the Majes-Colca watershed can be seen as an 'organic machine', which not only is a reflection of social divisions, but the site in which these divisions play out. Agreeing with Jensen and Morita (2017), who see infrastructures as 'ontological experiments', which reconfigure relations and environments, I suggest that infrastructures do not have physical, social and cultural *aspects* that can be understood as separate spheres. Rather, the dams and canals are made *with* cultural values and ideas, which shape the material physicality and also shape the impact on wider socio-ecological systems. Majes canal not only transformed the physical landscape that it runs through; it altered the relations between farmers and the state; between communities; between farmers, mountains and water springs.

Control over water can provide an effective means of consolidating power (Worster 1985). Influenced by both Marx and Weber, Karl August Wittfogel (1957) was the architect of the controversial 'hydraulic society' thesis, in which he postulated that large-scale irrigation systems, composed of ever larger dams and increasingly elaborate canal networks, lead to centralised coordination and administrative bureaucracies. Distribution of water requires high levels of organisation and cooperation, and necessitates regulations, manuals and bureaucratic details, and Wittfogel was concerned with the role of bureaucrats – those who 'rule through bureaus' – in governments that turn into despotic regimes (Wittfogel 1957). In a study inspired by Wittfogel, Donald Worster (1985) analysed large-scale manipulation of water in the arid American West, which generated a social order that he called 'a modern hydraulic society'. What Worster observed was a coercive, monolithic, and hierarchical system built on a sharply alienating and intensely managerial relationship with nature (Worster 1985). Water management in the Andes, and in Colca Valley in particular, has often been analysed in terms of opposition and conflict between state power and local governance; state intervention and control versus local user rights and resistance (Boelens 2009, 2015; Gelles 2000; Guillet 1992; Guillet and Mitchell 1994; Paerregaard 1994, 2013; Treacy 1994; Trawick 2003; Vera Delgado 2011). The MIP has been analysed particularly as an imposition of power, in which local needs were much neglected (Gelles 2000; Vera Delgado 2011). The stories and observations presented in this book confirm that the MIP was – and still is – a project of conquest and extractivism, and that in the same period the state has imposed regulations that come into conflict with communal water governance (Gelles 2000; Boelens 2015). However, although the state has often been imagined as a coherent, rational and stable entity, anthropologists have for some time criticised this view, focusing instead on state 'effects' (Mitchell 1991), practices and processes (Trouillot 2001), and forms of agency (Krohn-Hansen and Nustad 2005). In more recent scholarship, the state is increasingly being scrutinised and analysed as a configuration of dispersed and flexible practices (Pinker and Harvey 2015), and an aggregation of many levels of bureaucracies, agendas, offices and officials that may act in contradictory ways (Rasmussen 2015). Not only is the state an incoherent agent, but also the consequences of bureaucratic practices are arbitrary (Gupta 2012). However, since this book is more about world-making than state-making, I have looked to Rancière's thinking about the difference between 'police' and 'politics' to elicit the point that not only are the practices of statecraft multiple and emergent, but also that, by looking beyond the 'known' sphere of human activities, we can begin to understand the politics of multiple world-making projects. According to Rancière, what he calls 'police' is not the same as a 'state apparatus' understood as separate from 'society', but is about the configuration of the perceptible:

> The police is thus first an order of bodies that defines the allocation of ways of doing, ways of being, and ways of saying, and sees that those

> bodies are assigned by name to a particular place and task; it is an order of the visible and the sayable that sees that a particular activity is visible and another is not, that this speech is understood as discourse and another as noise. (Rancière 1999: 29)

In other words, policing is about shaping a uniform and normalised 'order', in which some bodies are acknowledged as having a legitimate place and voice. Politics, on the other hand, is a completely different activity: 'a mode of expression that undoes the perceptible divisions of the police order' (Rancière 1999: 30). What I will show below and in the rest of the book is that the boundaries between practices and processes of 'police' and 'politics' are not clear cut, and that politics is not always easy to discern and define since it can often only be glimpsed through ruptures, just as water leaks and flows through cracks and openings.

In this chapter, then, I suggest that although the official policies and legislation aim to curtail and contain local normative diversity in the Andes (Boelens 2009) – which singularise water in the process – the everyday practices of the engineers working in water management are complex. Arguably, the MIP has strengthened a managerial relationship to water in the Majes-Colca watershed, yet there is no monolithic and despotic hydraulic bureaucracy in complete control of the management of the watershed. Instead of seeing a Weberian ideal of an impersonal bureaucracy, which 'segregates official activity from the sphere of private life' (Weber 1978: 957), I observed engineers and bureaucrats whose lives were not sharply separated from the lives and irrigation practices of farmers (see also Stensrud 2019c). The work of the engineers and technicians in the hydraulic bureaucracy in the Majes-Colca watershed was embedded in ecological and social relationships, and they practised forms of care in their working relations with water users and hydraulic infrastructure. Care has usually been associated with loving and 'warm' human relationships, in contrast to 'cold' and rational technology. Following Mol et al. (2010), Stevenson (2014) and Yates-Dorr (2014), I suggest that care work can potentially be found anywhere, including in state bureaucracies and the work of engineers, and that caring practices – understood as a way of working and 'persistent tinkering' (Mol et al. 2010: 14) – can include water, technology and infrastructure.

Inspired by Lisa Stevenson (2014), who analyses different forms of care in the Canadian Arctic, I further understand care as the way something comes to matter – in this case water and water users – and the corresponding ethics that follow. Stevenson (2014) describes everyday forms of care in Inuit communities as keeping promises and practices of sharing that are not exclusive to the sphere of living humans, but often bind 'the living and the dead in ways that are not always straightforward or obvious' (Stevenson 2014: 3). She also explains how forms of bureaucratic care – informed by good intentions and an ethics of professionalism and anonymity – are tied to a colonial form of governance and surveillance. When water comes to matter in Colca Valley – both for users and the authorities – different forms of care are elicited in different relationships. Bureaucratic practices are informed by forms of care that are ambivalent – both controlling and enabling – and as I will show below, the divisions between bureacrats and users are often blurred. Thinking back to the quote that opened this chapter, I suggest that Zamalloa, as an engineer who was part of the construction of the MIP, wrote his book with careful attention to technical and personal details, as well as showing explicitly care for the continued shaping of the identity of the place and its people (see also Stensrud 2016c). Since Majes as a project mattered deeply to him, his work of archiving and writing also mattered, in which he not only showed his care but also attempted to control the narrative of what Majes is and should become, which will be explored in more detail in the next chapter. This chapter will mainly focus on the work of the engineers and how they intervene in the watershed. The first part will discuss the construction of the Majes canal and the tensions and struggles that this generated in Colca Valley in the 1970s and 1980s. After examining the neoliberal deregulation in the 1990s, and today's institutional plurality, I discuss the social embeddedness in the current management and regulation of water and water users, and the practices of care that I witnessed in the work of Miguel, José and other engineers in the Majes-Colca watershed.

Hydraulic dreams

> Engineers dream and plan as often and intensely as the rest of us. More than the rest of us, however, they believe that there is a calculated sameness between the planning and the dreaming.
>
> (Mrázek 2002: xvii)

As far as is known, the arid flat lands of Majes and Siguas have never previously been irrigated and populated.[2] However, the vast possibilities were obvious for the farmers who lived in Arequipa and in the nearby river valleys of the Majes and Siguas rivers. Since the climatic conditions and the location near Arequipa city and the Panamerican highway make it a strategic place for food production for various markets, the possibilities for irrigation and agriculture in this area have been envisioned for more than a century. According to Zamalloa's book, already in the 19th century farmers in the neighbouring province of Castilla expressed this desire to President Ramón Castilla (1858–62), to which he responded that this was 'a dream' (Zamalloa 2013: 23). When President Velasco finally introduced legislation to move the MIP forward, he said that this would 'make Arequipa's dream a reality' (Gelles 2000: 60). In 2014, one of the engineers in Autodema told me: 'This was a big dream from many years ago; to irrigate these pampas by directing water from the highlands of Arequipa, from the rivers in the high parts.'

The first engineer who took the dream seriously was Charles W. Sutton, a North American who in 1908 was asked by the government of Augusto B. Leguía (1908–12) to elaborate projects of irrigation in Peru. After specialising in irrigation studies in USA and working on the Panama canal, he returned to Peru, where he travelled along the coastline making proposals for possible irrigation projects. Several of Peru's large-scale irrigation projects were originally designed by Sutton, like Chavimochic in La Libertad and Olmos in Lambayeque. In 1946, based on detailed studies of water availability and land, Sutton made a proposal for a project that considered the use of water from the Colca River to irrigate the pampas of Majes and Siguas (Zamalloa 2013). The practice of engineering, aiming to control the environment by constructing infrastructure, is backed by a vision of development and modern statecraft. Civil engineering expertise in Peru was central to the rise of the modern state, not only in relation to the technical infrastructures – like roads, bridges, dams and canals – through which territorial integrity was imagined and materialised but also for the ways in which a sense of public benefit was consolidated around these arenas of state practice (Harvey and Knox 2015). Sutton supposedly insisted, 'the greatness of Peru would start the day that Peru decides to incorporate gradually, and without pause, nothing less that five thousand hectares per year to the national production' (Zamalloa 2013: 25). Indeed, there was little controversy around the importance of large infrastructural projects among the elite, and several presidents made studies and plans for Majes-Siguas: Bustamante y Rivero (1945–48), Odría (1949–53), Prado y Ugarteche (1956–62), and Belaúnde Terry (1963–68), before General Velasco Alvarado (1968–75) executed the project (Zamalloa 2013: 25).

In 1960, the Italian firm ELC Electroconsult made the project design, and the first Belaúnde government secured the financial part in 1967 by signing a contract with the General Mining and Finance Corporation Ltd. Robert Construction of South Africa. In 1971, the military left-wing government of Juan Velasco Alvarado (1968–75) started the execution of the 'Special Project Majes-Siguas' by taking up loans and creating the state entity Depema (Dirección Ejecutiva del Proyecto Majes), which in 1982 would change its name to Autodema – the Autonomous Authority of Majes. The Velasco government signed the financial and construction contracts for the first phase of the project with the International Consortium MACON (Majes Consorcio), which consisted of five companies from Sweden, England, South Africa, Canada and Spain. In the 1970s, the MIP was considered 'the world's most expensive irrigation project' (CIP 2013), and the total investment was US $630 million; 65 per cent of which was financed by MACON, and the rest by the state (Zamalloa 2013: 38). MACON built the Majes canal, consisting of 88 km of tunnels and 13 km of open canal through the districts of Tuti, Chivay, Yanque, Achoma, Maca, Cabanaconde and Huambo, and the water intake dam (*bocatoma*) in Tuti, where water from Colca River is dammed and directed into the

Figure 2 The Majes Canal leads large amounts of water from the headwaters, through Colca Valley and down to the arid pampa of Majes. Engineers do regular inspections of the canal and its valves.

tunnel-canal. Later, the Condoroma dam, with a storage capacity of 285 million cubic metres (MMC), was built at an altitude of 4,158 metres in Callalli district and finished in 1985.

Conquering mountains

In a speech held after signing a contract for completing the project in 1977, the CEO of the MIP, engineer Oscar Valdivia Ávalos, talked about the challenges they were up against seen from the state's modernising perspective. 'In Majes we are at war against a hostile and tough topography, against a nature that we must change, we are at war with the underdevelopment and this makes us impatient', he said (Zamalloa 2013: 36). The construction phase, which the CEO talked about as a war against nature, is remembered by many people in Colca Valley as a time of rapid change and intrusive encounters. Already in 1972, the work to construct the water intake in Tuti and Majes canal had started. MACON brought specialists from all over the world and workers from other parts of Peru, who were stationed in an encampment in Achoma district. In the years that they lived and worked there, the MACON workers, and especially the foreigners, were highly visible in Colca. 'That was the first time we saw *gringos*; there was no tourism yet', a man in his fifties commented. His name was Edwin and he told me that when he had been a young boy in the 1970s, the MACON *gringos*, also called '*los macones*', used to drink in his father's *cantina* (tavern). '*Los macones* have done whatever they wanted here', he commented. According to Paul Gelles, who did fieldwork in the community of Cabanaconde in the 1980s, most local people lamented the changes and abuses the project brought; stores were opened to meet the demands from a booming economy and 'everything became money'. The MACON workers abused the local people, and there were incidents of prostitution and rape (Gelles 2000: 61).

MACON offered temporary jobs to local men: low-paid manual labour in the construction of the dam, the water intake, the canal and tunnels. This work was dangerous and many lives were lost in the tunnels and the construction sites. One of Edwin's relatives was killed in an accident in Tuti when his poncho got stuck in machinery at night. In the eyes of many people, MACON challenged the respect for the powerful mountains as they used dynamite to make the Majes canal and the tunnels, and it was therefore necessary to make offerings (*pagos*) to avoid accidents. Accidents are often talked about as being eaten by hungry mountains (Gose 1994), or being lured by beings inside the mountains, called devils or *chinchilikos*. Old farmers who had worked as labourers in the making of the tunnels remembered the *chinchilikos*: small underground creatures, also called dwarfs, devils, miners or just 'small men with helmets', who appeared inside the mountains.[3] By offering you gold and silver, they can drag you inside the mountain and make you disappear. The daughter of a man who had met a *chinchiliko* in the Majes tunnel told me that when the devil drags you (*te jala*) it is the same as when the mountain eats you. In southern Andean Peru, it is a common practice to pay offerings and ask earth-beings for permission to make roads, tunnels and mines (cf. Harvey and Knox 2015). Although this was not (and could hardly be) part of the official work strategy of MACON, I was told that MACON workers also engaged in such practices. For example, Edwin told the story of a poor beggar who suddenly disappeared. A rumour said that the MACON workers had sacrificed him to the mountain to avoid accidents. The story went that they had made him drunk and after he had passed out, they put him in the *pago* and buried him alive. Another story told that 'they put a human foetus in the *pago*' before starting the construction of the water intake in Tuti, but it was never made clear to me who 'they' were. It could very well be both local people and MACON workers from other parts of highland Peru who wished to reduce the risk of fatal accidents.

These stories are not testimonies that give precise details about the past but serve to explain how situations and relations are perceived and how connections are made. The stories have broad resonance in the ethnographic literature from the Andes, for example in June Nash's (1979) study of how mine workers in Bolivia relate to *el Tío* – also associated with the devil – who is the owner of the mountain and to whom they must give offerings before taking out minerals (see also Fernández Juárez 2013). In Taussig's interpretation, making offerings to *el Tío* as the devil of the mine is a reaction to capitalist modes of production. In the pre-colonial Andes there was no conception or reification of an evil spirit: 'evil was neither reified nor fetishized, neither a thing opposed to good nor a thing spiritualized like the devil' (Taussig 1980: 169). The fetishisation of evil in the form of the devil was created after the Spanish Conquest, along with the new forms of class oppression (Taussig 1980). The earth-beings had to assimilate to the Christian religion or descend underground to the world within/below called *ukhu pacha* in order to become invisible, and some of these beings were identified with the devil (Cereceda 2006). Rather than understanding the *chinchiliko* as a symbol of Christian or capitalist oppression, I see it as an entity that emerged in encounters between worlds of different nature–culture constellations: a relational world where all living beings are connected versus a 'modern' world where nature is seen as a resource to be exploited or as a container from which value can be extracted.

The encounters with sentient mountains and *chinchilikos* are not part of the official story of the Majes Project. As in other histories of extractivist 'development' in the Andes, the earth-beings are denied real existence or are tolerated as indigenous belief or superstition (de la Cadena 2015). Yet, in Colca, the stories are told again and again, and not only by farmers but also by engineers working in different institutions. The arrival of MACON in Colca Valley was, and still is, perceived as a powerful intrusion that disrespected the humans living there as well as the sentient mountains. However, several of the engineers working in today's bureaucracy employ a more careful and sensitive way or working as they combine a technical approach with more relational modes of being. Some of them were born in Colca in the 1970s and, after their higher education in engineering, returned to work in the watershed, where they navigate and negotiate different values, tensions, practices and relationships.

Water struggles

Farming in the semi-arid Colca Valley has always been dependent on irrigation, and farmers are proud of their hydraulic infrastructure, which constitutes a complex network of canals and pipes, connecting the springs, lakes, glaciers, micro-dams, and reservoirs with the pastures and fields. However, water shortages have often led to conflicts among users and between communities. For example, in 1972 there was a dispute over the intersection of irrigation canals where water was divided between the villages of Yanque and Coporaque. It ended with a violent confrontation where stones where thrown: 'It was raining stones', as one man from Coporaque said. One man from Yanque died in the fight, and Yanque won the right to access the water (Benavides 1998; Brandshaug 2020). According to Juana Vera Delgado (2011), before the construction of the MIP, only four communities in the valley were able to more or less meet their irrigation needs (Chivay, Achoma and Maca on the left bank and Ichupamapa on the right bank). These communities had abundant sources of water – springs and wetlands. However, after the drilling of the Majes tunnel-canal, the three communities on the left bank also began to suffer from water scarcity, just like the rest of the valley (Vera Delgado 2011).

When the Majes canal was finished in 1982, the farmers in Colca suffered from an extreme drought while they watched the water flowing by in the canal. Their petitions to the government, soliciting access to this water, were ignored. Only after a group of eleven men from the village of Cabanaconde took action and blew a hole in the canal with dynamite, did the community of Cabanaconde get access to the water from the Majes canal to irrigate their lands. These men are still honoured as the 'eleven heroes' in Colca Valley (Gelles 2000). Vera Delgado (2011) describes how the rest of the affected communities on the left bank of the river felt encouraged and inspired by the Cabaneños example and organised a Defense Front for the interests of the Caylloma people. After many years of mobilisation and pressure from the local communities, Autodema agreed to open more valves alongside the canal in 1991 (Vera Delgado 2011). Today, the main marker of difference between the left and right side of the river valley relates to water access and agricultural production. There are 26 valves in the canal from which the villages at the left riverbank (*la margen izquierda*) – Canocota, Chivay, Yanque, Achoma, Maca, Pinchollo, Cabanaconde and Huambo – receive regulated amounts of water, and some farmer communities – in particular Cabanaconde – have expanded their areas of cultivation with the allocated water from the Majes canal (Paerregaard 2013, 2018).

However, the farmers living on the right bank of Colca River (*la margen derecha*) continue to struggle with water scarcity. After years of drought, the community of Coporaque carried out their own irrigation project in the 1980s, taking water downriver from the Tuti intake. After almost 20 years of collective work and continuous struggles, the Coporaque canal – including a 475-metre-long tunnel – was finished in 2003. The farmers in Coporaque, as in the rest of the Colca Valley, do all the maintenance work themselves and must struggle to get financial support from NGOs and the provincial municipality, while the state gives priority to large-scale projects such as the MIP. Autodema, which is the main operator of 'major infrastructure' (*infraestructura mayor*) in Arequipa, such as the Majes canal, the Condoroma dam, and the water intakes in Tuti and Pitay, is financed from the public budget. Autodema was transferred from the central to the newly formed regional government in 2004. Although the regional state has limited fiscal autonomy and no legislative or juridical power, the regions have a moral power associated with the wealth generated from local resources like water (Pinker and Harvey 2015). One of the things the regional government of Arequipa can do is administer public works like the MIP and manage the funds assigned to them to develop the region. Hydraulic engineers employed by Autodema are perceived as quite powerful because they operate the Condoroma dam and the Majes canal. Still, they have to coordinate with other water management institutions in the watershed.

Institutional plurality

A plurality of practices, entities, institutions and water users associations are involved in making the water flow in the Majes-Colca watershed. In Colca Valley, the approximate 10,000 farmers are organised in associations that used to be called 'irrigators' commissions' (*comisiones de regantes*) by the 1969 General Water Law (Ley general de aguas). The 2009 Water Resources Law (Ley de recursos hídricos), replaced the specific 'irrigator' with the generic word 'user', and today there are 31 water users commissions in Colca Valley. Some of the commissions are subdivided into several smaller water users committees (*comités de usuarios*), which are organised around single sources or canals. The General Water Law, which the Velasco regime introduced as a supplement to a radical agrarian reform, acknowledged water as public property and part of the patrimony of the state (del Castillo 1994). Oré and Rap (2009) have argued that the centralisation of the state's water management and the expansion of hydraulic infrastructure and public water institutions created what Wittfogel (1957) called a 'hydraulic bureaucracy' of engineers. By forming a professional culture and epistemic community through their education, trajectories and networks, these engineers have had a huge influence in Peruvian water politics during the past four decades (Oré and Rap 2009: 33). This hydraulic bureaucracy is, however, located mainly in the capital, Lima, where political and economic power is concentrated in Peru.

In the Majes-Colca watershed and neighbouring watersheds in Arequipa region, other regionally anchored bureaucracies have developed, following the policies of deregulation and decentralisation, where responsibilities of the central government and ministries were transferred to regional governments and private non-profit organizations such as the *Juntas*, the commissions and committees. The neoliberal Fujimori government (1990–2000) passed several legal decrees to deregulate the state's role in the management of water and hydraulic infrastructure. The deregulation had started already in 1989, when the functions of the state institutions in operation, maintenance and administration of the irrigation infrastructure were handed over to the water users boards (Juntas de Usuarios) (Oré and Rap 2009). In Majes-Colca there are two *Juntas*: one in Colca Valley (la Junta de Usuarios Valle del Colca, JUVC), and one in the irrigated pampa of Majes (la Junta de Pampa de Majes, JUPM). The *Juntas* are private non-profit associations that coordinate the water users commissions. Their responsibilities include the operation of minor hydraulic infrastructure, charging the irrigation tariff and distributing economic and material resources among the commissions, and mediation in conflicts over water.

In 2009, President García passed a new law on water resources, which was tailored to meet neoliberal interests that minimise the role of the state in economic and social politics (del Castillo 2011). One year earlier, in 2008, the management of all kinds of water in Peru – not only for agricultural use, but also industrial and populational use – was centralised in the National Water Authority (ANA, Autoridad Nacional del Agua), with offices in the capital Lima. The ANA is subdivided into regional Administrative Water Authorities (Autoridad Administrativa del Agua – AAA), referred to as 'triple A'. Colca Valley and the MIP belong to the AAA of Caplina-Ocoña, with an office in Arequipa city, which oversees seven local water administration offices called ALAs. Among them is the ALA Colca-Siguas-Chivay, which is responsible for the Majes-Colca watershed, including the MIP. Their main office is located in Villa El Pedregal, the main urban centre of Majes. The farmers living in Colca Valley seldom (if ever) went to this ALA office, because of the long journey: first, they have to travel by minibus to Chivay, then by bus to Arequipa city and finally by another bus to Villa El Pedregal.

Previously, when the Ministry of Agriculture supervised water management in 'irrigation districts', the administrative office of the Colca Valley irrigation district – the ATDR (Administración Técnica de Distrito de Riego) – used to have their main office in Chivay. The last bureaucrat to work in this office was Gabriel, who was born and raised in the nearby village of Achoma. After being relocated to the new ALA office, he moved to Villa El Pedregal with his wife and children in early 2010, and the office was left empty. In mid-2011, after being pressured by demands from farmers and the JUVC, the ALA director decided to send an ALA representative to be present in Chivay a couple of days a week. The designated employee was José, who was not educated as an engineer, but had experience from work in other water-related institutions such as JUPM. Having worked in the ALA for just a few months on a temporary contract, he was sent to the office where Gabriel earlier had worked as representative of the ATDR. José was supposed to be at the Chivay office every Monday and Tuesday, and also represent the ALA in meetings and inspections whenever necessary. His job was to provide the link between the local farmers and the ALA office in Pedregal, and he was supposed to coordinate work with the JUVC, the water users commissions, and with the Autodema staff stationed at the Tuti intake dam. Several of the representatives from different institutions knew each other from earlier collaborations. In Colca and Majes, most of the engineers and technicians worked on short-term contracts and circulated among different positions in different water institutions: the *Juntas*, the ALA, the AAA, Autodema, and the agricultural agencies in Chivay and Majes. Many of them knew each other from university or from having worked together at some point. As a result, some became friends and *compadres*: a reciprocal relation of sponsorship. Becoming *compadres* means engaging in a lifelong, unbreakable relationship between the parents and the godparents of a child or between a married couple and the godparents of their wedding.[4] Having a *compadre* or *padrino* (godfather) who holds a powerful position and has influence is beneficial in looking for a job and making a career. They are often willing to help in exchange for gifts or other services. Miguel who works for the *Junta*, for example, has one *compadre* in the ALA office and another *compadre* working for Autodema. José has a *padrino* from his wedding, who for a while held an important position in the regional government of Arequipa. For José, it was great luck to have a powerful *padrino* that he could turn to if he needed help, but this also meant that José had to be ready to be at his *padrino*'s disposal and help him with various tasks.

I went to see José on his first day in Chivay, a Monday at the beginning of June 2011, and I found him watching a movie on a small portable DVD-player. This was the day after the presidential election, and he was tired after having celebrated Ollanta Humala's victory together with his *padrino*, before leaving Pedregal at 3.30 a.m. to take the 6 a.m. bus from Arequipa to Chivay. The office was cold, dark and dirty, with unpainted concrete floor and walls, some shelves with files of old documents, two chairs and a desk. The computer was old and did not work; José commented that it seemed to be 'from the stone age'. Behind the shelves, I saw a single bed with some woollen blankets where he was supposed to sleep. Since the room was cold, with no heating, and an unsealed metal door that let the draft into the room, he would have to sleep with his clothes on. Three people came in while I was there. The first visitor that day was a farmer from Lari, a village on the right riverbank, who came to ask about a complaint that he had sent to the ALA a long time ago, regarding the water licence for a piece of land he had inherited from his mother. His niece had applied for a water licence for this land, but he stated that her claim was false because the land belonged to him. The second visitor was a young woman from the irrigation committee 'Miraculous springs' in the highland district of Tisco, asking whether a decision had been made in her application for a water licence. José called his colleague Gabriel in the ALA office in Majes, and told her to come back next week to receive a document with the answer. A man from Coporaque came to ask about his application to start a new water users committee. He had received a letter from the ALA with a list of the required documentation, but he said that he had already submitted everything except the water balance report. José told him that in addition to the map and the list of users, a report on the water balance is the most important part of an application. A water balance report consists of an inventory of water springs with their location marked by GPS and the volumetric flow rate (*caudal*), which is measured in litres per second. When the man asked how he should do this, José suggested that he talk to the engineer Miguel in the JUVC. José called Gabriel for advice, and then he told the man to return next week in order to receive a document with more information.

The need for information among the farmers was quite apparent; they appreciated having a person available who could answer questions. Many farmers find it hard to navigate among different institutions and regulations, and there is no easy access to the internet in Colca. Although there are '*cabinas de internet*' in Chivay, so far very few farmers have learned the skills to use computers, write emails and search for information. José's visitors on his first day had been given directions to the ALA office by the JUVC's secretary, Monica, who was alone in the *Junta* office that day because the manager, Miguel, and the accountant, Sara, had a meeting with a *comisión* in Cabanaconde. The farmers in Colca often go to the *Junta* office to ask about water-related problems. Since Chivay is the province capital and an administrative and commercial centre, they make sure to visit the *Junta* when they have other errands in town. Often, the *Junta* staff have to consult the ALA office in Majes, either by telephone or fax, in order to give answers to the farmers' questions. From now on, they would rather send people to José's office.

Caring for water and users

> 'The *Junta* has 31 children – the *comisiones* – and 15 grandchildren – the *comités*.' (Miguel, JUVC)

While the Majes canal divided the watershed between the beneficiaries and non-beneficiaries, *la Junta* (JUVC) aimed at gathering the watershed and uniting the water users by caring for all their 'children', as they sometimes call the *comisiones*. The *Junta* was led by a board consisting of a president, a secretary, a treasurer, an auditor, and two spokespersons, who were elected every three years by the general assembly. They held a monthly meeting where they discussed important issues, including how to comply with the new requirements of the Water Resources Law; how to solve water conflicts between commissions or committees; how to organise repair of infrastructure destroyed by rainstorms; or how to ask for help from the government in case of drought or other weather-induced disasters. Although they have more autonomy under the new law, they report to the ALA and regularly send them updated lists of water users, accounts, budgets and 'plans for operation and maintenance of the minor infrastructure', which included an inventory list of all the hydraulic infrastructure in Colca Valley. During my fieldwork in 2011, I attended many of their board meetings, where I observed their discussions around challenges and ambitions. For example, the *Junta* aimed at obtaining external support for projects to build micro-dams, improve canals and implement other inter-communal irrigation systems. Once a year, the *Junta* organised *el Encuentro*, an annual congress for all the water users commissions in the valley. The board members participated in inspections of water sources and infrastructure, and in meetings with commissions or with public authorities whenever necessary. However, the day-to-day running of the *Junta* office was in charge of the salaried staff: a technical manager, a secretary and an accountant.

When I came to Chivay in 2011, Miguel had worked as a technical manager (*gerente técnico*) for eight years. He was born and raised in Chivay, and trained as an engineer at the University of Arequipa. Having written his thesis about irrigation in Coporaque, he returned to Colca to serve his valley and his people. In spite of the relatively low salary that the *Junta* could afford to pay him, he took his work very seriously. It was not hard to see that Miguel cared deeply for his valley and its water and ecology, as well as the farmers. Since several of the water users were his family, childhood friends and *compadres*, he made an effort to be impartial and to show that he cared equally for all the users. He was especially concerned not to favour his father, who was board member in one of the commissions. When he attended the *Junta*'s office in an old building by the public plaza of Chivay, he always received visitors: farmers and leaders of commissions who sought advice and support. Some asked about the payment of tariffs, the interpretation of the law and its regulations, and how to apply for water licences or document land ownership. In 2011, Miguel and others in Colca were studying the new Water Resources Law of 2009, trying to understand it. 'The law is made for the coast, and does not fit well in the highlands; there are many holes in the law', Miguel commented, and continued:

> The people on the coast have made the law sitting at their desks, but if you go to the field it is different. So we adapt (*nos adecuamos*) and we mix the law with custom and base our work on internal agreements. For example, a water theft could result in a fine of 300 *soles*, but if the thief does not have money, he can pay with labour. People know this, we explain it in the meetings.

Before the new Water Resources Law was passed, Miguel had been invited to Lima to discuss the law proposal and to give his opinion. However, the arguments that he and other representatives from the Andean highlands presented were not taken into account. 'In Lima they look at us like *cholos*', he said, meaning that highlanders are discriminated against and seen as someone in-between the categories of indigenous and mestizo, rural and urban. *Cholo* is often used pejoratively in the cities about indigenous persons who are seen as 'unsuccessful' in becoming urban mestizos (de la Cadena 2000).

An important part of work in the *Junta* was to elaborate project proposals and apply for funding from the regional government in order to improve the hydraulic infrastructure. Miguel was also asked to attend meetings and events organised by commissions; to inform people about the Water Resources Law; to make inspections and give his opinions on construction plans, or to mediate in conflicts. He travelled several days a week in order to visit the 31 water users commissions in Colca Valley, sometimes accompanied by the secretary Monica or the accountant Sara. Since farmers work all day out in the fields, their meetings are usually held in the early morning (6 a.m.) or late at night (starting at 8 p.m.). Many of the villages were located several hours' travel away from Chivay, and Miguel usually used public transport. Therefore, he often had to get up in the middle of the night, and sometimes he had to spend the night away from home. In order to inspect springs, ponds and canals, he often had to walk for several hours in the mountains. In spite of the arduous travels and inconvenient working hours, he loved his job, and he was widely respected among the farmers who appreciated his honesty, efforts and modest way of being.

In April 2011, I was invited to join Miguel on a trip to a water users commission in Llanca village. Although Llanca is located in Choco district in the province of Castilla, the commission belongs to the *Junta* of Colca Valley. After taking the 4 a.m. bus from Chivay to Cabanaconde, Miguel and I climbed up on the cargo bed of a pickup truck that drove down the many curves of a dusty road to the riverbed in the deep Colca Canyon. Accompanied by two men from Llanca, we crossed the bridge in Soro and started to climb a steep path. Half way, we were given mules to ride the last part up to the village. When we finally reached Llanca at noon, the commission's meeting had already begun three hours before. After a short rest in the municipal building, where we were served sweet *chicha* (maize brew) to quench our thirst, the leader of the commission introduced us to the members. They were in the middle of a heated debate about a mine called Paula, owned by the Cedimin mining company. The mine was located about 20 km from the village, but the villagers explained that the mine's tunnels cut the underground water veins, affecting Llanca's supply of irrigation water. Many springs had already dried out, and the farmers explained that 'the fields are sad'. They had measured the volume of water that was missing, and now they wanted to demand that the mine should replace this water. The farmers told me this in the meeting after I had introduced myself and spoken about my research project, which focused on water scarcity and climate change. Understandably, the people in Llanca did not seem very worried about the changes in the climate because the mine was a much more direct cause of their water shortages.

Miguel had been invited to talk about the Water Resources Law, the water tariffs and the role of the *Junta*. Since the mine was the most urgent concern of the villagers, he started to talk about how the changes in regulations had allowed the mine to start its operations. Under the earlier General Water Law, the *Juntas* gave their opinion about the granting of water use rights to mines, he explained, but according to the new Water Resources Law, the ALA decides without asking the opinion of the *Junta*. This mine had received a permission from the ALA of Camaná in the downstream coastal area. However, the mine is located within the jurisdiction of ALA Colca-Siguas-Chivay, and the application should be decided by them. Miguel suggested that they demand to see the environmental impact report that was submitted to ALA Camaná, and that they should demand compensation. He explained that all mines are obliged to finance projects of social compensation that benefit the local communities. One of the farmers commented that the mine did not give them any benefits; it only took their water and brought more poverty. Miguel repeatedly promised that they would get support from the *Junta* in their fight against the mine and in their demands for compensation and social benefits. Miguel explained that the *Junta* has 31 children (the commissions) and 15 grandchildren (the committees), and both in words and action, Miguel wanted to convince the farmers that the *Junta* took good care of their 'children'. However, as they all knew too well, against big actors like the mining companies, they could not do much.

Later that year, the villagers of Llanca organised protest marches in Arequipa city, and, supported by the *Junta*, they presented their complaints to the president of the regional government. A delegation also had meetings with the mining company. In the end, however, nothing came of this. Every time I met the leader of Llanca's water users commission in Chivay, he said that they would continue their fight. When I returned two years later, Miguel complained that the mine had mocked the people in Llanca – *la mina se ha burlado de ellos*. As it turned out, the farmers had good reasons not to care about climate change: not only had the mining company denied responsibility for the water scarcity in Llanca, but they had also blamed global warming for the dry springs. In 2013, Cedimin was bought up by Buenaventura mining company, which one year later closed the Paula mine due to low profitability and lack of agreements with local communities.[5]

In the meeting in April 2011, Miguel explained to the farmers that the Water Resources Law is 'made by the big', and it does not take the opinion of the *Juntas* into account. Even if they do not like the law, however, they have to adapt their practices to it. After a late lunch, Miguel acted as an arbitrator in a case concerning alleged water theft. A married couple was accused of stealing water, because they had used some water from a canal to irrigate a new potato field without having applied for a permission and without having paid the irrigation tariff to the water users commission. The couple maintained their innocence and refused to pay the fine. After the meeting with Miguel, however, they agreed to pay a reduced fine. We see that there is a clear asymmetry in the *Junta*'s mandate and power to influence the distribution of water. Although the *Junta* has the power to sanction individual farmers for 'stealing' water, it has no means of sanctioning mining companies for large-scale water appropriation. Boelens (2009) has noted that the neoliberal state refuses to actively balance societal injustice, because according to (neo)liberal ideology, all water users are treated as 'equals'. Therefore, peasant and indigenous families are supposed to compete with transnational companies (Boelens 2009: 327).

By calling the commissions 'children', the *Junta* consolidated its paternalistic and caring power in the valley. Miguel acted as an intermediary, or broker and translator, between the farmers, the ALA and the law. He had the status and power of an engineer who cared, yet through his careful attention to relationships between water users, to farmers' concerns and complaints against the mine, and their doubts about the law, he created not only understanding but also compliance with rules and regulations. In the regulation of Majes canal, he was also acting as a broker between farmers, the ALA and Autodema.

The social life of valve regulation

The amount of water that is released from the Condoroma dam and directed into the Majes canal in the Tuti intake, is highly regulated. The amounts are decided in monthly meetings where Autodema, the ALA and the *Juntas* negotiate the distribution of water according to the supply in the dam and the farmers' demands, and the valves in the Majes canal are adjusted to specific flow rates measured in litres per second. In a monthly valve regulation (*regulación de válvulas*), the Autodema engineers inspect the valves in the Majes canal to ensure that the farmers do not use more water than they are allowed. In every *regulación de válvulas*, representatives from the JUVC, the ALA and Autodema have to be present, since the three entities have different roles to fulfil. As the operator of the large-scale infrastructure, Autodema is responsible for the functioning and maintenance of the Majes canal. In the *regulación* their representative has to control the water flow rate (*caudal*) from each valve, adjust the flow according to the amount allocated to each water users commission, and make sure that the canal and the valves are working. In short, the Autodema representative should make sure that the farmers along the canal do not take more water than they are allowed to, and thus ensure that enough water reaches Majes. As representative of all the water users commissions in Colca Valley, the JUVC has to attend the *regulación* in order to defend the rights of the farmers and ensure that the commissions get the water to which they are entitled. Since the ALA represents the state and holds ultimate authority over water in the watershed, its role is to supervise the whole *regulación* and ensure that regulations are followed.

In September 2011, I was invited to join a *regulación* with a group of engineers and technicians: José from the ALA, Jorge from Autodema and Miguel from the JUVC. The driver, Luís, worked at the Autodema water intake station in Tuti. We left Chivay at 4.30 a.m. and after two hours, we reached the district of Cabanaconde, where the inspection began at valve number 21. The engineers measured the water flow rate in the two canals coming from the valve: one canal had 85 litres per second (lps) and the other had 50 lps. The allowed flow rate for this commission was 130 lps, and the engineers agreed that it was not necessary to adjust the valve. After eating breakfast in the village of Cabanaconde, we met Alberto and Roberto – the president and vice-president of one of the water users commissions. Bringing two bottles of soda, which we shared, they came with us to the next water out-take, where they opened a padlock to grant access to two valves. Luís and Alberto used sticks to measure the height of the water coming out of the valve through a standard size triangular hydraulic outlet, and Jorge measured the length in centimetres and calculated the flow rate by consulting a chart. The flow rate was too low in both valves. Alberto and Roberto complained that 'the water is decreasing' because of algae blocking the flow through the valve, and asked the engineers for a solution. The engineers discussed how the valve could be moved to a better location, but in order to do this, Autodema would have to stop the flow of water in the canal in a so-called 'water cut' (*corte de agua*). However, they had already had three water cuts this year in order to do repairs and maintenance work and could not cut the water again until next year. Jorge admitted that other villages had also complained, asking Autodema to 'not send so much algae'. There is more algae this year because of the warmer climate, he explained. Previously, workers in the Tuti water intake removed all the algae before the water entered the Majes canal, but now it was too hard due to the large quantities. Luís confirmed that the algae flows down the Colca River 'like blankets, and that one of the workers in Tuti had gone crazy because of the algae and now they call him '*locoalgas*'. The growth of algae is only one of the climate change effects in Colca Valley; a more serious problem is the changing rainy season, decreasing water supplies from glaciers and springs, and stronger heat, which increases the need for irrigation water and makes farming more difficult. Some farmers from Cabanaconde have acquired a piece of the irrigated land in Majes, and Roberto told us that his brother had a small farm close to Villa El Pedregal. It turned out that José knew him: José's cousin was the son-in-law of Roberto's brother. 'We are family, then', Roberto said, and José promised to visit him the next time he came to Cabanaconde.

Back in the village, Alberto wanted to discuss some issues with the engineers, and invited us to a small shop where he bought three big bottles of beer. He served beer in a glass and invited all the engineers to drink with him. In the Andes, social relationships are strengthened through sharing food and drink in sessions where everyone drinks from the same glass, one at a time, and acknowledges each other by respectful toasting as well as giving a few drops to the earth mother (see for example Allen 1988). The glass went around while he talked about recent problems in his commission. Although Alberto had tried to improve the water distribution, some farmers complained that they had been allocated less water. Especially one man was always bothering him – 'he makes my life impossible' – and Alberto admitted that he wanted to withdraw from his position. The engineers advised him to call a meeting to explain the problem for everyone and to invite a representative from the authorities. Alberto bought another round and they agreed to have the meeting in a month's time, and that Miguel from the *Junta* and a representative from the ALA should be present to support him.

The inspection continued, valve by valve, while the engineers were telling each other jokes and laughing. Some valves had a meter which showed the flow rate, while in others the engineers had to use sticks, measuring tape and the aforementioned chart. Sometimes, they measured by simply 'looking': jokingly, they called this the 'eye-meter' (*ojímetro*). All the results were carefully written down. If the water flow was lower or higher than what was allocated, they adjusted it. Miguel was the keeper of all the keys to the valves (the presidents of the commissions also had keys), but in some places the padlocks had been changed, which meant that they had to destroy them. In one valve, the flow rate was 30 lps higher than permitted, so they destroyed the padlock to adjust the flow via eye measure. Miguel said that they always had problems with this particular water users commission: 'They don't show respect; they destroy the padlocks and increase the water flow. The ALA should sanction them, but they don't.' At one point, Miguel and José disappeared behind the bushes to look for a cactus fruit that was in season. While they were gone, Jorge said to me: 'We are supposed to be enemies, but we seem more like friends.' He was particularly referring to José, who was often distracted from his supervisory duty because he was concerned with making and maintaining relations of friendship. However, in the weeks to come, it became clear to me that this was not a one-time incident of socialising; the statement also revealed the degree to which engineers who worked in different entities were socially entangled.

After checking valve number 6 in Yanque, we went to see the president of a commission because the engineers had promised to discuss some matters with him. At his house, we stumbled upon a farewell party for a couple who had got married the day before. The president and his wife were godparents for the couple, and they served us huge glasses of *chicha* while the *huayno* music played in the background. Afterwards, it was hard to continue the inspection of the last five valves. After eating dinner in Chivay, the engineers went to a bar to drink beer. They were joined by two engineers who worked in a World Bank programme for the modernisation of irrigation, and by another engineer who was employed in another state-sponsored development programme and who also was the son-in-law of José's godfather.

Management of water and hydraulic infrastructure takes place within social encounters and relationships, which in the Andes are constituted and consolidated through the sharing of food and drink. The obligation to accept whatever you are offered and to reciprocate in one way or another is extremely strong. Therefore, the formal 'division of power' between the institutions in terms of regulatory matters is seldom transferred neatly to on-the-ground regulations. In this case, the overlap of social and professional relationships implied that boundaries between institutions were often blurred and confrontations were avoided. In the relationships between engineers and farmers, however, the sharing of food, drink and advice were asymmetrical, and often strengthened the asymmetries of power that exist between farmers and state officials, who often are people with higher education and in privileged positions. Among most farmers in Colca Valley, the figure of the engineer invokes mixed feelings of awe and submissive anxiety. However, not all engineers are the same; they differ in social background, local knowledge and in their relationships and dealings with farmers. The MACON engineers were foreigners or mestizos from the Peruvian urban coast without any knowledge of the social conditions and cultural values in Colca Valley, and hence they aroused both admiration and fear. When someone born in Colca returns after having studied and worked in the city, like Miguel and Gabriel, they can more easily gain the farmers' trust. Nevertheless, they have to always show their worthiness and earn people's trust by accepting invitations to drink and keeping promises.

Conclusion

In this chapter, I have extended care to include some of the engineers' work practices, like the careful maintenance of relationships among water users. Understanding 'good care' as a 'persistent tinkering in a world full of complex ambivalence and shifting tensions' (Mol et al. 2010: 14), we can see that the ways the engineers tinkered with the padlocks, measuring sticks, valves, forms and documents, were part of caring about doing a good job. Also, the ways they wrote down numbers, talked to people, gave advice, accepted drinks and made friendly relationships, were different modes of caring. Similarly, I observed how Miguel and others carefully inspected sources and canals, and analysed problems and documents before making decisions, and how they would explain rules and regulations to farmers and other water users. Through these actions, they were not only aiming to take care of the water, but also the water users, by trying to enable a fair water distribution within the limitations of the law and structural inequalities. However, they seemed to be unable to control and sanction the most powerful users like mines and agribusiness companies, who were also the largest potential perpetrators. Furthermore, the care provided by the *Junta* was a bit ambiguous: the explicit aim was to improve the water flow, distribution and access for farmers, yet by convincing them about the necessity to comply with the law and pay the tariff, the care was also an exercise in paternalistic control and care-power. As an intermediary who carefully translated and mediated, Miguel allowed for multiplicity in practices at local levels, yet as he helped people to apply for user licences and other documents, the effect was rather to create standardisation, consolidate state control and produce singularity. Nevertheless, the following chapters will show more complexity, as the notion of care will be further extended to include ponds, canals and tractors, which are in constant need of repair, and springs, lakes and mountains, which are enacted as living sentient beings.

Infrastructure is often associated with the sense of shaping modern society and creating progress (Larkin 2013). As projects of modernity, however, large-scale infrastructures cannot be seen as separate from coloniality, which is not only the heritage of colonialism, but constitutive of modernity (Mignolo 2000; Escobar 2007; Maldonado-Torres 2007). In the next chapter, I will discuss the coloniality inherent in the modern quest for progress in Majes, where land was conquered and transformed by the implementation of new technology and the labour of settlers and workers.

2
Colonising the Desert

> The Special Project Majes-Siguas, today [known as] Majes District, generous and friendly land of singular beauty because of her soil, earlier desert and today green savannah, the enviable climate that makes her own [people] and strangers consider it a greenhouse, land considered as the promised land where milk and honey flow, thanks to the arrival of the water and the effort of the first settlers who came to these pampas, until it came to be considered today as the leading milk-producing district of the south region of the country and leader in agro-exports.
>
> (Zamalloa 2013: 1)

Far away from the water springs and the Condoroma dam in the highlands, and unaware of the trouble caused by the Majes canal in Colca Valley, farmers in Majes praise the water that arrives in the desert, offering possibilities for progress.[1] People living in Majes call the Majes canal their 'umbilical cord' since it provides them with the vital force that they totally depend on. Before the canal was built, the arid and flat pampa of Majes, located between the Majes River and the Siguas River, was not populated by humans. People settled here to irrigate and cultivate the land after the water started to flow in the grid of canals spreading out in the desert in a carefully planned pattern of lines and squares. During the time I lived in Villa El Pedregal, the main urban centre in Majes, I visited some of the settlers in the farms and listened to the stories told by them and their now grown-up children about their experience of coming to a new place, where 'there was nothing'. They all built up new lives from scratch, aspiring to a better future in the 'land of milk and honey', where the expectations of work, income and business were great. It was not always easy, however, as the following story will show. In the marketplace 'New Hope' (*La Nueva Esperanza*) in Villa El Pedregal, I met Martina who was born in Colca Valley. I often stopped by her market stall to drink mango juice, listen to music from Colca and chat. As the daughter of a farmer who came with the third group of settlers, Martina has first-hand experience of the hardships of making a living in Majes. In 1990, when she was 10 years old, Martina travelled from Achoma village in Colca Valley to her parents' new farm in 'section C' in the MIP. She vividly remembered the night that they walked from the bus to the new farm, under a full moon and in a suffocating heat she was not used to. They walked through 'section B', where the fields were already sown, to 'section C', which was still a desert. Along the way, she saw baskets with lights out in the fields. Her father told her that they were not baskets, but houses of straw mats where people lived. She was thirsty when they arrived to the farmstead, but she was surprised to find that the water coming out of the tap was warm and tasteless, and very different from the cold and sweet water that she was used to from the highland streams. Her parents had moved there a year earlier to prepare the land and build a house, and she and her brothers had stayed with their grandparents in Achoma while they waited. They had been imagining how Majes would be like: green fields and alfalfa growing metres high. When they arrived, however, they encountered a different reality than they had seen in propaganda films on the TV screen in the village shop. The first months had been very difficult, as they didn't know people and they had to walk far to buy supplies. Since fruit rotted quickly in the heat, they got used to eating dry food, like the dried roasted corn *canchitas*. She walked through the desert to school, and on the way home she used to hitchhike with the milk trucks that collected milk cans from the farms. Her parents woke up every day at 3 a.m. to put out the sprinklers to irrigate the alfalfa fields and milk the cows by hand. After a few years her mother's hands grew stiff from exhaustion, and they finally bought a milking machine. According to the advice given by the agricultural engineers and the experts from Europe, her father bought good cows, of foreign race and with big udders. A cow named Antonia had an udder so huge that it touched the ground. But her first offspring died. According to Martina, they lacked technical support and guidance:

> 'We didn't know how to do it, it was different from the highlands. When the cows were ready to give birth, [we] should help getting the offspring out, but [my parents] didn't know that. In the highlands the cows give birth by themselves, they don't need any help. But these [were different], that's why the first calves died. Only one calf survived.'

Her parents dedicated themselves solely to work; they never went out to parties, and she grew up in that environment and learned to work hard.

Her father was not only a farmer, but also a merchant who sold groceries from a market stall in Villa El Pedregal. When his potato harvest failed three times in a row and the prices fell, he fell into debt. He is still carrying these debts until today, Martina told me: 'The interest is very high; you pay off and you pay off, but you never finish paying the debt.' She continued: 'People suffer here also. Not everyone has access to credit and capital to work, they have debts.' Seeing how her father struggled with debt, and how almost all farmers and merchants depended on credit to work, some of them taking loans from two or three different banks, she decided to start a business without any bank loans and credits. Her business has grown little by little, and today – ten years later – she and her husband are the owners of a market stall in Villa El Pedregal where they sell juice and sandwiches, and also CDs and DVDs with popular Peruvian music. Chatting with Martina over breakfast at her stall, I mentioned that people in Colca talked about people in Majes as 'rich'. She agreed: 'Yes, there they think that we have money. I see how they look at me: "She got money, therefore she is aloof and does not talk to us" … and I'm there all shy! They don't know that we also suffer. I live off my work!'

This chapter will show that Majes is not only a 'leader in agro-exports', which is taking the lead in achieving economic growth and development in Peru. I will show that Majes as a place to live and work has emerged – and is still emerging – as a heterogeneous assemblage of soil, water, technology, labour, capital, seeds, cows, farm buildings, factories, and financial institutions – in coordinated relationships that are being mediated by governmental policies and international agreements. The relationships between these entities are not symmetrical in terms of power, however, but increasingly unequal. Since the start in 1983, these inequalities have emerged 'from heterogeneous processes through which people, labor, sentiments, plants, animals, and life-ways are converted into resources for various projects of production' (Bear et al. 2015). During the last four decades, Majes has become the home of thousands of people with diverse backgrounds, among whom a few have prospered while many still struggle to survive. There is not one singular and complete history of Majes, but different and partially overlapping stories told from various positions and perspectives. As inequalities are increasing, it is important to remember that inequality is not only about economic differences, but is embedded both in the intersectionality of social class, race and gender (Strønen and Ystanes 2018) and in the 'sticky materiality' (Tsing 2005: 1) of soil, water, technology, alfalfa seeds, cows and milk. The chapter will also discuss the ambiguities of dependency and risk, which I suggest are inherent to life in Majes. After decades of neoliberal policies, farmers have become increasingly dependent on the global food market, which is associated with volatility and risk. At the same time, life in the irrigated desert is totally dependent on the supply of water from the Majes canal; the water that facilitates the hetereogenous connections from which Majes emerges. These connections are not symmetrical in the sense that they are all equal in terms of power of causation; water is the force that moves, enables and facilitates other entities and relations that are hierarchically interconnected. Like the unidirectional flow of the Amazon River that shaped the rubber economy, giving it a specific pattern or form (Kohn 2013: 160–3), the vital force of the water flow in Majes facilitates the dairy- and agro-export economy in Majes.

In recent years, however, in the wake of climate change, drought, earthquakes, and risks associated with the 30-year-old crumbling canal, in addition to claims from people in the headwaters, they have become more aware of their vulnerability. Hence, rather than only portraying Majes as a leader that is 'advancing' and distancing itself from the poorer highland provinces, I emphasise the importance of seeing Majes as inherently dependent on the water supply from the headwaters.

Figure 3 Farmland in the Majes Irrigation Project where drip irrigation has just been installed. The owner planned to sow quinoa on this land in 2014. A few cows are grazing on a small piece of grassland, and behind is the arid and uncultivated pampa of Majes.

Land for those who work it: the pioneer settlers

> You forged yourself between stone and stone,
> And grew with a view to triumph,
> Transforming the desert into beautiful fields,
> With hope, love and freedom.
>
> Great men are your strength,
> Ranchers and farmers,
> Who are cultivating the furrow of progress,
> With the effort of Villa el Pedregal.
>
> First two verses of 'Himno de Majes' ('Hymn of Majes')
> by Edgar Zamalloa (Zamalloa 2013: 346)

At the entrance of Villa El Pedregal – the main urban centre of Majes – you are met by the impressive statue of General Juan Velasco Alvarado, the president who started the execution of the Special Project Majes-Siguas in 1971. After a coup-de-état in 1968, Velasco's military regime – inspired by Marxist ideas of equality and redistribution of resources – aimed to bring Peru out of feudalism and poverty and into an era of modernity and progress. As a part of this effort, the MIP was presented as a programme of regional development aimed at creating agricultural and industrial production and employment. *Los colonos* – the settlers – played a key role in this regional development, and especially in the first phase of colonising the desert through irrigation and cultivation. In today's Majes, the settlers are praised for their hard work and sacrifice in monuments, speeches, poems and songs, like in Zamalloa's 'Himno de Majes', where they are represented as male mestizo pioneers and brave frontier men. In the main urban centre Villa El Pedregal, the monument of the settler – *el Monumento al Colono* – has a central place: a statue of a male farmer holding a milk can. Although female settlers undoubtedly did a great part of the work on the first farms, they have not been given a statue on their own; instead a woman is included in the Cow Monument – *el Monumento a la Vaca* – which is a statue of a cow being hand-milked by a milkmaid, placed in front of the water administration office, the ALA.

The MIP was implemented soon after the 1969 agrarian reform, which came after years of peasant struggles and land invasions, and dramatically changed relations of property and power in Peru. Four decades earlier, the Peruvian Marxist José Carlos Mariátegui (2001 [1928]) identified the unequal distribution of land property as the main problem in Peru, where powerful hacienda owners (*hacendados*) controlled all the resources, including water and the labour of indigenous people within their territories. Before 1969, 3.9 per cent of the population controlled 56 per cent of the land (Seligmann 1995). In 1968, the left-wing Velasco regime started to nationalise land, water and industry. Posters with slogans such as 'Land without masters' put forth an emancipatory vision of a 'new Peru' (Cant 2012: 3). Hence, the MIP was from the start constructed in a political climate with visions of national progress for all Peruvians (Collier 1978). In less than a decade, Velasco's land reform succeeded in ending the dominant power of the *hacendados* and introducing a system of cooperative farms (Collier 1978). However, many peasants who had been active in reclaiming their land from the haciendas, found that the reform constricted their autonomy and were reluctant to join the cooperatives and thus enter new relations of dependence (Smith 1989). The agrarian cooperatives were largely managed by public-sector technocrats and bureaucrats and soon encountered huge problems: corruption, clientelistic relationships and internal conflicts (Hunefeldt 1997). Lack of planning, technical support and training were some of the other reasons that the reform mainly failed (Rénique 1991). The shortcomings of the reform contributed to the massive increase in migration from the highlands to the urban coast. A major part of the current population in Majes come from the regions of Puno, Cusco and Apurimac, where the agrarian reform had profound effects on peasant livelihoods.

However, before the MIP was completed and before the land was distributed to the first farmers, the economic policies started to change. The turn toward neoliberal policies began with the military government of Morales Bermúdez (1975–80), which after pressure from the United States and the International Monetary Fund (IMF), started to reduce the role of the state and enhance that of the market (Klarén 2000: 359). This policy was strengthened under the second presidency of Fernando Belaúnde Terry (1980–85), who, backed by a team with backgrounds at the University of Chicago, implemented the free-market doctrines of Milton Friedman, removed tariff protection and encouraged private foreign investment (Klarén 2000: 374). A new approach of 'agrarian developmentalism' implied that state subsidies were eliminated and the focus of policy makers changed from land distribution and social justice to a concern with efficiency and higher output rates. Following a worldwide trend, liberal technocrats believed that the only way to increase productivity was through private ownership (Hunefeldt 1997: 112–13). The establishment of the family farms on 5-hectare parcels in Majes coincided with a change towards privatisation of land and the dismantling of the associative enterprises from the agrarian reform.

The first group of 592 settlers (*colonos*) started to cultivate their land in 1983, after the water arrived in the pampa (Zamalloa 2013). The land was distributed through a state-sponsored lottery. Of the 5,000 people who applied for the programme, only 914 were declared suitable, and these were categorised according to different classes: landless peasants, agricultural workers, smallholding farmers and professionals (mostly agronomists, but also doctors, lawyers and engineers). Then, a certain number of applicants were selected from each category through a lottery (*sorteo*), and the lucky ones had the opportunity to buy 5 hectares of land, which was considered a basic family unit, at a subsidised price with a loan from the state-owned Agrarian Bank (Zamalloa 2013). This land had to be worked from scratch, and sacrifice, hard work and suffering has a central place in the narratives of the first settlers. Those who succeeded tell stories to convey their strong will to endure the solitary and arid environment of stones, dust, wind, the hard manual labour, and the stubborn dedication to making the land productive.

Juan Rondón is famous in Majes for being the very first settler who arrived in Majes, when there was still nothing there, not even water. He used to work as a farmer in Arequipa, where he rented land. Juan enjoyed the farm work very much and dreamt of working on land that was his own. He applied for the programme at the Ministry of Agriculture and after winning the lottery, he formally received his property in July 1982. He was 42 years old when he came to his assigned property in 'section A' on 28 October 1982, two months before the water came. 'There was nothing here and we had to bring supplies', he told me when I interviewed him in 2014. His wife stayed behind in Arequipa with six of their seven children, and they came two years later, when the first school in Majes was built. Meanwhile, and together with his oldest son and a group of hired workers, Juan prepared the land by removing stones, levelling, and preparing the subsoil. They started work at 5 a.m. every day. After taking a break from 10 a.m. to 2 p.m. because of the strong winds, they worked again from 2 p.m. until nightfall. He was the first to sow alfalfa in March 1983 and was proud to show his already green fields when President Belaúnde arrived on 28 May 1983 to inaugurate the 'mother canal' (Canal Madre). At that time, there were only three settlers living on their land, and Belaúnde had the honour of opening the water hydrants and the sprinklers on the other two farms. All the settlers started by sowing alfalfa, a plant that nourishes the land with nitrate and is used as cattle fodder. In the first months, they received help from foreign engineers who gave them advice and technical support. Engineers from Israel, who have gained a reputation in Peru as world experts in the irrigation of arid areas, brought irrigation equipment and taught them about agrarian techniques and technologies: how to clear the terrain with horses, how to apply the fertilisers, how to sow, and how to irrigate.[2] Each family farm was connected to the grid of water canals and pipes, and the farmers learnt new ways of irrigating the land with modern technology: pivot, sprinkler, and drip irrigation systems. Although everyone ideally should install drip irrigation, which is the most water-efficient but also the most expensive system, most of the first farms installed sprinkler systems. A total area of 15,800 hectares was irrigated during the first phase of the project, and most of this land was divided into family farms. In addition, there are some agribusiness companies, for example the Pampa Baja Group, that own 1,288 hectares of land, where they installed drip irrigation from the start.

According to 1979 regulations, all water users had to be organised in committees, commissions and boards (*juntas*), according to different irrigation districts, and these were dependent on the National Water Directory of the Ministry of Agriculture. These regulations were supplementing the 1969 General Water Law, in which water was nationalised and water management was centralised and brought under state control (Oré and Rap 2009: 36). As the first settler, Juan took the initiative to create the first Irrigation Committee, named after their irrigation channel '2R La Colina', on 18 December 1984. The Water Users Board of the Pampa of Majes, JUPM, was founded in 1988. In 2014 there were 2,600 farmers organised in the JUPM, divided into 26 users' commissions (*comisiones de usuarios*). Each commission managed the canals in its area; they had their own budgets and supervisors and set the irrigation tariff according to their investments. Farmers pay for the volume of water, but there are no gauges, instead the volume in cubic metres is calculated by land size and water flow (measured in litres per second). In 2014, JUPM had 60 employees, including 30 water allocators (*tomeros*), who opens the gates of the ponds, each of which contains 20,000 cubic metres of water. The *tomeros* used to work for the commissions, but today they receive their payment directly from the JUPM. Since water management is of key importance in Majes,

Autodema and the public water administration also have offices in the MIP area, in addition to their main offices in Arequipa city.

Searching for life and making a home

When I first came to Majes in June 2011, it was to visit the office of the water administration, the ALA, where I had scheduled interviews with several of the administrators, engineers and technicians working there. After a formal interview with the ALA director, who explained to me the various challenges of regulating the Majes-Colca watershed and the changes introduced by the 2009 Water Resources Law, he called José, who I already knew from his visits to Chivay. The director asked him to give me a tour around Majes to show me the area and especially the irrigation infrastructure that makes life in the desert possible. Sitting on the back of the motorcycle that José drove through the desert, I was amazed by how different this landscape was from Colca. In contrast to the tiny fields scattered in the Colca mountains, everything here was large-scale and linear, and it was quite easy to imagine how the canals, ponds and square standard-sized 5-hectare farms had been planned and drawn on a map by architects and engineers, inspired by the ideals of modern statecraft and 'high modernism' (Scott 1998). As I explained in chapter 1, the state is no monolithic and unified entity, but can rather be studied through dispersed and contradictory practices and effects. Nevertheless, the main project and aim of modern national states is to strive towards order and control of territories and populations. Although total control is only an ideal and far from a reality, this ideal has influenced many large-scale projects in the world, including the MIP. Seeing the irrigated and cultivated landscape of Majes, it was almost like a materialisation of the 'striated space' described by Deleuze and Guattari, who also refer to Wittfogel's thesis on the importance of large-scale waterworks for the building of empire:

> the State needs to subordinate hydraulic force to conduits, pipes, embankments, which prevent turbulence, which constrain movement to go from one point to another, and space itself to be striated and measured, which makes the fluid depend on the solid, and flows proceed by parallel, laminar layers. (Deleuze and Guattari 2004 [1980]: 400)

The imprint of squares and lines on the desert landscape became even more obvious when I saw it from the aeroplane a few weeks later, making it clear how this striated space is much easier to oversee and regulate than the diverse small-scale livelihood activities in Colca. The hot, dry and sandy environment was another sharp contrast from the highlands with its cold weather and fresh air. I remembered how my friends in Chivay – who perceived Colca as a healthy place to live – talked about Majes as a potentially bad place, where there was a big risk of being polluted by chemicals and of moral degeneration through greed. The fields of Majes produce a lot more than in Colca because of the warm and stable climate, yet they also have to use a lot more chemical-based pesticides and fertilisers. In Majes, most farmers produce for export, either on contract with an agribusiness company, or selling directly to a intermediary trade agent. In Colca, where most farmers produce for local and regional markets, I often heard references to the farmers in Majes as if all of them were rich. A reason for the growing dissatisfaction expressed by water users in Colca is the fact that farmers in Majes use water coming from the Colca headwaters. They make big money on 'our water', political leaders in Colca would say. I soon discovered, however, that people travelled from Colca to Majes regularly: not only to fix paperwork related to water user rights, but also to visit family, to work and trade, or 'do business'. As one of my interlocutors told me, nostalgically, earlier people used to travel by foot to the fertile Majes river valley, with their mules loaded with salted and dried meat to be bartered for fruit. Today, people go by bus to the irrigated pampa of Majes to make money as seasonal agricultural workers. Some families stay as squatters in the desert while they search for work on the farms, in agro-industry or in the informal economy, looking for 'progress' and what they see as a better life and future for themselves and their children.

Ever since the first *colonos* arrived in 1983, Majes has been populated by people from all over the country. The first out of four population centres (*centro poblado*), Santa Maria de La Colina, was founded on 29 January 1983 by the president of the Senate, who asked the inhabitants for their 'effort and work for its development'.[3] In the following inauguration ceremony, a priest took possession of the land with a cross in his hands and by declaring: 'This is the promised land like the one Jesus prepared for his people' (Zamalloa 2013: 94). Despite the religious rhetoric, however, the MIP is a project born out of modern engineering and science. Both agricultural and urban areas in the MIP were carefully designed by engineers who also designed the Condoroma dam and the Majes canal. However, not everything went as planned. The engineers designed the urban settlements for 40,000 inhabitants, and today's population, an estimated

120,000, is spreading out into the surrounding desert. Since Majes became known as a bustling place of farming, engineering, industry and business, it attracts new people every day who come in search of work and money. The squatter settlements grow at an accelerated speed, causing a sense of 'chaos', which land traffickers are taking advantage of, while the municipality struggles to provide the population with safe drinking water (see chapter 6).

Shortly after I returned to Villa El Pedregal in January 2014, José took me for a visit to the abandoned Water Monument (*el Monumento al Agua*) in the outskirts of Majes. The Water Monument is a large concrete construction that was inaugurated by President Belaúnde in 1984. It was supposed to honour water as a life-giving resource, but was left incomplete and dry, overlooking an area called *la Ciudad Perdida*, 'the Lost City': 'It was all lost, it would no longer be a city', José said, after explaining how the planned 'Majes City' (Ciudad de Majes) could not be built in the designated area after the engineers found out that the soil was shifting and sinking, and not suitable for two-storey buildings. A few buildings with cracked-up walls were left behind and the planned Majes City was moved to the other side, José told me, while pointing towards an extensive area filled with houses, but yet without infrastructure. He proceeded to point out all the sectors that could be seen from the Water Monument and named them: 'There you can see *bloque* 5, that was the first *invasión* (illegal squatting), and after that the *módulo* G in Ciudad Majes.' He also directed my attention to the settler areas where farmers had transformed the desert into fertile soil:

> There is E8, E3, E4, E5, E6, and there is the *zona especializada*, where the university has fields for research, and in the back are B1 and C1, and in the middle B2 and C2; in the back to the right is C3 and below is B4. On the other side we can see the *sección* D: D5, D2, beyond the *panamericana* [highway] is D4 and in the back is D3.

I was amazed by his ability to remember all these letters and numbers, which for me seemed impersonal and random. However, I soon realised that these were names of places that had been settled by farmers in several stages, and that for him, they were place names that he had grown up with.

José arrived in Majes as an 11-year-old boy in 1983 and grew up as the oldest son of a *colono* who worked hard to transform the desert into fertile soil, but then lost his land in the 1990s. Because of a series of misfortunes and 'bad luck', José's father was not able to pay his loan to the bank. The debt accumulated and he was forced to sell the farm. José's three uncles still have their farms, and sometimes José works with his cousins in the fields; he helps to rent machinery, to buy seeds, and to sell the harvest. To make a living, José has worked in all kinds of jobs in different public offices, mainly as a driver or assistant, on temporary contracts. Steady employment is hard to find, and many people try to start businesses of their own. Precariously employed on short-term contracts, José was constantly searching for ways of making money to sustain his family. His sister told me with pride that he was a *buscavida*, in the sense that he is always searching for ways to survive through business, work and income to sustain his family. At the time when we visited the Water Monument, José was considering an offer to collaborate in a business project in the 'Lost City', where extensive areas were being 'invaded' by squatters taking possession of land in order to start small businesses. The idea of José's friend was to set up a brick factory. He did not go forward with this idea, however, but José never lacked business ideas and projects.

A few weeks after the visit to the Water Monument, José and his wife Melissa bought a microbus on credit with the intention of making money in the transport business. After driving the vehicle home from Arequipa City, they asked the local priest to baptise it with holy water. Then, they asked me to be the *madrina* (godmother) of the car, and they asked one of Jose's many friends, who was also the owner of a car repair shop, to be *padrino* (godfather). We brought some accessories as gifts for the car, and a crate of beer. In a ceremony called *t'inka* in the back yard, the *padrino* and I sprinkled beer on the vehicle, so that it should work well and make money for the owners, and afterwards we celebrated by drinking together.[4] After asking for advice from their friends in the public transport section of the municipality, they filed an application to work on one of the new bus routes in Majes City. When they finally obtained permission to put the microbus to work, however, they soon realised that the income was not enough to pay the debt and have a profitable business. They ended up selling the vehicle. To survive as a small-scale 'precarious entrepreneur' in the semi-formal urban economy in Peru is a risky endeavour and the probability of failing is high (see also Stensrud 2017).

Spending a lot of time together with Jose and Melissa, I saw how they were always searching for new ideas to start a business and also making and maintaining a network of relations. 'Friendships are important here', José told me, 'not only knowing people, but friendships; you have to take care of them and cultivate them.' Extensive networks of friends, family and *compadres* are not only a precondition for starting a business, but also to connect to the grid of water pipes. Like most families living outside of the urban centres, José and Melissa were looking for the possibility of getting access to safe water in their house. Since the urban population in Majes expanded beyond the planned urban settlements and into the new settlements in the desert, it is a constant preoccupation to get the municipality to build the infrastructure of water and electricity as fast as possible. People living in the new settlements organise in housing associations and elect leaders who are constantly knocking on doors in the municipality in order to obtain electricity and water. Houses are connected to the grid of water pipes both as a result of collective struggles and individual efforts. Meanwhile, many families take water from the open irrigation canals and boil it before consuming it. Some households, like José and Melissa's, have their own systems of purification, where the water is filtered before it is boiled. Those who live far from the irrigated areas and out in the newly squatted areas, buy water from trucks that come once a week. Those living relatively close to the grid of potable water pipes, without having a formal/legal connection, sometimes find other – informal – ways of connecting, often with the help from personal connections.

In spite of the short history of Majes, the place has not only grown rapidly in terms of numbers, but it has also become a home for thousands of people with diverse background who have come from various parts of Peru. The generation who has grown up here, has grown with the place, and for many years families have also been burying their dead here. In 1998, José's grandmother was buried in a cemetery in the arid outskirts of Majes, where the number of graves was steadily growing. Each year, her husband, children and grandchildren visit the grave on her birthday, and I was invited to join them in 2014, when José's grandfather was 102 years old. After cleaning the grave and decorating it with flowers, they brought a case of beer and sprinkled some drops on the grave, for the grandmother, and on the ground, for the earth-mother. Then they sat in a circle around the grave, sharing bottles of beer, drinking, talking, joking, laughing and advising each other. One of the women commented that the grandmother was watching her children and that she would be glad to see that they were happy and united. Burying and remembering the dead make affective connections to the land and a hinge between the past and the future. Visiting the graveyard and acknowledging the presence of the ancestors' souls and the earth-mother as a sentient being creates a sense of continuity amidst accelerated change.

Majes was seen as a 'promised land', in the sense that peasants got the chance to own their own land and create a better future for themselves. 'A better life' implied not only social mobility, however, but also an elevated status in the hierarchy marked by ideas of ethnicity and 'race'. In one of José's family reunions with his grandfather, parents, uncles, aunts and cousins, they talked about how their lives had changed. When they lived in the Caylloma highlands, they had been the poorest peasant family in the village. The grandparents only had a tiny piece of land and a couple of cows, and they had to work as labourers for others in order to provide for their nine children. When the Majes project opened, all of these children – who were adults by then – registered, and four of the brothers got farms in 'section A'. The brothers' farms were not next to each other, but they helped each other in the work. Instead of hiring help like others did, they joined forces and worked together in all of their fields; 'like in *ayni*', which is a Quechua word that means reciprocal work exchange: in rural communities, *campesinos* (peasants) work in *ayni* on each other's fields in times of sowing and harvesting.[5] José says that they were all dreaming about coming here and changing their lives, and 'to earn another way of being'. When I asked whether they had accomplished this, he said that his grandfather was very pleased by seeing that his sons were doing well, and that 'they are not despised, that they are not treated badly'. Indigenous peasants in the Andes have been oppressed and exploited since their land was colonised and dominated by the owners of large estates, and discrimination based on social class and ideas of race is still a problem in Peru.

In Colca Valley, peasants were never dominated by large haciendas (Guillet 1992), however they still have experienced marginalisation. The reasons that many people from Colca have migrated to Majes are mainly related to poverty and socio-economic inequality, and in later years also the marketisation of agriculture and climate change. In Majes, they hope for better lives: more income opportunities, better education and careers for their children, and higher social standing. In Peru, geographical and social mobility is inherently connected to cultural identity and ethnic classification and marginalisation. Since the Spanish colonisation, the Andean highlands have been marginalised, while economic and political power has been concentrated on the coast. The Peruvian project of modernisation is intrinsically tied up with geographies and hierarchies of 'race', culture and class, and linked to the desire to escape a stigmatised indigenous past (de la Cadena 2000; Ødegaard 2010). This escape requires hard work since ethnic identification is closely linked to socio-economic status. As part of the reformation of Peruvian society, the Velasco government officially replaced the ethnic and racial term *indio* (Indian) by the class-related term *campesino* (peasant). However, this was not enough to uproot racial discrimination (Seligmann 1995). The owners of 5-hectare farms in the MIP call themselves 'farmers' (*agricultores*) and 'smallholders' (*minifundistas*). Conceptually, they distance themselves from the 'peasants' (*campesinos*) in the highlands (*sierra*). In Peru, 'peasants' is a historically charged term with cultural connotations of indigeneity coloured by racist assumptions of 'backwardness'. In 1955, Eric Wolf described peasants as those aiming for subsistence, not reinvestment, while a farmer, in his definition, 'views agriculture as a business enterprise' (Wolf 1955: 454). The farmers who have moved to the MIP from the *sierra* work hard to escape the stigma of peasanthood by taking part in modern agriculture and progress.

In Peru, 'modernity' has, since independence, been based on a vision of 'order and progress' modelled after a European ideal. The ultimate goal is to become like Europe, and the Peruvian government also asked European countries for support and expertise in order to develop a modern economy. Hence, in addition to a state-sponsored access to new land, the farmers in Majes also received support and help from engineers and modern technology from abroad, particularly from Israel. In the period 1984–92, the farmers of 'section A' in the MIP were supported by the EEC (European Economic Community), and received financial help, technical assistance, technology, equipment and machinery, breeding animals and training (Zamalloa 2013: 57). Among the technical solutions were artificial insemination of cattle and a factory for production of concentrated cattle fodder. Settlers that I interviewed often emphasised the external funding and technology that they received, and talked with pride about the modern irrigation technology from Israel, and the genetically improved cows from Holland and Germany. The MIP became a flagship of modern agriculture and progress, led by proud pioneers and hard-working farmers who owned their own land. To show his support, President Belaúnde came to visit Majes not just once, but three times: first, to open the 'mother canal' in 1983, then to inaugurate the Water Monument in 1984, and finally, in 1985, after having inaugurated the Condoroma dam, he came to inspect the agrarian development of the first 3,000 hectares that had been irrigated (Zamalloa 2013: 77).

Since the first settlers arrived, they have been encouraged and pushed to transform themselves into business-minded entrepreneurs (*empresarios*). As Zamalloa writes in the first chapter of the book on Majes:

> One of the principal effects that is achieved in the development process of the Majes Project is the change of attitude and mentality of the settler, who stops working in the traditional way and transforms into an entrepreneur (*empresario*), thanks to the determined participation of the European Economic Community (EEC) through the agreements of technology transfers that have been achieved. (Zamalloa 2013: 6–7)

The discourse of entrepreneurship as the way to end poverty and hasten progress intensified in the 1990s. The promotion of entrepreneurship was concomitant with the neoliberal turn away from agrarian reform. However, not all settler stories are stories of success; not all the settlers were as resourceful as Juan, and some came from very poor backgrounds, ending up with other life trajectories. In the process of transforming their family farms into businesses, many farmers struggle to survive and sustain their families through increasing their self-exploitation and by combining farming with incomes from other sources, and thus the difference between peasants and farmers is not so clear today (Stensrud 2019a). Many of the farmers in Majes lost their land during the years of market liberalisation and price volatility, which took off in the 1990s. Juan said that he had seen many of his fellow farmers lose their land, and that of the first group of settlers, only half were left in 2014. The next section will take a closer look at what happened during the neoliberal decade that started in 1990.

Neoliberalism, volatility and precarity

> It was supposed to be an agro-industrial project. The alfalfa was just to prepare the terrain; it was transitory. But the farmers have gotten used to it and they have continued with alfalfa [cow fodder]. And who benefits from milk production? Gloria! And the farmers? Instead of taking risks and orienting the crop to exports, they continue with alfalfa and cattle, and they are satisfied with what Gloria pays for the milk every two weeks. The cultural level here is very low. People don't accept change.
>
> (Daniel, hydraulic engineer, 6 February 2014)

Daniel, who had worked as an engineer in Majes for 30 years, told me this a bit dejectedly during a conversation in his office, and thus revealed some of the tensions that have arisen in Majes during the past three decades. The purpose of the MIP was to develop an industrial export-oriented agriculture, but many – farmers, engineers and politicians alike – complain that this has not happened. Many of the engineers and political authorities I talked to emphasised the importance of taking risks, thinking like entrepreneurs and taking advantage of the newest irrigation technology available. They seemed to blame the farmers for being too traditional and afraid of change. The farmers themselves, on the other hand, knew too many examples of farmers who had invested all their money and taken up loans to sow cash crops and then had lost everything because the price had plummeted. The broad availability of high-interest credits and loans, in combination with the fluctuating product prices on the 'free market', as well as a lack of coordinated planning and subsidies in the agrarian sector, have led to a situation in which most farmers in Majes describe agriculture as a 'lottery' where one can either win or lose everything (Stensrud 2019a). In everyday conversations, farmers talk a lot about how the prices of their products increase and decrease. This situation is in many ways a result of the neoliberal structural adjustment programmes that were promoted by the IMF and the World Bank in the 1980s and 1990s. These programmes dismantled national agricultural agencies and eliminated subsidies and price guarantees throughout the global South (Sage 2013).

When Alan García from APRA (Alianza Popular Revolucionaria Americana) was elected president in 1985, he refused to abide by IMF rules. He tried to reverse the process of neoliberalisation through a 'heterodox' economic policy, which meant more state intervention, price control, and an attempt to appeal to the popular classes and to solicit participation of local capital (Pastor and Wise 1992). During the first two years, agriculture benefited from a stronger urban demand, as well from the greater availability of credit. Those who gained were not the poor peasants in the highlands, but the 'producers who were the most integrated into the market' (Klarén 2000: 389), like the farmers in Majes. The first settlers tend to remember the short-term economic boom in agricultural prices in 1985–7, although in the end this mini-boom proved unsustainable (Crabtree 2002: 138). When García in 1987 announced the nationalisation of banks (Velasco had already nationalised 80 per cent of them, and García would take the remaining 20 per cent), the private sector began to disinvest. In 1988, inflation soared to almost 7000 per cent, and the ensuing devaluation and increased prices and taxes was not enough to restrain inflation (Klarén 2000: 393–5). The result was a deep economic and social crisis, with rising unemployment, shortages of staples and malnutrition among children, at the same time as the war between the military and the Shining Path guerrillas intensified (Klarén 2000).[6]

Alberto Fujimori, an agricultural engineer of Japanese descent and founder of the populist right-wing party Cambio 90, was elected president in 1990.[7] He moved quickly to implement a radical shock treatment of higher interest rates and taxes, as well as a slashing of price subsidies and social spending: this became known as the 'Fuji shock'. As a result, food prices rose 500 per cent and gasoline prices soared 3000 per cent. The shock was followed by deregulation of markets, massive privatisation and incentives for international investment (Klarén 2000; Crabtree 2002). Fujimori's neoliberal reforms were the most rapid and radical programme of structural adjustment in Latin America (Solfrini 2001). In agrarian policy, the neoliberal restructuring of the state in the 1990s entailed a total reversal of the agrarian reform; the cancellation of all forms of subsidies and special credit to farmers, and the dismantling of the state apparatus that had dealt with agrarian reform and rural development. The last vestiges of protectionist agrarian laws were removed, allowing unlimited private property (Mayer 2009). The 1995 Land Law (Ley de tierras) promoted the titling of individual land ownership, abolished the previous upper limits on personal landholding and allowed the state to sell land currently in public ownership. Hernando de Soto, director of the free-market think-tank Instituto Libertad y Democracia, was Fujimori's adviser and his ideas of individual title deeds as key to development were influential (see also chapter 6). The new law opened the way to the capitalisation of agriculture by enabling title-holders to raise mortgages (Crabtree 2002: 142). In Majes, the consequences for land transactions have been long-term. In recent years, the increasing demand for land has caused the price of a 5-hectare parcel in the MIP to increase from US $100,000 to US $400,000. Without subsidised prices and affordable loans, most people from the highlands can no longer afford to buy land in Majes. Hence, most of the newly arrived migrants earn a living as labourers for landowners and the large-scale agribusiness that was welcomed in Majes in the 1990s. One example is the Pampa Baja Group, which bought 1,288 hectares in a public auction in 1998. Today, the company employs 2,000 workers and produces avocado and citrus fruit for export to Europe, the United States, Mexico, Canada and Asia.[8]

Farmers' ability to plan cultivation and future incomes was also affected. Among Fujimori's first moves was to scrap price controls, allowing these to be set by market forces. He also closed down ENCI (Empresa Nacional Comercializadora de Insumos), the institution that controlled imports of food and fertiliser, and eliminated the Agrarian Bank as a source of subsidised credit to producers (Crabtree 2002: 141). Private lenders have been reluctant to lend money to smallholders due to the high risks involved, which is reflected in the high interest rates that they charge. Farmers are also extremely aware of the high economic risks and insecurity involved in food production because of the market volatility. A farmer who was one of the first to arrive in 1983 and who has been combining dairy farming with different crops told me about the so-called free market:

> Well, now we have the law of *el chinito* [Alberto Fujimori]:[9] the law of supply and demand [...] so the market manages itself. When the production is high – boom! – [the price] falls. When there is low production, [the price] increases a little bit. For example, just now the onion is at 2 *soles* [per kilogram], and when it reaches the top, it plummets to 20 *centavos*, to 10 *centavos*. So then there is an atrocious loss for the farmer.

Fujimori's law of the free market has indeed deeply affected the everyday life of the farmers and the choices they make regarding their land, their cows and their future. The following presidents – Toledo (2001–6), García (2006–11) and Humala (2011–16) – continued on the neoliberal path and negotiated numerous free trade agreements, like the bilateral agreement with China, which entered into force in 2010. In Majes, many farmers earned a lot of money in the 'boom of red pepper (*ají paprika*)' that started in 2005 and lasted five years before prices plummeted due to worldwide over-production and the competition from China. Juan mentioned the *ají paprika* as a specific example of the boom-and-bust of the free market:

> The prices always fall, when everyone sows potatoes, the prices fall [...] In 2009, there was a good harvest of *ají paprika*; then the price fell from US $2.80 per kilo to 0.80 cents. The same happened with the onions [...] There is more risk now than 30 years ago; now there is free market. Earlier we had stable prices, but Fujimori made [the] free market. [...] The financial institutions that give loans take a lot of interest; 18 per cent and up to 30 per cent! Some get indebted because the intermediaries don't pay for the products that they have bought and taken away. (17 February 2014)

The 'good old days' that Juan remembers were his first years in Majes during the last years of Belaúnde's second presidency and the first years of García's first presidency. Although the economic liberalisation had already started, the farmers in Majes still benefited from subsidised prices and cheap loans from the state-owned Agrarian Bank. More importantly, in this period the settlers received extensive support as part of an agreement between Peru and the EEC. This agreement ended in 1992, the same year Fujimori instigated a self-coup with the support of the armed forces, and dissolved the Congress. Since Fujimori removed the last remains of state support and price control, farmers tend to lay all the blame on him for problems related to the 'free market'.[10]

Dependency and risk

Today, the majority of the 2,600 farmers in the MIP rely on low-income but stable dairy production, and 70 per cent of the crops in Majes are cattle fodder: alfalfa and maize. A standard 5-hectare farm unit can sustain between 15 and 20 cows, and each cow can give around 15 litres of milk per day. Most of the dairy farmers sell milk to the Gloria plant, which is owned by the Gloria Group, one of the largest companies in Peru, whose owners – the Rodriguez brothers – are among the few Peruvian billionaires on the Forbes lists. Since 1941, the company has expanded, with centres for fresh milk collection and production plants on various sites all over the country, and in 1996 Gloria constructed a milk plant in Majes. In 2002, they built a new industrial plant with modern equipment where they receive 870,000 litres of milk daily from dairy farms in the MIP and the surrounding provinces. In 2016, Gloria produced a range of dairy products for the national market, and exported evaporated milk to 40 countries (Gloria SA 2016). The mayor of Majes district boasted of the quantities of milk produced, and the commerce and 'economic movement' that this production stimulates. In my interview with him, the mayor highlighted the existence of four banks and twelve financial institutions as an indication of a booming local economy: 'We are a pilot centre of economic development [...] The monthly movement here is US $30 million. This place has the highest economic growth rate on a national level. Or maybe in the whole world.'

Milk money is said to be the petty cash (*la caja chica*) of the farmer because it is a continuous and reliable income. When farmers sow potatoes or other crops, they must wait four months for the harvest. In contrast, Gloria pays for the milk regularly every two weeks: on the 8th and 23rd of each month. On these payment days, there are long lines of people outside the banks, farmers spend their milk money on supplies and merchants come to town to do business. At night, the bars and streets of Villa El Pedregal are filled with people drinking beer and partying. However, in spite of these milk money parties, many farmers do not feel that they share in the economic growth. The president of the JUPM pointed out that he had seen all the changes during his 26 years in Majes, but that the quality of life had not improved much. His main point was that, although many farmers had improved their lives through hard work – 'by their own effort' – the possibilities for improvement were more limited for smallholders today than they were three decades ago. Because of the banks' high interest rates, many farmers are indebted and several have been forced to sell their land. Although dairy farmers see milk as a safe income, as opposed to the unstable crop prices, they complain about the Gloria Group's low payments. While production costs have increased, Gloria has not increased the price paid to farmers; it continues to fluctuate between 0.95 and 1.09 *soles* per litre, which is below the production cost. The farmers organised massive protests in 1992 and 2008, where one man died. In March 2015, the farmers spilled 5,000 litres of milk outside the Gloria plant in another protest against the low prices. With prices like that, it is impossible to make a profit with 15 cows, and most farmers have to sell the calves to survive. Both farmers and engineers talked about dairy farming as 'enslaving' (*esclavizante*) and 'precarious' (*precario*) because of the hard work and the low income.

Therefore, most farmers try not to depend solely on income from milk production. Rather, they usually combine milk production with high- and medium-risk cash crops. Most crops are sold to intermediaries who sell the products to exporters in Lima. Another option is contract farming for export-oriented agribusiness. Several farmers are providers to one of the agro-industrial companies in Majes: the Peruvian company Open World Export and the Danish-Peruvian company DANPER, which produce canned artichokes and red peppers for export. One of the farmers who has worked for the DANPER agribusiness company is Sergio. In 1996, he bought a farm from a *colono* and started with alfalfa, cows and milk production, as most farmers in Majes do. Then he started sowing potatoes, onions and artichokes, and became a 'provider' (*proveedor*) for DANPER, which meant that he produced according to their demand. He produced 18 tons of artichoke per hectare a year, and DANPER paid US $0.5 per kilo.

It was not a bad deal. The problem was the heavy workload of the continuous harvesting: the artichokes have to be harvested twelve times a year. Companies that integrate processing with export, like DANPER, transfer quality requirements to contracted farmers like Sergio, which helps to establish flexible labour processes (Narotzky 2016).

Producing on contracts for Gloria and DANPER implies safety and dependency. In contrast, the farmers who independently grow crops for global and national markets must do so at their own risk, and they depend on middlemen and the uncertain 'lottery' of the market. Despite this risk, it is tempting to leave contract farming when there is a boom going on, like the 'quinoa boom'. Quinoa is an Andean grain crop with edible seeds that has gained worldwide popularity as a high-protein and gluten free pseudo-cereal with a remarkable nutritional value. In 2006, the demand from US and European markets started to increase rapidly, and from 2010 to 2014, the global price doubled from US $2.96 to US $6.74 per kilogram (Statista 2018). Like many others, Sergio decided to change to quinoa in 2013, and at the same time he invested in a drip system, which is the most efficient irrigation form. He explained this by comparing quinoa to artichokes: 'It is easier because it is only one harvest', he said, and it also gives much more profit. Of course, he would now be dependent on the market, with the elements of 'gambling' that this implied. From the first harvest he got 20,000 kilos from 2.5 hectares and sold it for 11 *soles* per kilo (around US $3.85) to one of the intermediary traders who were buying quinoa from farmers in Majes. From 2013 to 2014, Peru's production of quinoa surged from 44,046 tons to 114,342 tons on a national level, and production on the coastal plains, including Majes, increased from 1,603 to 45,270 tons in the same period (McDonell 2018). In 2014, Sergio was preparing more land to sow quinoa. Yet, although he was certainly hoping the price of quinoa would continue to increase, he still kept 1 hectare with alfalfa and a few cows. As it turned out, it was a good decision to be careful. Already, by the end of 2014, prices began to decrease. In 2017 the average global price had dropped to US $1.66 per kg, only rising slightly to US $2.32 per kg in 2018 (Statista 2020).

New water uncertainties

We see that although global markets are associated with risk, farmers also depend on them to sell their produce. They are also completely dependent on a stable water supply, which for many years was taken for granted. In the past few years, however, there has been a growing awareness of the threat of global warming and climate change, and less certainty about the future water supply. Farmers in Majes are more aware of the fragility of their dependence on the 30-year-old Majes canal, which is showing signs of deterioration and needs maintenance. In fact, it has already been broken twice because of earthquakes, leaving the Majes population in a state of crisis for shorter periods. Plans have been made to set up an alternative water supply from the Siguas River in emergency situations. What is more difficult to control is the threat of climate change. Life in Majes is dependent on continued rainfall in the highlands, where the drought periods have become more frequent. In 2014, the water levels in the Condoroma dam sunk to 60 per cent of its maximum capacity of 285 MMC. In January 2016, an Emergency Coordination Committee was established in Majes and, in agreement with the National Water Authority, it was decided that the discharge from Condoroma should be reduced from 9.5 m^3/s (cubic metres per second) to 6 m^3/s from 1 February 2016. The farmers needed to reduce their crops according to the available water (Stensrud 2016a).

In Majes, from the start, water was seen as a valuable economic resource that has to be used rationally and 'efficiently' to produce for the market. The senior ALA employee Daniel explained to me that in the original plans, the farmers were supposed to get 0.5 lps of water, but instead they have received 0.75 lps. Today, the majority of farmers have shifted from sprinklers to drip irrigation, which uses water more efficiently, and therefore the amount of water has been reduced to 0.62 lps. Still, this has led to complaints and protests from farmers. Daniel was shaking his head when he told me about this in his office, and said that the private agri-business company Pampa Baja uses only 0.33 lps to irrigate their 1,200 hectares of land, by using the famous drip technology from Israel. The small-scale farmers argue that they don't have the money to invest in expensive foreign equipment. In Daniel's opinion, however, these farmers are not as poor as they claim, and they have elevated their socio-economic status since they started cultivating their 5-hectare farms, which is more land that most peasants own in the highlands. In the original design, the MIP was supposed to cover 23,000 hectares, but after three decades, only 15,000 hectares were irrigated. Therefore, as explained earlier, in 2014 the regional government, Autodema and the ANA were planning to expand the irrigated areas little by little, until they fulfilled the original plan. Since the 8,000 hectares that were left should be irrigated without increasing the amount of water running in the Majes canal, the only way to achieve this goal was to reduce the amount of litres per second given to each farm. Hence, all farmers would be forced to irrigate more efficiently. The farmers, represented by la JUPM, were not surprisingly opposing this idea and demanded more water to expand the irrigation.

The MIP, like other irrigation projects in arid plateaus on the coastline, has also caused unforeseen ecological consequences in the form of landslides. The problem is that the water that is not absorbed by the plants seeps into the ground, down to a dense layer of clay, where it gathers and accumulates. After twenty years or so, the underground water started to destabilise the land, causing landslides along Siguas River. A lot of land has been lost already, threatening not only farmland but also the Gloria milk plant and the Panamerican highway. A recent geological study documents the long-term effects of modern intensive farming and irrigation on the erosion of arid deserts in the Vitor and Siguas river valleys, using 40 years of satellite data. The study demonstrates that irrigation initiated very large slow-moving landslides, affecting one-third of the valleys (Lacroix et al. 2020). In 2014, this problem was heatedly debated among the hydraulic engineers in the ALA. While the farmers got most of the blame because they used too much water, the proposed solutions were purely technical. One proposal was to drill deep holes to measure the amount of underground water and pump it out. Since this was salinised wastewater, however, it could not be re-used.

Conclusion

Every year, during the anniversaries of the district of Majes and of its *centros poblades*, the brave pioneers and resourceful, hard-working and entrepreneurial settlers are celebrated in heartfelt speeches and songs. Today however, hard work is no longer a guarantee of success. Majes is full of *buscavidas*, searching for and creating different life-projects in the desert, anticipating a 'better' life for the next generation: better housing, better education, better jobs. However, future histories contingent on water are uncertain and unpredictable (Randle and Barnes 2018; Ballestero 2019b). What many of my interlocutors worried about, was that the development of Majes happened in an unorganised and disorderly way. The intended and unintended consequences of the project are piling up as the population grows and the place changes at an accelerated speed. Most people find that the changes are beyond their control: the farmers are concerned by unstable prices for their produce, the engineers are struggling with the crumbling infrastructure, the landless workers are searching for jobs in a precarious labour market, the self-employed entrepreneurs are chasing money in a highly competitive urban informal economy, the politicians attempt to control the illegal squatters in the surrounding desert, and everyone is concerned by the threat of climate change and drought in the highlands. The role of Majes in the watershed is ambivalent: privileged and powerful, yet dependent and vulnerable at the same time. In addition to concerns related to climate change and drought, there are also increasing worries among farmers regarding the threat of water privatisation and more expensive water tariffs. The next chapter will look into how irrigation and water distribution is organised higher up in the watershed, particularly in Colca Valley, and discuss how water payments have been introduced, received and combined with other kinds of 'payments' to the animate landscape.

3
Water Payments

Early one October morning at 5.30, I met Aurelio by one of Chivay's water reservoirs, called Estanque Tataccocha (Father-lake tank), which collects water flowing from the spring called Manantial Mamaccocha (Mother-lake spring) and from a valve in the Majes canal.[1] Since the spring water mixes with the canal water in the tank, this water is called 'combined water' (*agua combinada*) and it is used for irrigation of fields in the sectors called Huito and Patacca in 'Urinsaya', which is the lower part of Chivay. The water users in these sectors pay the tariff price set for 'combined water', which is more expensive than spring water, but cheaper than the 'regulated water' from the Majes canal. Aurelio was a man in his fifties who was elected *regidor* – water allocator – by the water users commission in Chivay Urinsaya. The *regidor* is elected for one year at a time, and it is a position that all farmers should hold at least once in their lifetime in order to serve their community. His work as a *regidor* consisted in distributing the irrigation water as fairly as possible among the 450 farmers in his commission. On this particular day, seven farmers were going to irrigate with water from the Tataccocha tank. Therefore, Aurelio opened the valve by turning the wheel 15 times, to let sufficient water into the Población canal, which goes through the village and down to the fields in Chivay Urinsaya. He knew exactly how many times to turn the valve wheel in order to let out sufficient water for the number of users who had asked for water that day. 'If I let out too much water it's in vain; the water overflows and goes to the river', he explained. Some of the farmers were waiting by the tank to make sure that they got their share of the water today. One of them was going to irrigate in a field above the tank, and Aurelio gave him permission to open a valve uphill. He also asked Aurelio for a little water for another field that he had just levelled but not sowed yet. 'Just give me a little bit of water', he pleaded, and the others laughed. 'Just a little bit? You should just urinate, then', said an old man jokingly, 'one little drop a day!' – making the rest of the group laugh.

Aurelio left to inspect and direct the water flow, and I walked with him along the canal to the fields. Cement blocks covered the part of the canal that passed through the village, but when we came out in the open landscape, we could see and hear the water flowing and whooshing through the canal. As the sun rose, beams of sunlight started to warm the cold air and the dry earth. The canal divided into several smaller branches going in different directions, in between the small fields of various sizes and sown with different seeds. All the canals had names; one was named Totoroccocha and on the other side, we could see the Puka Puka, channelling water to another sector. Aurelio started to open and close small gates in the intersections in order to direct the water to the right fields. Only two or three farmers can irrigate from the same minor canal on the same day, and each farmer had the right to use the water for a certain number of hours that day. The farmers irrigate by furrows (*por surco*), Aurelio explained: 'it is more practical; you have more order and the water flows beautifully'. The *regidor* distributes and controls the use of the irrigation water, and he also ensures that nobody takes water without permission. Aurelio said that as *regidor*, he imposes order, and prevents the strongest man taking most of the water. The work of the *regidor* is especially difficult in the months of October, November and December, when the plants are starting to grow and they are waiting for the rain. Previously, the rain used to start in October, but in recent years the rainy season has started later and water is even scarcer than it used to be in these months.

We arrived at Umalaquishua, which was called 'the distribution place' because it was where the water users made their irrigation requests to the *regidor*, who allocated irrigation times. Eight farmers were waiting there. This was a Thursday, and most of them asked for water for Friday and Saturday, and another for Monday. Aurelio carefully noted all the names, fields and times in his little black notebook. The farmers had all brought their *libretas de control*, which were booklets used to control the user rights and obligations. The *libretas* had the name of the water users commission printed on the front, and inside there were columns to fill in crucial information about payments of the tariff and attendance at *faenas* (collective work), with signatures and stamps. This was in addition to the official receipts of the water tariffs issued by the *Junta*'s accountant. On this day, the president of the water users commission of Urinsaya had also shown up to ask for water; he was planning to irrigate three *yuntadas* (equivalent of 1 hectare) on Friday. The president said that those who have paid the tariff have the right to irrigate every day if they want to, but if they have not paid the tariff, they cannot have any water at all. He wanted to make a point because there were a few users who asked for water although they had not paid the tariff. He had recently had a quarrel with one of them; a woman who afterwards had wrongly accused him of stealing cement from the commission. Nobody irrigates a field every day, however; the frequency of irrigation usually varies between 8 and 15 days, depending on the plant, Aurelio explained. Peas endure; they can get water every 20 or 30 days, but beans need water every eight to ten days. Most farmers have small fields in different locations that are sown with different seeds according to the micro-climatic conditions, which vary a lot between the riverbed and high up on the mountain slopes.

According to Aurelio, there are always problems to sort out. For example, a user had asked for water one day, but did not go to his field and the water spilled over and went down to the river. Others take water from each other. That is why Aurelio takes a look at midday, to check that everything is okay: 'I am imposing order', as he put it. The *regidor* is not only responsible for negotiating with the farmers, however; he should also maintain good relations with the water sources and water bodies, and make the appropriate *pagos*, which literally means 'payments' yet is often translated as 'offerings', to the mountain-lords (*apus*) and springs (*pukyos*), ponds and canals. Since Aurelio also was a *paqu* – a ritual expert who knows how to read coca leaves and make *pagos* to houses, shops and water sources – he performed the payments himself, and was also often hired to do this for other commissions. The water from the Mamaccocha spring is not only used to irrigate large parts of the agricultural fields in Chivay, but it also supplies the population in Chivay with drinking water. Aurelio is in charge of making the *pago* to Mamaccocha twice a year, on 1 January and in the month of August. When he goes up to the spring, he brings the *vara* – a staff of authority that belongs to the office of the *regidor*. After being elected, the new *regidor* receives the *vara* in a ceremony, and before starting to execute his office, he should make a *pago* to the *vara* out of respect. If it is not given a *pago* and 'cleaned' with incense, it can grab you and make you sick. 'The *vara* has powers', Aurelio explained.

In this chapter, I will discuss different forms of water payments, from which different, yet partially connected water-worlds emerge. Not seeing realities as preceding practice, singular and a priori, and acknowledging that worlds are messy and multiple, enacted in and through material practices and human–non-human interactions, implies the need to look more closely at the particular practices from which realities or worlds emerge (Mol 2002; Law 2004; Tsing 2015). The different payment practices – tariffs and *pagos* – enact different assemblages, which are often seen as directly opposed: one relating to the state and the market versus a collective of mutually constituted entities and beings. On the one hand, paying tariffs consolidates relations between water users (mainly farmers) and water producers, that is, the operators of hydraulic infrastructure and state bureaucracy (the *Junta*, Autodema and the ALA) in terms of a contract based on a monetary logic. On the other hand, making *pagos* maintains relationships between humans (people) and other-than-human beings (springs, mountains, earth, water) in mutually constitutive relationships. The question here is how these assemblages can coexist and be partially connected?

Bill Maurer (2006) has shown that modern money is often seen as a universal and homogenising force: 'according to Marx, Simmel, and Weber, capitalist moneys render everything quantifiable according to one scale of value and permit previously unthinkable comparisons among objects, persons, and activities' (Maurer 2006: 20). The spread of a global capitalist, monetary economy has been imagined to lead unavoidably to universal commodification (see for example Taussig 1980). According to more recent scholarship, however, money's homogenising effects are not as complete as once believed (Maurer 2006: 21). Rather, seeing that money can be incorporated and encompassed in different modalities of exchange allows us to see multiple monetary repertoires with which people engage (Maurer 2006; see also Guyer 2004). In practice, tariffs and *pagos* as modes of exchange do not exclude each other, and are pragmatically combined. Although these assemblages work according to different logics, they are not incompatible. Tariffs are legitimised by an extractivist logic that reduces and singularises relations between water and humans to contractual relationships between a resource and its users, and *pagos* make sense according to a relational logic, in which humans and multiple water-entities and beings mutually engage in relations of reciprocity. Nevertheless, tariffs and *pagos* are not mutually exclusive precisely because they do not compete but are practised in different registers of life.

Consequently, the worlds that emerge from these practices are not separate but partially connected (Strathern 2004 [1991]). As Marisol de la Cadena (2015) explains it, life in the Andes does not consist of different 'units' that are separate but sometimes interact, such as 'mestizo culture', 'indigenous culture', or 'capitalist economy' versus 'peasant pre-capitalist economy'. Rather, worlds are made in the encounters and emerge continuously from encounters and practices related to different ways of making a living and making life. Thinking with Rancière (2010: 37), who defines politics as 'the manifestation of dissensus as the presence of two worlds in one', I suggest that these encounters of different – and partially connected – practices, can be seen as everyday politics of world-making, or 'pluriversal politics', which allows the presence of other-than-humans and earth-beings in the public sphere (de la Cadena 2010). Writing from the Peruvian Andes, de la Cadena refers to this as 'indigenous cosmopolitics': the appearance of indigeneity and earth-beings demanding a place in politics, which also implies putting into question the alleged universality and singularity of 'Nature', which science has the monopoly to 'objectively' define (De la Cadena 2010: 346).

In the rest of the chapter, I first analyse the organisation and distribution of irrigation water and payments for it – how tariffs are calculated and how water is distributed – and, second, I will explore how the worlds of monetary and scientific practices are entangled with the world-making practices that enact water and earth as living beings.

Neoliberal policies and water tariffs

The farmers in Colca Valley have to navigate through the plurality of customs, institutions and regulations that are part of water governance, and this includes making the right kinds of payments for different uses and sources of water. According to the Water Resources Law, all water users have to pay different water taxes and tariffs for different water uses – agricultural, industrial and human consumption – to different institutions. The payments began as a result of the liberalisation of markets that took off in the 1990s, when the Fujimori regime implemented massive privatisation and economic deregulation. When the Supreme Decree 037-89-AG was passed in 1989, the functions of the state institutions in operation, maintenance and administration of the irrigation infrastructure were handed over to the *Juntas de Usuarios*. To finance this work the *Juntas* were to charge a tariff and were allowed to increase it in order to have financial autonomy from the state. The decree is seen as the first step towards privatisation of water, and one of the promoters behind it was Absalón Vásquez, who was the vice-minister of agriculture in 1989. Three years later he became Minister of Agriculture in the Fujimori government, and large numbers of state functionaries in the water administration were fired in this period (Oré and Rap 2009: 46–7). During the 1990s, Vásquez made several attempts to pass a new water law that would privatise water and create a water market, inspired by the Chilean Water Code that was actively promoted by the World Bank and the Inter-American Development Bank. This process towards commodification of water was part of a global trend that started with the 1992 Dublin Statement, in which the need to recognise water as an economic good was declared (Franco et al. 2013). The Fujimori government passed several legal decrees to give the irrigation organisations a more 'modern optic and business bias' (Cupe Burga 2001: 1).

The *Junta* of Colca Valley started to charge farmers the irrigation tariff in the 1990s. The tariff is calculated according to the area of land and the source of the water: whether it is regulated water from the Majes canal, unregulated water from natural springs and streams, or mixed water from both sources. The tariffs are not payments for the water per se, since water is public property by law, but for the use of infrastructure. Therefore, the water that comes from the Majes canal is the most expensive (between 26 and 40 *soles* a year per hectare), while unregulated water is cheap in comparison (between 12 and 15 *soles*). The tariff price of 'combined water' is between 15 and 26 *soles*. The *Junta* pays Autodema, which is responsible for the maintenance of the Majes canal, for the regulated water. All farmers in Majes pay the highest tariff for regulated water, while a farmer in Colca might pay one tariff for the irrigation of one field, the other for another, depending on the source of the water. When the tariffs were introduced, the *Junta* was met with strong sentiments of distrust and opposition among the farmers. Miguel, the technical manager of the *Junta*, told me:

> People saw the *Junta* as an entity that only collected the water tariff, and they didn't want to pay the tariff. People didn't understand why the *Junta* was charging for the water; they were saying that the water is given to us by God or the mountains, so why should we pay for something which is ours? But little by little we have been changing this, by generating trust through courses, teaching, visits to the commissions, and supporting projects for building irrigation infrastructure.

The farmers in Colca engage in mutual relations of reciprocity with mountains, springs and lakes, which in these practices emerge as living, sentient and responsive beings (cf. Gelles 2000; Stensrud 2016b; see also Allen 1988; de la Cadena 2015). People receive water from the mountains and reciprocate by 'paying' food, coca leaves, alcohol and other items. Similarly, when the farmers pay the tariff to the JUVC, they expect something in return – cement, services and support – as part of a mutual reciprocal relation. When Miguel explained the work of the *Junta* to a group of visitors from another watershed, he emphasised that: 'We have to give service to the farmers; if we don't, [people] say that the *Junta* does not give us anything and why then should we pay?' Without the tariff, we would not have any organisation and no means to repair and improve the canals and water intakes, Miguel pointed out.

In the end, the Fujimori government failed to privatise water due to strong opposition from the irrigation organisations (Oré and Rap 2009; Oré et al. 2009: 52–3). Nevertheless, neoliberal thought continued to influence policies of water governance, not only during Fujimori's regime, but also in the governments that followed. In 2007, the García government started to adapt the water law to the Free Trade Agreement (del Castillo 2011: 94–5). Two years later, in 2009, the García government passed the Water Resources Law (Ley de recursos hídricos), which emphasises the economic value of water and the need for efficiency and modernity in water management (ANA 2010). Although the water law still explicitly acknowledges water as state property, it has been adapted to a neoliberal project that induces the state to downplay its role in economic and social politics. Hence, the law gives ample space for private companies to intervene and invest in water management (del Castillo 2011). One of the first things Miguel said when I asked him about water legislation was that he liked Velasco's 1969 water law because it nationalised water and supported local organisation. The new law on water resources (2009), on the other hand, seeks privatisation, he said. According to the law, if the *Junta* do not charge the tariff and work efficiently, it can be replaced by private companies that will operate the infrastructure and manage the water distribution according to a business model. A private operator would undoubtedly charge a more expensive tariff. However, Miguel was not worried because the *Junta* in Colca Valley was regarded as the best *Junta* in the Peruvian highlands since between 60 and 70 per cent of the farmers paid the tariff. In other parts of the highlands, the majority of the smallholders still refused to pay.

The presidents of the commissions and the *Junta* work voluntarily, without pay. The *regidores* are also volunteers; they work hard, but do not receive any payment. A few commissions have started to pay their *regidores*, however: a monthly payment of 450 *soles* in the five most critical months from August till December. In these months, they spend every day supervising the irrigation, and in Miguel's opinion, they should all be paid for this work. The only problem is that then they would have to increase the tariff, which will make the farmers complain. The state does not give anything, Miguel explained; it just tells the *Junta* to charge the tariff. The *Junta* receives the tariffs from all the farmers and distributes the money: a small part to the National Junta, some for the water tax to the state (*canon hídrico*), some to the ALA, and some for amortisation to Autodema for the use of water from the Majes canal. A large part was sent back to the commissions, for the supply of cement and other materials and the hire of extra labour power when needed. The rest was used for daily expenses, office materials and staff salaries.

The tariff is estimated according to land area, which in Colca Valley is measured in relative measures like *topo* and *yuntada*. A *topo* refers to the amount of land a team of men wielding a foot plough can prepare in one day, and a *yuntada* is the amount of land a team of oxen can plough in a day. The amount of land that can be ploughed in a day varies by plot shape, slope, soil type, and distance from the village. In irrigation matters, relative measures are preferred, since two fields may measure the same in area under the metric system but have quite different water absorption rates. Relative measures allow proportional allocations of water and labour to be negotiated and adjusted to fit individual cases (Guillet 1992: 33–4). Farmers in Colca Valley mostly use traditional irrigation methods based on gravity and furrows, and the water is measured in time: how many hours it takes to flood a field. This time also depends on several factors, like the soil type, slope, and on the volume of the water flow coming from the water source or irrigation canal. This water flow volume is today often measured in litres per second. Both land and water are thus measured according to labour force and movement in time, and the focus is on the accomplishment of a task: how long it takes for humans, animals or water to enable land to produce food. These relative measures, however, are not very convenient in the building of a nation state or in inter-regional market transactions. Standardised units of measurement make scalable projects – be it of business, development or state building – possible, and measurement of land and water have to a large degree been standardised with units of size, volume and time, such as metres, hectares, litres, minutes and seconds. When the accountant in the *Junta* calculates the tariff, she translates 2 *yuntadas* into 1 *topo*, and 3 *topos* become the equivalent of 1 hectare.

According to the regulations of the commissions, all water users have the obligation to participate in meetings and collective work, and those who cannot attend should send another person in his or her place, or pay a fine for not attending. Users also pay fines for breaking the law, for example, for water theft. Some fines are determined by the law, but as Miguel repeatedly pointed out, the law had many holes and gaps, because the geographical and socio-economic conditions in the highlands were very different from those on the coastline. For example, in the highlands, where people raise alpacas for a living, one farmer might own 100 hectares of pasture. But if we charge 15 *soles* per hectare, it would be 1,500 *soles*, which no alpaca farmer could possibly pay. Moreover, how can we 'cut' the water, as the law dictates, when the water comes from the springs, Miguel asked. However, if we agree on charging 1 *sol* per hectare in the highlands, it would be 100 *soles*, which it is possible to pay. Miguel also had another anecdote to show how they adapted the law to their social context. One farmer in Coporaque had irrigated his field of beans, and afterwards he had closed the hole in the canal with a stone. However, during the night, the reservoir had filled up, the water had spilled over, and the stone had fallen out of the hole in the canal. In the morning, the *regidor* saw that the field was wet, and accused the man of water theft. According to the law, the fine should be 300 *soles*. As the farmer did not have that money, however, they agreed that he should give away a part of his harvest.

Collective work in las comisiones

In order to have the right to use water, all water users are obliged to participate in the collective work parties (*faenas*) organised by the commissions, when they clean and repair ponds and canals. In Chivay, there are three *comisiones de usuarios*: Anansaya (upper part), Urinsaya (lower part), and Ccapa ('rich' part, which means the part of town where the main market and most businesses are located).[2] Apart from the presidents, secretaries and treasurers who are elected according to state regulations, the *regidores* are also elected on an annual basis. Although women do much of the irrigation and other kinds of work in the fields, most leaders, board members and *regidores* are male. Women seldom hold positions of authority in rural communities (Li 2008; Vera and Zwarteveen 2007). Yet, most men could not perform their duties as presidents and *regidores* without the consent and support of their wives, and women participate in meetings and *faenas*. In these *faenas*, farmers do most of the construction and maintenance work, and they pay most of the costs of materials and extra labour through the tariff, although they also make efforts to get funding from public institutions or NGOs for the construction of new infrastructure. In contrast, the Majes canal is administered by Autodema, which is financed from the public budget with an annual amount of US $33 million: $8 million for infrastructure insurance, $22 million for staff (Vera Delgado and Zwarteveen 2008: 17–18). Miguel once noted that by paying the tariff, farmers learn how to give economic value to the water. However, the farmers in Colca already know that water has great value. Since the valley is semi-arid, the water users commissions are important actors in local economic and political community life. The leader of the commission in Yanque Urinsaya explained that the farmers and the water are interdependent – there is no life without water and humans need to work to make the water flow: 'The commission is the only solid organisation here, because the water unites us. [...] Everyone attends the meetings and everyone participates in the collective work, because the water obliges us to.' Irrigation is an inherently collective activity, where success is achieved through cooperation both among farmers and in their relation to the water as a sentient being. John M. Treacy, who studied irrigation in the neighbouring village Coporaque in the 1980s, reported that the *coporaqueños* described irrigation as teaching the water to flow over an uneven surface: *yaku karpay, yaku yachachiy* means 'to irrigate is to teach the water' (Treacy 1994: 113).

As described at the beginning of this chapter, every water user has a *libreta*; a control book, where key information about the membership and water rights is written down: mandatory attendance at meetings and for collective work, and the tariffs, licences and fines that have been paid. Documents and written words have a key importance in community life and politics in the Peruvian highlands. Salomon and Niño-Murcia (2011) have shown how literacy has been a tool of power in the Andes since colonial times, and how literacy is closely associated with dignity and respect in Andean villages; it is seen as a 'self-defence against fraud and abuse' (Salomon and Niño-Murcia 2011: 25). In all the meetings of the different water users commissions in Colca Valley, the secretary always wrote the minutes meticulously in a 'book of acts' (*libros de acta*), where all participants had to sign to approve its validity. Rasmussen (2014, 2015) has analysed books of acts and other documents as 'dry technologies' that are important tools in the organisation of water users in the Andes. But what is it that the *libreta* and the writing enact, as a socio-material object and practice? I suggest that *la libreta* can be seen as part of the assemblage making the water flow in Colca Valley. Seeing how water users always kept their *libretas* close and how they carefully kept them in plastic bags so that they would not get wet and dirty, they clearly saw them as important. The *libretas* were the physical evidence that they had fulfilled their obligations and that they had the right to use water to irrigate their fields. The *libretas* carefully documented all their payments of tariffs and fines, their participation and contributions, and as such they were evidence of the 'water citizenship' (Paerregaard et al. 2016) through which a person is member of a community as a water user. As the leader in Yanque Urinsaya said, the water obliges people to participate, and the *libreta* is the material and cultural device that proves their participation in the collective of water and people. We could say that when the practices that people are engaged in (like cleaning canals and irrigating) are written in a *libreta*, the obligations and rights are enclosed in it, and it also singularises the users' rights in terms of what is regulated by the law. However, there are also practices that are mandatory in Colca in order to receive water, but which are not written in the *libreta* and these are the ones involving reciprocal relationships with other-than-human beings.

The *regidores* have the responsibility for maintaining good and respectful relations with the mountains, springs and lakes, as well as with the ponds, reservoirs and canals. Twice a year they offer *pagos* – also called *iranta*[3] in Colca – consisting of herbs, coca leaves, fat, sugar, alpaca foetus and other items in addition to alcohol, to the most important water sources. The main offerings are organised by the president and the *regidor* in collaboration with a ritual expert (*paqu*) during the annual cleaning of reservoirs and canals. While most of the water users clean the infrastructure, ritual experts make *pagos* to the mountain springs and the reservoirs and canals. One of the presidents explained:

> I go with the *regidor* and we make our *iranta* by the springs, and we pay (*pagamos*) and sprinkle with wine, and afterwards I make all the people pray [...] We also go to the irrigation ponds (*estanques*) to clean them on another day, and then we also make our *iranta* there [...] We respect them so that they will supply us all year; so that there will be enough water in the ponds to sustain all our agricultural fields.

The irrigation systems also necessitate cooperation between communities. For example, the farmers in Yanque receive water from the neighbouring districts. People in Chivay jokingly call the *yanqueños* 'water thieves' (*yaku suwa*) and the farmers in Yanque respond that they don't steal but borrow the water. Each year in August, they organise collective work to clean the long irrigation canals from the Huarancante Mountain in Chivay and the canal Mismi, which runs for 25 km from Mount Mismi in Tuti district, through Coporaque district and down to Yanque. Every August, which is the month before the start of a new sowing season, each water users commission organises the annual 'canal cleaning' (*escarbo de acequia*, or *yarqa aspiy* in Quechua), when water is cut off and all members must participate in the cleaning and maintenance of reservoirs, ponds and canals. In Yanque, the cleaning work takes four days for the group of farmers who go up to the source and descend on foot, cleaning the canal with shovels as they go. Before starting the work, it is important to make *pago* to the mountains so that no accidents or deaths will happen. Proper offerings also have to be made to the ponds and canals that are going to be cleaned and repaired. The night before cleaning the main pond in Coporaque (an old earthen tank called Estanque Santa Rosa in Spanish and Mama Qocha in Quechua) in 2011, the two water users commissions each made a *pago* to the pond. They put the *pagos* in a box buried deep in the earth beside the gate, where they also keep small miniatures of llamas that are taken out to be 'read' and interpreted before they are returned. The wine goblet should be empty – this means that the earth-mother of this place and this pond is content – before it is filled with new wine. According to Catherine Allen, ritual practices in the Andes are 'premised on a principle of consubstantiality, the assumption that all beings are intrinsically interconnected through their sharing a matrix of animated substance' (Allen 1997: 75). Hydraulic infrastructure, such as ponds and canals, cannot be seen as separate from the entangled world of soil, water, earth-beings and other animated entities in the surroundings.

When the maintenance and ritual work in Estanque Santa Rosa was done, the water was released into the cleaned canals and slowly filled up the reservoir as people welcomed the water with joy and awe. The *regidores* drank the water and poured *chicha* into it, and others danced around the canals and inside the *estanque* while a band played festive music. The annual cleaning and celebration is sponsored by the *regidor*, and on the last day, he hands over the staff (*vara*) – and the power and responsibility that comes with it – to the new *regidor* who has been elected for the coming year. Finally, all participants celebrate with food, drink, music and dancing. Different variations of these festivals of cleaning the irrigation canals take place in all the communities of Colca Valley (see among others

Paerregaard 1994; Gelles 2000). These relations to water can be seen as evidence that land and water are not just commodities to farmers in Colca Valley. Not only is water not considered a commodity, however; through these world-making practices, water and water-beings are also enacted as living non-human persons.

Figure 4 A *pago* is being prepared to the living springs and mountains above Chivay. The *paqu* is carefully assembling the ingredients on a woven cloth placed on a flat stone. On the stone is also a dried starfish, which is sprinkled with alcohol and covered by cotton, a bag with coca leaves, and tiny goblets with wine for the spring.

Sentient water and water-beings

In August 2011, the president of the water users commission Chivay Ccapa invited my partner, who was visiting from Norway, and me to accompany a group of men up to the mountains to make *irantas* to the high springs, located higher than 4,000 metres of altitude. The president introduced us to the *regidor*, who was in charge of the trip, and instructed us to meet them outside of his house at 4 a.m. on the next day. On our way up the mountain next morning, we met the *paqu* and a couple of other board members who joined us. The *paqu* was Aurelio, who was *regidor* in Urinsaya that year. By each spring, there was the same procedure: the *regidor* made a fire, while the *paqu* sat down by a stone table where he would prepare the ingredients of the *iranta*. First, some herbs were put on burning coal on a stone plate, and we all blew the smoke to the table, the spring, the rock and the hill. Then, Aurelio put an alpaca fetus on the table and gave out pieces of llama fat (*untu*) to everyone in the group. Each person rolled a ball of *untu* and blew their *samay* (breath, life-essence, vital force) into it and gave their *samay* to various beings by invoking their names: to the place, to the spring, to the Lord Santiago (who controls the lightning, so that he will not send a lot of lightning, but only rain), and finally to the *machulas* (the ancestors). Thereafter, we all made bouquets of coca leaves called *k'intus*, into which we also blew our *samay* while invoking the same beings. Next, the *regidor* served us tiny cups of wine, and we made *t'inka*, which according to the main Quechua dictionary means the sprinkling or spattering of liquid matter (Academia Mayor 2005) and which is often translated as 'libation',[4] to the spring, the mountain and the *iranta*, which by now was finished. They placed the *iranta* package in the fire, and the wood made a crackling sound. That sound indicated that the earth received the *iranta* and that they had done it well. 'When it starts to burst, it is a proof, a sign that the earth is receiving,' one of the men explained to me. After burning the *iranta*, Aurelio placed tiny ceramic goblets with *chicha*, sweet wine and holy water in a box in the earth beside the spring. He explained: 'It is for here, for the spring, to drink. This will be preserved here and it is for the whole year. It is ... how should I put it ... it is [her] *pago*. Like we sometimes toast [drink], they are also thirsty.' In these world-making practices, springs (*pukyos*), lakes (*qochas*), mountains and other water- and earth-beings have names and personal characteristics, and they can feel thirst, hunger and respond to human action. These beings are not inherently benevolent or malevolent, but they are powerful and can be quite capricious and dangerous, especially when they are hungry. They demand proper respect and gifts (*pagos*) and in return provide water, plants, fertility and well-being (Allen 1988; de la Cadena 2015; Gelles 2000; Gose 1994).

Water also emerges as a sentient and responsive being. Farmers in Chivay told me that the common name of water is Yakumama, which means 'water mother', but that they also use the name Mama Choqueshisha 'out of respect' (*de respeto*). Hence, when people in Colca say that 'water is life' they are not speaking metaphorically. Water – in the rain, springs, streams, rivers, lakes and the ocean – is not a passive element that is acted upon by humans; water takes part in sociality and work activities. Water is essential for the production of food and bodies and is related to as an animate substance and a female life source that connects humans, plants, animals and spirits.[5] Valderrama and Escalante, who studied water in Yanque in the 1970s, say that water is 'a vital force, principle of life, a living being which, like ourselves, participates in the universe' (Valderrama and Escalante 1988: 206).

Water can also respond when it is called upon by specific techniques. 'To call the water' (*llamar al agua*) is a technique that performs the hydrological cycle in order to call the water from the ocean and make clouds and rain. On our tour of making *pagos* to the springs that provide the fields of Chivay Ccapa with water, Aurelio performed this calling in each spring before burning the *iranta*. He used seawater that had been brought in a bottle all the way from the Pacific Ocean, and he poured it into a small container, covering it with a piece of cotton. After *t'inka* and invocations, he placed these items – together with a starfish from the ocean – into the spring. Aurelio told me that the seawater 'will call for more water', and explained that the cotton was 'clouds, so that there will be rain'. He continued: 'This is water from the ocean. It will be absorbed by the mountain and all of this spring, so that the water will continue to come out.' By focusing on these world-making practices, the world itself appears as emerging, as always becoming in different versions; as multiple realities. These worlds are partially connected; they are fragmented and partial in the sense that they are enacted through practice and thus always subjected to potential change.

Mediating water-worlds

As daily manager of the *Junta*, Miguel not only mediated between the state and the farmers (as seen in chapter 1) but also between the partially connected worlds of modernity and relationality. As an engineer who was constantly seeking to understand how the world worked, he tried to find scientific evidence for why 'calling the water' and other practices seemed to work. When Miguel grew up in Colca Valley, he learned how everything is related, connected and alive, and when he studied engineering at the university of Arequipa he learned how to take everything apart in units that can be examined, counted and reassembled. On the one hand, he relates to water and water-bodies as living beings. Miguel told me that the springs have life and powers; he knows stories about things that have happened at particular springs and he is cautious when approaching them. On the other hand, he relates to water as fluid matter that can be quantified and counted in units of litres per second. However, he does not move from one world and back, and he is never in-between. Rather, he lives in both simultaneously, yet always partially, since they overlap and cannot be clearly separated in real-life experience and practice; we could say that he lives in more than one but less than two worlds (Strathern 2004 [1991]; Haraway 1991; Mol 2002; de la Cadena 2015). This dual reality is perhaps best described by the Aymara concept of '*ch'ixi*', which Silvia Rivera Cusicanqui (2012) uses to describe how indigenous and mestizo worlds can be combined without being mixed. *Ch'ixi* has many connotations and reflects the Aymara idea of something that is and is not at the same time. Hence, the notion of *ch'ixi* can illuminate the 'motley' (*abigarrada*) quality of Andean society, expressing the parallel coexistence of multiple cultural differences that do not extinguish, but instead both antagonise and complement each other (Rivera Cusicanqui 2012: 105).

These worlds emerge from his different practices in everyday life at home and at work, and there seem to be constant tensions and attempts at making coherence, for example by trying to find a scientific explanation for why the calling of rainwater works. He told me the following:

> In the time of the Incas, it is told that the *chasquis* [runners] went down from the mountains to the ocean, where they did a *pago* to the ocean. Afterwards, they took seawater in pitchers, and they put one pitcher on each mountaintop, from the ocean to the highlands. And then rain clouds were formed, and the clouds followed the seawater to the highlands, where it rained. Today, when they make *pagos* to the water springs, they put seawater in [the spring]. They bring water from the sea in bottles. There must be a scientific reason; we should look for a scien-

tific explanation. For example, when the clouds follow the seawater, it could be that the seawater contains ions?

By suggesting that there are ions in the seawater that attract the rain-clouds, Miguel attempts to explain why it works in a way that science could accept. In his work as an engineer, he tries to subordinate one world to another, but he does not quite succeed. As long as he lives and works in Colca and participates in different world-making practices, the worlds will be connected, although only partially. His effort to make connections can also only be partially successful, because the two worlds can never be the same. There will always be excesses that cannot be encompassed in both worlds. This does not mean that one world will eventually extinguish the other; on the contrary – new worlds are constantly being enacted in the interface and in encounters across local, regional and global scales (see Zhan 2009; de la Cadena 2015; Tsing 2015).

On another occasion, in 2013, Miguel told a story about two tractors. Some years earlier, the *Junta* applied to the regional government for funding to buy vehicles for transportation and work and, in 2011, I saw how Miguel and the board members were waiting, soliciting, knocking on office doors, and had endless meetings with politicians and bureaucrats. Therefore, when I returned in 2013, I was happy to hear that the *Junta* had finally received a donation of vehicles from the regional government; a car, four motorbikes and two tractors. The tractors – one red and one blue – were owned by the *Junta* and rented out to the water users. However, they had noted a difference between the tractors. The blue one had worked well since the beginning and it had produced an income for the organisation. The red tractor, on the other hand, for a long time had caused nothing but trouble; it broke down all the time and they had to spend money on repairs. Miguel, together with the accountant Sara and the secretary Monica, figured out that the problem was a lack of *t'inka*, also called *ch'alla*. When they received the blue tractor, they had made a proper *ch'alla* by pouring six big bottles of beer over it while invoking the local mountain-lords and other earth-beings, before they started to use it. However, when the red tractor arrived, they had been very busy and had not prioritised making a *ch'alla*. As soon as they decided that this must be the problem, Sara and Monica took charge, bought beer and made the *ch'alla* for the red tractor. 'After this, it has worked well,' Miguel said with a smile; 'it seems like a lie, but that's how it is' (*parece mentira, pero es así*). Through his statement, Miguel implicitly told me that he knew that I would think about this as a 'lie', or just a funny story, and he was probably also saying that he also thought of it in those terms sometimes. As an engineer working with projects of development, he participates in the world of science, which he refers to in terms of technicalities and methods for measurements, or when he insists on finding 'scientific' explanations for 'non-scientific' practices like the 'calling for water'. However, he also participates in practices that make other worlds emerge: worlds made of entities, beings and relations that are not acknowledged as real by science and the modern Peruvian state. The story shows the complexity of contemporary life in the Andes, where 'indigenous' and 'modern' worlds are not separate units, but emerging realities and always overlapping and partially connected (de la Cadena 2015). It is important to notice that when he translates between these two worlds, he translates from the relational world of Colca and into the language of science, for example when he explains the 'calling for water' with 'ions', and not the other way around. This illustrates that different knowledge systems, worlds and realities are not symmetrical in terms of power, they are organised in a hierarchy where some ways of knowing are more legitimate and are recognised as 'true'. Hence, Miguel was very much aware that, seen from a scientific perspective, what he told me was impossible and not a valid explanation for the functioning of a tractor, yet on the other hand it happened and it was real (Stensrud 2016d).

I translate the *t'inka*, *ch'alla* and *iranta* as communicative and relational world-making practices from where humans and other-than-humans (earth-mothers, water-mothers, mountain-lords and other beings and bonus-things like the tractor-with-*ch'alla*) emerge in the practice. These practices enact the possibility of fertility, goodwill and protection: the possibility of harvesting potatoes, safeguarding the water supply in a spring, or making sure that a tractor will endure and work well. State actors and engineers working in development projects usually see these practices as the cultural spice that adds colour and flavour to life in the Andes – cultural idiosyncrasies that have to be tolerated when working with Quechua-speaking peasants. Miguel is an engineer who not only recognises and tolerates but also engages with different world-making practices in his daily work and life. Through these practices, realities emerge. How can we imagine a tractor with *ch'alla*? It is not the same as a tractor without *ch'alla*; it is something more and something else. It has become a different and better entity, a 'thing-with-bonus', because it has become so with the protection and force from the earth-beings. Miguel knows this, but he also knows that the existence of tractor-with-*ch'alla* is not accepted everywhere; it cannot be included in official paperwork and bureaucracy or in reports from development projects. These tensions have to be negotiated on a daily basis, and through these negotiations, the worlds that Miguel lives in are continuously being made; it is not a question of either this or that world, but of the relationships that Marilyn Strathern (2004 [1991]) calls 'partial connections'. The worlds are partially connected because they are 'neither singular nor plural, neither one nor many' (2004 [1991]: 54). It is like thinking of water; partially connected worlds do not exist side by side, and are not identical, but are like streams of water flowing down a rocky hill: sometimes together, sometimes apart; at times joining and mixing, and at times diverging. What *la Junta* calls 'mixed water' comes from different sources, but can never again be separated into spring water and canal water.

Different practices enact different worlds; these worlds can be fragmented, uncertain and contested (see also Cepek 2016); they can be overlapping and changing, and they can all coexist as part of each other through negotiation. The negotiations and the tensions involved in them are what make world-making practices 'politics of the everyday'. To understand why the practice of *ch'alla* and other indigenous world-making practices are instances of everyday politics, we must see how the dominant Peruvian society regards these practices. In the dominant discourse of modernisation and progress, indigenous practices are ridiculed and seen as 'ancient' customs that should be eradicated because they are hindering progress and economic growth. This view was publicly stated by president Alan García in an interview on national television in 2011:

> [we] must defeat the absurd pantheistic ideologies that believe that walls are gods, that the air is god, the return to these primitive forms of religion, where they say do not touch that mountain because it is an apu and full of a millenarian spirit [...]. That we are advancing does not mean that all our ancient forms of thought have been overcome. (*Los Andes* 2011)

The state tends to see indigenous practices as obstructions to development that should be overcome by education, economic persuasion or force. In 2007, President García made social protests and strikes illegal, and the same year, he published an article in a national newspaper, where he called the opponents of extractive industries 'dogs in the manger'. Hence, he was saying that since indigenous people and environmentalists do not want to use the resources in their territories for economic gain and since they do not want anyone else (transnational companies) to exploit these valuable resources, they are lazy, jealous and angry. In a denigrating way, he accused indigenous and social movements of obstructing progress due to old ideologies, laziness and inertia, and because of the 'demagogy and deception that say that these lands cannot be touched because they are holy objects' (García Pérez 2007). Since the national economy of Peru is growing thanks to the extractive industries, any practice, project, community, way of life or organised movement that opposes the logic of extractivism is perceived as a threat.

Conclusion

State policies of water management seek to standardise water, to make it legible, measureable and possible to control, and to convert water into a commodity. However, when water and nature are defined as a singularised resource, and only that, then all the excessive meanings of water are peeled away. These meanings are then translated into the language of religion, as when *pago* is translated into 'offering', *t'inka* into 'libation', or when Alan García calls lands and mountains 'holy objects' (cf. de la Cadena 2015; Li 2015). Hence, these practices are defined, bounded, and put safely to rest in the category of 'indigenous religion'. I argue that paying water tariffs and taxes to the *Junta* and the state versus paying food offerings to the mountains and springs reveal fundamentally different ways of engaging with the environment. On the one hand, the practice of charging money comes from an extractivist logic, which separates humans from the environment and nature from culture, and which singularises water as only an economic resource. On the other hand, relational practices and logics of multiplicity, in which nature is inseparable from culture, allow different practices, entities and beings to emerge and participate in pluriversal collectives. That these logics – or epistemic-ontological regimes – are different does not prevent them from overlapping in everyday practices. All people – whether categorised by society as indigenous, mestizo or other – may engage in both extractivist and relational practices, and there is a need to get away from dichotomising modernity from indigeneity. There is no contradiction in participating in both worlds; there is no necessity of an either-or (de la Cadena 2015). Looking at people's actual practices in Colca reveal continuous efforts to maintain relations to earth-beings *and* to make coherent worlds.

Bruno Latour noted that if *cosmos* is to mean anything, it must embrace, literally, everything – including all the non-human entities making humans act. He argued: 'Cosmopolitans may dream of the time when citizens of the world come to recognise that they all inhabit the same world, but cosmopolitics are up against a somewhat more daunting task: to see how this 'same world' can be slowly composed' (Latour 2004: 457). This reminds us of the need to complicate the concept of 'nature'; to rethink the idea of nature as a singular entity that can only be 'interpreted' by culture. Understanding nature as multiple and emerging from practice, and composing a world in which humans are not seen as separate from the environment, and where plural (water) practices and beings can exist together, requires constant negotiations and careful attention to different kinds of relationships. In the next chapter, we will see that the changing weather and insecure water supply increase the importance of irrigation and *pagos/irantas* to mountains and springs, and that relationships to mountains might acquire new meanings in light of climate change.

4
Water Uncertainties and Disasters

For World Water Day on 22 March 2011, water users from all over the valley came to Chivay to take part in a march and a meeting where they would discuss climate change, how it affects water supply and how they could adapt. The water users came from almost all of the 33 different water user commissions in Colca. They brought painted and embroidered banners with illustrations and messages about water, like 'Water is life – do not waste it!' and 'Water should not be sold – water should be defended', and they marched around the public plaza so that all could see their messages. The water march and the following meeting was organised by the Junta de Usuarios, the NGO Desco Sur, the state irrigation programme PSI (Programa Subsectorial de Irrigaciones), and the municipality. The organising committee also had announced a banner competition, and a winner was chosen by two judges representing PSI and Desco, who came from Arequipa city. The winning banner was made by the water users commission of Chivay Urinsaya, and their message was written in Quechua: '*Mamaccochata sumacta ttincaricusun hashcata yacuta ccohuananchispacc*'. A translation to English would be something like this: 'We must give a good *t'inka* [ritual offering] to Mamaccocha so that she will provide us with a lot of water'. The judges liked that the message was written in the indigenous language Quechua and represented the cultural tradition of Colca. However, for the farmers in Chivay Urinsaya, the message was very real: the water supply from their 'mother spring' Mamaccocha was decreasing, and they had to treat her well to maintain the cultivation of the land and their lives as farmers. Keeping a good relationship with Mamaccocha required respect and reciprocity, and they made sure that she received proper *pagos* twice a year. However, Mamaccocha as a sentient being was not included in the meeting and discussion about possible responses to climate change that took place in the municipality hall after the march. The meeting focused on the effects of global warming on water: the reduction and disappearance of glaciers, springs and water streams.

In this chapter, I will look more into the consequences of decreasing water supplies and changing weather patterns. How does climate change affect the world and the beings inhabiting different places in the landscape, and the relationships among the beings and the places? How do people live with increasing uncertainties related to climate change and the future of water? These questions became a matter of concern for both farmers and political leaders in Caylloma province during the first decade of the 21st century, and this chapter shows how people in Colca respond to environmental change, both by working hard in their fields and in other income-generating activities, and by engaging intensely in relationships of reciprocity and care with mountain-beings and springs. The last part of the chapter, I discuss how these world-making practices become public and political.

The main topic of the World Water Day in 2011 was precisely 'climate change and adaptation', mirroring the discursive turn towards the concept of adaptation as a priority for research and policy in the 21st century. *Climate change adaptation* has been popularised through UNFCCC (United Nations Framework Convention on Climate Change) and has become the new buzzword in development. In his critical review of the term, Ben Orlove (2009) argues that it directs attention towards the problems that can be easily measured (such as economic well-being) and away from the problems that cannot be easily measured, such as people's concern for animals and mountains. Hence, the term excludes many aspects of life that are not seen as relevant or important, like the relationships to earth-beings.

After the water march around the plaza of Chivay, there was a meeting for all the water users in the assembly hall of the municipality, where they would discuss how climate change affected them and how they could adapt. These questions were perceived as extremely urgent because only a few days earlier, the political authorities in the province of Caylloma declared a state of emergency after a month of extreme weather in the province: 70 per cent of the population had been affected by the torrential rainfall and heavy snow in the highlands, as well as unexpected frost in the valley; 25,000 young alpacas had died, 400 hectares of cultivated land were lost, and several irrigation canals were destroyed. The mayors of Caylloma's 20 sub-districts estimated the losses to exceed US $1.5 million (*Perú 21* 2011: 7). The first speaker at the meeting was an engineer who was invited to talk about his work on improvements of water sources and hydraulic infrastructure in other parts of the southern highlands. His presentation started with a short film about what a future without water would look like in 2070. By seeing the images of desert land with no life, the onlookers were supposed to wake up and realise that the water resources are being depleted and that the outcome will be devastating if nothing is done. He then presented different measures that could be undertaken, like making inventories of water sources and critical infrastructures and taking measures to improve water efficiency. The film served as a confirmation of what water users in Colca were already observing in their daily life and work, as they would soon give testimony.

The meeting proceeded to discuss the present situation in Colca and future scenarios. The two questions that guided the discussions were: How do you see the current situation of water and climate change in our area? and What would the alternative be to find solutions to the problems? To discuss these questions, the organisers had invited representatives from different state institutions, development agencies and NGOs working in Colca Valley (Agricultural Ministry, AgroRural, SierraSur, PSI, and the NGO Desco Sur), in addition to the *Junta* and the water users commissions. First, the members of the water users commissions were invited to present their testimonies about how climate change affected them, and the commissions had representatives from the different climatic zones in Colca: Tisco and Caylloma represented the highlands (*parte alta*), Lari and Coporaque represented the middle valley (*parte media*), and Cabanaconde and Huambo represented the lowlands (*parte baja*). The main message that came across from all representatives was that the mountains have lost their glaciers, the springs have dried, the water level in the rivers has decreased, and the soil has eroded due to heavy rain and lost its capacity to store rainwater. The representative from Cabanaconde emphasised how the decreasing water supplies from glaciers and springs make farmers even more dependent on the Majes canal. The man representing Huambo told us that the amount of water passing in the Colca River, fed by springs and streams from the surrounding mountains, has decreased from 600 litres per second to only 100 litres per second. This was referred to as 'evidence' that water is no longer coming out of the mountains because of global warming. The representative from the pastoral community Tisco, in the highlands above the altitude of 4,200 metres, talked about how the mountain peat bog lands (*bofedales*) used to be like sponges holding the rainwater. The glaciers used to store the rainwater and feed the *bofedales* with meltwater. Today, however, the water runs over the surface of the eroded and dry soil. Blaming climate change, he predicted 'after some months we will no longer have any water and the springs will dry'.

The testimonials confirmed the dominant climate change discourses presented by 'experts', namely that global warming led to the disappearance of glaciers, which again led to water scarcity and soil degradation. Almost all the speakers were middle-aged men, leaders in their communities, and they spoke with big words about global warming, repeating the scientific discourse on climate change and sustaining their claims with 'facts' based on water measurements. At the end, a young woman spoke, and she focused on a very specific problem in her community. She represented a new user committee called 'Miraculous springs' that was established two years earlier in a highland pastoral community. They had constructed a pond to harvest water, but in the extreme weather that had occurred in that year's rainy season, their pond was destroyed by the torrential rain, and she pleaded for help and support. While not mentioning the driving causes behind global warming – which may seem hard to tackle from their position – the water users focus on how to deal with the effects of climate change, which are making their lives and livelihoods increasingly hard.

Emergencies caused by extreme weather have become more common in the last decade. After 2011, similar emergencies caused by heavy snow, torrential rain or long drought periods have occurred every year (*RPP Noticias* 2012, 2013; *El Buho* 2013). In 2014, authorities calculated that the drought and frost had caused an economic loss of 14 million *soles* (US $4.9 million), affecting 5,284 families in the province (*RPP Noticias* 2014). In the highland districts, the new-born and young alpaca (*crías*) died because of scarcity of rain and fodder, while in the valley, 6,000 hectares of cultivated areas were affected by the irregular frost, and more than a thousand hectares of beans, potatoes and maize were lost (*RPP Noticias* 2014). Unlike the occasional snowstorm or drought periods that happened earlier, these extreme events and emergencies are disrupting the known seasonal cycles, and they are becoming more frequent and normalised. Contrary to other environmental disasters in the Caylloma highlands and Colca Valley, like earthquakes, volcanic eruptions and landslides, the consequences of climate change are slow and seem to be perpetual. As Kirsten Hastrup (2009) argues, climate change is a chronic disaster; it is diffuse and long term, but it fundamentally alters the foundations of people's lives.

In the past two decades, new concerns have emerged as many farmers have noted changes in the weather, the landscape and the water supply:

melting glaciers, irregular rainy seasons, more extreme weather (drought and frost), springs that disappear and dry pastures. In the same period, international NGOs and national public agencies have introduced the narratives of global warming and climate change, which resonate and give meaning to the observations that many farmers make in their everyday life. The narrative of global climate change gives scientific authority and legitimacy to the local observations, and there is funding for programmes and projects that focus on climate change adaptation. At the same time, these narratives foster and nurture a sense of fear of a waterless future without the possibility of life. As Kirsten Hastrup points out, one of the challenges for anthropologists working with climate change is to explore new senses of causality that may embrace several scales at once, and see that global imagery is part of local experiences (Hastrup 2013a).

The peasant farmers in Caylloma, however, do not experience climate change as an isolated phenomenon, but as one of many issues that smallholders have to deal with. Several scholars have shown how changes in glaciers and water supply are entangled in socio-economic structures and neoliberal policies (Oré et al. 2009; Carey 2010; Lynch 2012; Rasmussen 2015; Boelens 2009). Furthermore, as shown in this book, water practices are not only embedded in sociality, politics and economic life, but also in relationships with the sentient landscape. Water and water-related practices are thus inseparable from the different world-making practices from which multiple and inter-related realities emerge (Zhan 2009; Tsing 2015). In ethnographic research, there are different scales of attention and modes of perception (Hastrup 2013b), and it matters what kinds of questions we ask and what we look for. Anna Tsing (2015) has shown us that scales are not ready-made but always constructed and contested. As Susan Gal argues, 'scaling is a relational practice that relies on situated comparisons among events, persons, and activities' (2016: 91). If all we search for are structures in what we recognise as 'economy' or 'politics', then this is what we will see. However, the multiplicity of worlds, and their entanglement across scales, becomes discernible for those who care to pay attention.

As argued in chapter 3, the state-sponsored water-practices, including tariff payments and measuring in litres per second, which I call practices of singularisation, do not necessarily exclude other-than-modern beings and practices. Instead, they overlap and are partially connected in a dynamic web of relationships between water sources as sentient beings and water as measurable liquid and economic resource. Following from this, I suggest that climate change – both the effects and the responses – is also embedded in the multiplicity of relationships. In Colca Valley, climate change also affects the other-than-human beings, and measures of adaptation and mitigation also take these beings and relationships into consideration. Maintaining relations of respect and reciprocity in relation to the powerful beings in the surroundings, who respond to human action and interaction, is being done as part of a range of practices aiming to live well in a place and avoid misfortune, and to maintain the social well-being and sustainability of a place and its people.

Responses to climate change that emerge from indigenous and 'other-than-modern' life-projects in particular places have often been interpreted as symbolic and cultural representations (see for example Orlove et al. 2008; Adger et al. 2009; Crate and Nuttall 2009; Crate 2011; Boelens 2015). I argue that these responses are not only 'cultural', a view that hinges on a separation between nature as objective and singular and culture as subjective perspectives and construction of meaning. Instead, responses emerge from and are entangled with practices that make worlds in which 'nature' and 'culture' as separate spheres do not make sense (Kohn 2013; de la Cadena 2015). These practices are not only representational, but also enact 'emplacement', or what Blaser (2019) calls 'emplaced collectives', which are not best thought of as 'cultural' communities living in 'natural' places but as heterogeneous assemblages of human and non-human entities 'with unique configurations that "take place" in specific locations' (Blaser 2019: 84). Blaser argues that the politics of emplaced collectives is marked by 'strong mutual obligations that make it difficult from within them to privilege the needs of some of their components at the expense of others without risking the whole collective' (2019: 84). This is similar to de la Cadenas' analysis of being 'in-*ayllu*', which describes how 'humans and other-than-humans are inherently connected' (de la Cadena 2015: 101) and their relationship is also part of them (2015: 102). Similarly, water and its users in Colca Valley are part of a mutual composition of place, but they are also part of translocal and global relationships (Cruikshank 2005; Zhan 2009; Hastrup 2013a; Li 2015; Tsing 2015). In other words, people, land and water co-constitute each other in everyday practices and translocal encounters. When these relationships and compositions are altered and thrown out of balance, this fosters uncertainty and people need to perform different kinds of work – relational, ritual and constructional – to make the water flow.

Communicating with the water-giving mountain-beings

'The *apus* are our godfathers and godmothers (*padrinos y madrinas*)', Maria said. Cotallaulli is the name of the *apu* that is looking over Chivay; she is a sleeping volcano with hot springs, and she is a woman. Her friend Miriam claimed that Mt Mismi (a bigger *apu* between Tuti and Coporaque) was courting her. The words that Miriam used, as well as her tone, indicated that she was teasing Cotallaulli. 'Careful, don't annoy her', Maria said. 'But she is a bit naughty', Miriam responded; 'she says she will burst, but it never happens.' With a worried look on her face, Maria pleaded to Cotallaulli: 'Please don't listen to her.' It was in everyday conversations and small-talk like this, as well as in the small actions and interactions in daily life, like pouring drops of beer on the ground, that the reality of mountains, earth-places and springs as living beings emerged. In these small moments, I became aware of their presence and immediacy in people's lives. My friends in Chivay also made me realise that the *apus* are also affected by global warming, which is reminiscent of other ethnographic accounts of climate change and sentient mountains, glaciers and weather phenomena in other parts of the world (see for example Cruikshank 2005; Bolin 2009; Leduc

Figure 5 There is very little left of the glacier on Mount Hualca Hualca, rising 6,025 metres above sea level. In 2011, the peasants from Pinchollo village went to the place where the meltwater starts to flow to respectfully acknowledge the presence of Apu Hualca Hualca, by making pagos, singing and dancing.

2011). Two of the most majestic mountains in Colca are Hualca Hualca and Ampato. Both of them can be seen from Chivay and they used to be covered in snow. As Miriam and Maria said, 'Hualca Hualca and Ampato always used to wear their white ponchos – always! Now they look blue.'

For people living in the town of Chivay and for the farmers working their fields in Chivay Urinsaya, Mt Hualca Hualca (6,025 metres) and Mt Ampato (6,288 metres) are part of the horizon when they are looking towards Yanque. However, these *apus* are more than just part of a scenery, which has lost some of its beauty now that the mountaintops are no longer snow white. They are also powerful protectors and guardians who demand respect. People might summon them and offer gifts, which they may accept or not. They can be capricious and dangerous if they are disrespected. Both Hualca Hualca and Ampato have a more immediate significance to the villages that receive water directly from them. Hualca Hualca provides water to various communities, among them are Cabanaconde and the smaller village Pinchollo, which is part of Cabanaconde district. Gelles (2000) describes how Hualca Hualca gives water and life to the fields of Cabanaconde and accepts 'her children's many offerings, responding vengefully when the latter are insufficient or made in bad faith' (Gelles 2000: 84).

This kind of reciprocal relationships and vengeful or capricious responses are prominent in ethnographic descriptions from the Andes (see, among others, Allen 1988; de la Cadena 2015; Gelles 2000; Gose 1994). However, these relationships are not static. As political, economic and environmental conditions change, so do people's relationships with their surrounding entities. Based on ethnographic research in Tapay and Cabanaconde since the early 1990s, Paerregaard argues that the Majes canal has altered farmers' relations to the mountains as living beings, and that making offerings to the *apus* is not as important as it used to be (Paerregaard 2013). As discussed in chapter 1, the Majes canal has certainly brought many changes to the Colca Valley. I will argue, however, that the canal does not necessarily mean that the *apus* lose importance as providers of water, animals and protection. For most people, there is no necessary paradox in engaging in ritual relationships with the mountain, while they also receive water from the Majes canal and participate in state programmes of formalisation and technification of water use, although the different practices are grounded in diverging conceptualisations of nature, including whether 'nature', as a category different from society, is meaningful at all.

The changes that have followed the Majes canal and other development interventions notwithstanding, I found a continuous concern to maintain good relations with the mountains among the water users along the canal. In Pinchollo, where 40 per cent of the irrigation water comes from the Majes canal, they did for some years cancel the practice of doing an offering at the top of Hualca Hualca, which used to be an annual event with all villagers participating. However, a few years before my fieldwork in 2011, they had re-started the practice, with the support of the NGO Desco. This NGO had also made a film, which not only shows the collective rituals, but also a re-enactment of an old custom of sacrificing a young girl to the mountain. The film shows how the community members accompany a beautiful girl in a white dress and how she enters a water spring called 'the window', which is like a little cave going into the mountain.

Practices may be reshaped when facing new challenges, such as climate change and melting glaciers. More than two decades ago, Paul Gelles described Hualca Hualca as a 'striking mountain, with its snow-covered base peaking in a jagged rocky crest' (Gelles 2000: 84). Today, there is little left of the permanent ice and snow, and this is partly blamed on global warming and partly on a more local source of heat: the neighbouring volcano Sabancaya, who occasionally spews ashes. After a big eruption some years ago, glacial meltwater rushed down from Hualca Hualca, destroying irrigation infrastructure and cultivated fields. Since then, the glacier has not recovered because of increased temperatures. Some days, Hualca Hualca can be seen covered in snow, but it soon melts away. The farmers in Pinchollo still depend on the glacial melt water from Hualca Hualca to irrigate 60 per cent of their fields, and hence they are deeply affected by the disappearance of Hualca Hualca's ice.

After the regular supply of meltwater decreased substantially a few years ago, the Pinchollo farmers started to go up to Hualca Hualca every year to offer *pagos*, hoping that the water supply will increase. In October 2011, I was invited by the water users commission to join the villagers of Pinchollo going up to the foot of the Hualca Hualca glacier, in order to offer gifts to the mountain and to clean the water channels. The irrigation commission organised the event, with the support and participation of the local authorities: the mayor, the justice of the peace, and the leader of the peasant community. After a Catholic mass in the church, all went in a procession around the plaza, led by San Isidro Labrador, the patron saint of the farmers, and the priest, who sprinkled holy water on the participants. San Isidro, who was carried by several men, accompanied the water users to the road where they started the walk towards Hualca Hualca, and the saint bade them farewell. Most of the water users walked on foot and some rode horses up the steep and rocky paths for several hours until we reached the campsite. After dinner, we gathered around a bonfire for a meeting to discuss the following day's events and to hold a serenade for Hualca Hualca. I was told that tomorrow was the day of Hualca Hualca, 'like his birthday'. A group of musicians had brought their instruments – harp, guitar and mandolin – and they sang a song for Hualca Hualca called '*Apu* Hualca Hualca, powerful mountain'. Early next morning, after a good night's sleep and breakfast, we walked uphill to the foot of the glacier where the meltwater starts flowing down towards the village. However, there was hardly any ice left to see, just a thin piece of ice crawling down in the middle of a broad rocky mountainside. The scant meltwater that dripped from the ice started a small stream flowing downwards and making some green patches along the way. Apart from celebrating Hualca Hualca's 'birthday', the water users' visit had a very particular purpose, which the leader of Pinchollo's peasant community explained to me:

> This is a ritual that we make for our *Apu* Hualca Hualca. We, the authorities, watch over our people in Pinchollo. The organisers in the irrigation commission, together with the mayor, and the leaders of the peasant community, we make an offering, a ritual, so that he [Hualca Hualca] will receive with a lot of goodwill and affection, and so that we will not lack water in the next year. The water is fundamental for us, for our plants, for the humans. We live from the water, and that is why we make this offering, with a lot of affection and devotion. And I know that tomorrow, the water will increase with 3 or 4 litres per second. We have this hope and every year we do this.

The leader of the irrigation commission was in charge of presenting the *iranta*, that is, a package of alpaca foetus, llama fat, maize, coca leaves, sweets, fruit, flowers, wine and maize brew, to Hualca Hualca, asking him not to forget the people, to give them more water and to protect the village. Suddenly, a huge amount of ice fell down from a rock overhang, startling the onlookers. One of the elderly men in the water users commission explained to me that this was common; some ice always fell down when they made offerings. He explained that it was like when someone visits you on your birthday and you get excited. This was Hualca Hualca's way of showing excitement and affection: he makes the ice fall in order to say 'Here is the water!'

Afterwards, the water users made more offerings (many had brought their own alpaca foetus and other special ingredients) and libations (*t'inka* and *ch'alla*), by sprinkling alcohol in the air and pouring *chicha* that was coloured red on the rock and the ice. While some were dedicated to the assembling of *pagos*, others made virgin mother figures of the ice that had fallen down. All were sharing drinks, and some started to dance while the musicians were playing music and singing in honour of Hualca Hualca. People's spirits were lifted making a festive atmosphere, and it felt like being at a birthday party. Before going back to camp for dinner, some of us had a photo session where individuals and groups posed with the ice. Manuel was one of the elderly men in the group, and he had been smiling all day. Manuel had done his best to keep the good spirits up among all the participants since we departed from Pinchollo. He explained to me. 'Without *Apu* Hualca Hualca, without the snowcapped mountain, there is no water. If there is no water, there is no life. Without Hualca Hualca our village would not exist. That is why we make the *t'inka*.' His friend added, 'The *Apu* Hualca Hualca gives us the vital liquid; the water that my wife drinks, that my children drink'.

The next day, after a cold night's rest in the camp, we went to the spring called 'the window' to make *iranta* and *t'inka*. The villagers talked about the human offerings made in ancient times: in times of crisis, a young girl would be chosen to go into the mountain through 'the window' as *Apu* Hualca Hualca called upon her. The group of musicians, sang their song:

Apu Hualca Hualca	Lord Hualca Hualca
Cerro Poderoso	Powerful mountain
Desde aquellas nieves	From those snows
Bajan nuestras aguas	Our waters flow down
Para el regadío	For the irrigation
De nuestra campiña	Of our lands
En el sitio de Achumani	In the place of Achumani
Hay una ventana	There is a window
Donde antiguamente	Where they in the old times
Pagaban al Apu	Paid to the Lord
Con una doncella	With a maiden
Al Apu Hualca Hualca	For the Lord Hualca Hualca

The farmers in Pinchollo recognise the mountain Hualca Hualca as their source of life. They are worried because the permanent snow is disappearing and there is less water in the springs. Manuel expressed his concern about Hualca Hualca: 'If the glacier disappears, there is no life any more; there is no village any more. The mountain supports us. Who will contain the thaw? Earlier the snow of Hualca Hualca reached the foot of the mountain. Now there is little snow.'

On their way down from the mountain, women and men cleaned and repaired the canals with shovels so that the water would flow more easily down to the village and the fields. While the effects of global warming are perceived in very material and physical ways, the causes behind seem abstract and out of reach, impossible to solve. Even the mighty *apus* like Hualca Hualca are affected by the chronic catastrophe of global warming and may become less powerful as a consequence. When their life source loses power, people do what they can to keep the water flowing, by maintaining good relationships with the water sources and to maintain the channels to sure that water reaches the villages. I suggest that the increased intensity in affective relationships with earth-beings and increased ritual activity is partly a response to the increased uncertainty related to a complex interplay of market forces and climate change in recent times.

Belated rain and dry springs

In Colca Valley, global warming is mainly talked about through water, both related to the changing supply and demand of water. In the past couple of decades, people living there have increasingly been observing changes in weather and environment, like the drying springs and pastures, and the irregular incidents of frost in the supposed rainy season. During my first stay in 2011, most of the farmers I talked to told me about their worries regarding these changes. What they talked about most frequently, was the irregular rain: belated rain, less rain, torrential rainfall and rainfall in the dry season (Stensrud 2015). Many expressed their concern, like my friend Maria, who said: 'The rain comes when it feels like it.' The expected points of the beginning and end of the rainy season are strongly connected to the agricultural cycle, which should start with the sowing in September and end with the harvesting in May (Treacy 1994: 56). This cycle has developed over generations and has been adapted to the local environments and the weather seasons. When I asked leaders of the water user commissions in the different villages in Colca Valley about recent changes, they all talked about how the rainy seasons had changed since they were children. While the rain 'used to accompany us in the sowing' in September, now they had to wait until the end of the year, and sometimes it only rained from mid-January to mid-March. Others emphasise that, some years, the rain continues into the months of April, May and June, which are considered part of the 'dry season'. Maria told me that the rain that comes too late, in April and May, 'destroys the harvest; the rain makes the potato rot, and we must dig them up in the rain'.

Rapidly shifting weather is not unusual in mountain environments. However, what most farmers in Colca observed, was a dramatic increasing irregularity and uncertainty regarding the seasons. The leader of the water users commission in Yanque Urinsaya expressed the uncertainty related to the new irregularities: 'Each weather had its period, we used to know when it would rain, but now we don't know, at any random moment it rains and that harms us, there is a lot of variation.' Drought is not a new phenomenon in Caylloma, but people say that earlier generations had methods to predict whether the coming year would be a good year with sufficient rain or not, and they would prepare themselves accordingly. The mayor of Canocota village, who also is a farmer, told me that people used to know how to 'read the signs of nature', as he phrased it:

> Earlier, if there would be a dry year, we the people took precautions, because we knew, we knew how the nature expressed itself, for example in the plants or in the earth [...] or in how the fox cries. The animals and the plants manifest themselves, and the Andean man observes, and he knows what is going to happen and he prepares.

The people who still know these signs, look at the earth beneath the stones, observe the flowering of the plants, and listen to the crying of the foxes. If a farmer observes green algae in the river water, he knows that it will be a good year, and he knows that if the seagulls fly up the river from the ocean, they are bringing the message that the rain is approaching. Treacy (1994) has described how the farmers in Coporaque in the 1980s would take into account the strengths of the rains in September and October, the amount of snow on the mountains, and the early flowering for the plants as climatic indicators (Treacy 1994: 56). Many of my interlocutors, however, complained that much of this knowledge has, to a large degree, been lost.

The idea of lost knowledge, in addition to daily observations of changing environment and weather patterns and the narratives of global warming and climate change, add up to an increasing sense of uncertainty and fear of a future without water and no possibility of life. When I asked farmers about the future, they would talk about how water will disappear: '15 years from today, the water will decrease, and we will no longer be able to supply ourselves; with so little water, we will lose harvests and animals'. Statements such as this one bear witness to the fear that life is not sustainable in Colca (Stensrud 2015). These fears are nurtured by images and films from African deserts that are shown in the powerpoints of engineers and NGO workers who talk about climate change in different meetings and workshops organised for water users. However, the predictions of a waterless future are also connected to observations made in daily agricultural work, and they are explicitly linked to the lack of rain. When there is no rain to feed the springs and the glaciers, and the short and intense February rainfalls cause soil erosion, the conditions for drought are created. The irregular rain and the drying springs lead to practical problems of irrigation and distribution of water among users. Since farmers in many communities now have to sow before the rain comes, there is a greater need for irrigation water. The temperature is also higher during daytime, and one water user in Cabanaconde commented that 'the heat affects us; we used to irrigate every 40 or 45 days, but now, after only 30 days the plants are dry and ask for more water'. The increased demand for water made the work of the *regidores* (the water allocators) more demanding, like the daily work of Aurelio, who was *regidor* of Chivay Urinsaya in 2011 (see chapter 3), who made his rounds regularly to maintain order in the intricate system of canals, fields and *libretas* (control books).

Two of the members of the water users commission in Chivay Urinsaya were Miriam and Pedro, a married couple who lived in a house very close to where I lived in Chivay. I often visited them in the morning or in the afternoon, after they came home from the fields that they had inherited from their parents and where they cultivated broad beans (*habas*) and maize. One day Pedro told me:

> The water is decreasing little by little.... We notice. Earlier they allocated water to 15 farmers a day [in my section], but now they give it only to 8. There is not enough water. Mamaccocha is drying up. There are no springs like there used to be; they have dried up. On my father's

land there used to be two springs that gave water, and there was a little garden there. Now they are dry.

Pedro and Miriam lament the decreasing water in Mamaccocha, not only because they must work harder to irrigate, but also because the water is very important in making Chivay their home. One afternoon in early May 2011, I helped Miriam to sort the last batch of broad beans (*habas verdes*) that she and Pedro had harvested that day, seven bags in total. We separated 30 kilos for an aunt who owned a restaurant, and the rest they would sell on the market for between 80 centimos and 1 *sol* per kilo. They kept some beans to cook for themselves, and Miriam invited me to eat a bowl of boiled fresh beans with cheese. It tasted delicious, and Miriam said that in her opinion, the *habas* in Chivay have a better flavour than in other places. The *habas* taste sweeter here, she said, and explained that probably it was because the water here provides a special flavour. Many years earlier, Miriam and Pedro had moved to Arequipa city in order to offer their children better education, and they lived there for several years. Many families migrate from Colca to Arequipa to have better access to schools, jobs and health services. However, when their children were adults, with jobs and families on their own, Miriam and Pedro moved back to their beloved Chivay in order to cultivate their fields and live a quiet and good life. They were tired of the stressful life in the city. However, they found that farming was not like it used to be when they were younger; the ecological and socio-economic conditions had changed.

When I returned to Colca after two years absence in November 2013, the rainy season was supposed to start, but once again all the farmers were waiting in vain. I went to visit Miriam and Pedro in their house. In order to find them before they went out, I went early in the morning, but Pedro had already gone out to irrigate one of their fields. Miriam took a break from her sewing machine, where she was making garments and purses in vivid colours and patterns to sell at the market, and invited me to have some hot tea and bread for breakfast. Like so many times before, we talked about the weather, and Miriam updated me on the abnormal seasons in the past year: it had rained in the dry season, and the frost continued into (the supposed) rainy season. 'The world is upside-down', Miriam noted thoughtfully. She continued: 'earlier the seasons were respected … but the climate has changed, and it affects the agriculture. The earth has transformed too much.' She was worried that their bean plants would get the 'chocolate illness' that blackens and ruins the beans. The most notable changes were the frosts that suddenly arrived at times when it should be warm, and the extreme heat during daytime. 'The sun seems to be closer to the earth', Miriam said. A few hours later, I met Pedro coming home from the fields. He complained that they must irrigate more often because the heat makes the earth dryer than usual. Farming involves harder work and they risk losing the harvest because of frost or illnesses.

Money cannot be eaten: new insecurities

During the past couple of decades, the conditions for small-scale farming have worsened and it has become harder to survive as a peasant farmer in Colca Valley. 'We used to cultivate to consume, but now everything is money', Miriam told me. Having returned to Colca to escape the money-chasing in the city of Arequipa, she soon discovered that the processes of marketisation and commercialisation had also arrived in Chivay. To survive economically, Pedro and Miriam had other sources of income in addition to farming. Pedro took odd jobs for the municipality and others, and Miriam had a market stall where she sold clothes and small purses and boxes, some of which she embroidered herself in typical Colca patterns. I often visited her at her stall, where we could chat in the quiet periods of the day, while waiting for customers. At the marketplace, I also got to know other women selling clothes, shoes and artisanal items in the surrounding stalls. Maria sold factory-made cotton clothes, Cirila sold shoes, and Hilda sold hats and bags that she embroidered in the beautiful colourful patterns from Colca.

Agriculture is still the main economic activity in Colca, but it has been undergoing a transition from subsistence farming to market production of potatoes, quinoa, beans and maize. Private banks and financial institutions offer micro-credit and loans to farmers at high interest rates of between 18 and 30 per cent. The money is spent on fertilisers, pesticides, herbicides, and new seeds. New standardised types of potatoes have to a large degree replaced local varieties. In 2014, farmers in Chivay told me about a new potato called La Única, which had been introduced five years earlier. While they used to harvest potatoes seven months after sowing, La Única can be harvested after only four or five months in the highland climate, and therefore it is more efficient to produce for market sale. La Única is a potato variety that, after being developed by the International Potato Centre (CIP) was first released in Peru in 1998 and has since spread to many parts of the world.[1] However, several people, both farmers and others, in Chivay pointed out to me that La Única does not taste good and it cannot be kept for a long time. The smaller potatoes they used to sow earlier, like the black potato, Sika, had a better flavour and could be kept for longer. Miriam's friend Cirila talked about the fear of new illnesses because of the chemicals used in food production: 'Earlier they used natural fertilisers from the cattle pen, but now they use [artificial] fertilisers and hormones. That's why the potatoes get big. And this produces cancer. The cancer is due to the fertilisers, the hormones they put in.'

Since farmers often take up credit loans to buy seeds and fertilisers, they are left with nothing but debt if the harvest fails. After losing her harvest two years in a row, Cirila was paying off her debts by selling shoes in Chivay, where she rented a market kiosk beside Miriam's business. When I talked to her in November 2013, she was considering whether she should sow potatoes again. Potatoes are usually sown in the beginning of the rainy season, but the rain had not yet come. The fluctuating market price was another factor to take into consideration. Cirila said: 'When there is a lot of potatoes the price falls, and when there is little potatoes, the price increases. And the farmer cannot guess …' When I met her again in March, after four months of drought and frost periods, she told me that she had not sown anything this year and had instead chosen to focus on her shoe business in the Chivay market. She was happy with that decision when she considered how her neighbours had lost a large part of their beans and all the potatoes were ruined.

As farmers make plans for the coming season, they have to anticipate the weather and the market. Both have become increasingly difficult to predict in the past couple of decades: the weather is more unstable because of climate change and market prices are more volatile because of deregulation policies. Farmers respond to this exacerbation of uncertainties in different ways. Many people move to the city because farming is no longer considered to be 'profitable', which in this context, means that it is almost impossible to earn a living as a small-scale peasant farmer. When I interviewed the leaders of water users commissions, they often pointed to the empty fields during our conversations: 'Look at those abandoned fields', they would say, before they talked about how changing climate and markets affected livelihoods and relationships in the valley. One change that many noted was the increased costs of labour. Earlier, farmers in the valley usually performed tasks like sowing and harvesting collectively and reciprocally: farmers helped each other and mutually exchanged services.

Today, it is more common to hire landless people – often migrants from highland communities – as day labourers (*peones*).

The leader of the Junta de Usuarios in Colca Valley was concerned that all the young people wanted to be merchants and businessmen instead of producing food. 'What are we going to eat?', he asked rhetorically, 'Money cannot be eaten.' The concern is not only about food security, but growing individualism and social inequality as a consequence of market liberalisation. The effects of marketisation also exacerbate the impact of climate change on households. In March 2014, I interviewed the mayor of Lari district, where all of the 320 farmers had lost on average 60 per cent of their harvests after drought and frost had ruined the supposed rainy season. He explained that they were in a crisis because most of these farmers had borrowed money from micro-finance agencies and now they would have to refinance their loans. 'The micro-finance agencies have made us forget certain customs', the mayor of Lari said. He explained that in his opinion, farmers should go back to doing communal work and *ayni*, in order to stand united as equals: 'this is a way of mitigating'. A proposal to return to *ayni* – which is a form of labour exchange based on mutual reciprocity (Allen 1988; Mayer 2002) – is a way of envisioning the future as in need of commonality and mutuality. Such visions of a better future evoke certain imaginations of the past as different; not necessarily easier or more just, but quieter and more predictable.

One quiet morning at the market, I talked to Miriam, Maria, Hilda and Cirila about how Chivay had changed during the past couple of decades. Miriam talked nostalgically about her childhood, about fifty years ago:

> It used to be calmer. My father sent my brother and me to bring the cow from the mountains, and since we knew the names of the mountains, we found [our way]. It used to be nice, all the world was [made of] fields [*chakra*]. There were only about a hundred people living in Chivay, and just a few houses. The plaza was like everyone's backyard, with hens and pigs walking around. There was no piped water, in each street there was a water canal made of stones, and we went to the springs to fetch water in buckets. […] The nutrition was healthier. They did not use insecticides; they used ashes from the *yareta*, which they used as firewood.[2] Now there is almost no *yareta* left. It grows like green mushroom in the hills and it is good to burn.

Hilda added that the *yareta* 'grows like a human being; it takes time to grow'. All four women talked, confirming and complementing each other's thoughts and memories. They talked about how they could not buy milk or eggs, but they could barter from those who had cows and hens. They remembered that there used to be plenty of beans, maize and barley, and that people came from Huambo with salt to trade for beans. From the high parts, pastoralists brought alpaca meat and wool to trade. In those times, there was no electric light and people lit candles in their windows at night, while outside in the dark night, there were ghosts roaming in the shadows. The women warned me that humans should not walk through desolate unknown places; it could be very dangerous. Especially where the mountains don't know you, then you should be careful to show the proper respect.

Climate cosmopolitics

Most *irantas* and *pagos* in Colca Valley are made privately. Depending on the purpose, they are made within a house – either a family home or a business locale – or on a field, or by a water spring, with just a few selected members of the water users commission present. Ideally, the humans should not watch and disturb while the earth-being eats, out of respect. A few rituals are performed with the whole community present, like the celebrations of the water-mother Yakumama after the cleaning work of the irrigation canals in August, as described in chapter 3. However, the main *pago* is usually made the night before, with just a few persons present.

In later years, more rituals have come to be performed publicly in the Andes, either as tourist attractions or in support of indigenous political movements. In Peru, the Andean indigenous movements have not had the same force in the last two decades as in Bolivia, where Evo Morales was elected as the first indigenous president and the rights of Pachamama were incorporated in the constitution. Morales has famously celebrated the earth-mother Pachamama with huge public offerings and festivities. The mayor of Caylloma province often highlighted the Qollana-Cabana culture and the pride in the cultural traditions of Colca, like the different fiestas and rituals connected to sowing, irrigating and harvesting. The famous Wititi-dance, which is danced by people in colourful Colca dresses in the fiesta of Virgin Asunta in August and in the fiesta of Concepción in December, was included as cultural heritage on UNESCO's list in 2015.

Figure 6 On the World Water Day in 2011, peasants – called water users – from all over Colca Valley met in Chivay to march and to discuss climate change and water. In the march, they carried flags and banners, and the women were dressed in hats and *pollera* skirts with the distinct design of the different Colca communities.

As seen in the beginning of this chapter, earth-beings were not directly a part of the World Water Day in 2011, although Mamaccocha was mentioned on the winning banner. Three years later, however, in March 2014, the celebration of the World Water Day included a public offering to Yakumama and Pachamama, performed on the plaza of Chivay. The idea of enacting the *iranta* publicly was partly intended to acknowledge the existing local water cultures. Gabriel, one of the engineers working in the state administration of water – who, like Miguel, was born in Colca Valley and educated in Arequipa city – was one of the first to post pictures of the *pago* and the rain on Facebook, commenting: 'After the *pago*, a rain from God, like a blessing.' Under another picture he wrote: 'The *pago* to the water, which was carried out successfully and afterwards a good rain fell, in the locality of Chivay, yesterday 7th of March, we hope that the rains continue, to ensure the water resources for the present crop year.' What happens when these world-making practices and relations to earth-beings are made public? Do they hold a cosmopolitical potential, in the sense that they create new collective modes of being together and allow a diversity of worlds to coexist? Do they enact pluriversal worlds? I suggest that it depends on *how* they are made public and on whose premises. When they are presented in the language of religion and cultural representation, like on the municipal Facebook page, where they were described as 'ancestral culture', the practices are in a way made harmless and irrelevant because they are bounded, defined, and put safely to rest in a known category that refers to the past. Hence, they are presented as unchanging and, by implication, unable to create change and rebel against the hegemonic order of things. I noticed how people often distanced themselves from these practices when talking to others, by placing the practices safely in the past: 'This is what our ancestors used to do.' The reason for this need to assert distance was probably because of the social hierarchies that are legitimised by ideas of race and levels of education, as well as discrimination against indigenous people throughout public life in Peru.

However, I suggest that this explanation is not sufficient. It could also be a way of preventing expected misunderstandings, or what Viveiros de Castro calls 'equivocation', which is not just a failure to understand, 'but a failure to understand that understandings are necessarily not the same, and that they are not related to imaginary ways of "seeing the world" but to the real worlds that are being seen' (Viveiros de Castro 2004: 11). Equivocations are inherently implicit in all kinds of encounters, and are therefore also – perhaps not intentionally, but still – taken for granted by those whose world is being misunderstood. Looking at people's actual practices reveals continuous efforts to maintain relations to other beings and to make coherent worlds. When the other-than-human beings – like the Pachamama, Yakumama and *apus* – are invoked, consulted and supplicated in search for a solution to a specific problem (in this case drought), then their presence as *real beings* is acknowledged. When emerging as parts of the public space, they are also making politics. Rancière's definition of politics is that of breaking with the configuration whereby parts are defined and making a place for 'the part of those who have no part' (Rancière 1999: 30). He explains:

> This break is manifest in a series of actions that reconfigure the space where parties, parts, or lack of parts have been defined. Political activity is whatever shifts a body from the place assigned to it or changes a place's destination. It makes visible what had no business being seen, and makes heard a discourse where once there was only place for noise; it makes understood as discourse what was once only heard as noise. (Rancière 1999: 30)

Making world-making practices and relations to earth-beings visible in the public, is close to what Rancière sees as the *political*, which 'consists in re-figuring space, that is in what is to be done, to be seen and to be named in it' (Rancière 2010: 37), and 'making what was unseen visible' (2010: 38).

A public *iranta* is in many ways the same as private *irantas*, but at the same time they are very different, simply because they *emerge in the practice*: different people participate, different pleas are made and for different aims and purposes. In fact, no *iranta* is the same as another; each is unique in that it is always performed by a specific person for a specific purpose. Since the earth-beings are enacted in practices, they will inevitably also change through new practices. Hence, the earth-mother, the mountains and the water also become different in these public encounters. Furthermore, all practices – and thus all worlds – are different and continuously changing. Being flexible and pragmatic is what makes practices and worlds endure, and this also includes negotiating with representations of the past in the present and relationships to ancestors, as when the municipality framed the *pago* as 'ancestral'. Understanding world-making as filled with uncertainty, humour, diversity of opinions, and negotiations, as is argued by Cepek (2016), strengthens – in my opinion – the view of emerging worlds as continuously enacted through practice. Hence, while agreeing with Cepek that we should acknowledge these uncertainties and contestations (as a politics of world-making) and being always aware of the danger of romanticising indigenous worlds, I disagree with his claim that this insight somehow undermines the argument made by various scholars associated with an ontological approach. Recognising that there are multiple turns and twists within the so-called 'ontological turn', and that some might just replace the word 'culture' with 'ontology' (as discussed in Carrithers et al. 2010), I propose rather to imagine 'ontological openings', as suggested by de la Cadena (2014), which will enable us to critically examine disagreements and the politics involved in making worlds.

Conclusion

In Colca Valley, the responses to the effects of climate change are embedded in emplaced collectives and relatedness, in which water is part of other constellations that disrupt singularisations. What are the implications of allowing Yakumama and Pachamama and *apus* to intervene in the public celebration of World Water Day? These beings and worlds were not invited into public discussions about the impact and possible responses to climate change, however. I suggest that although earth-beings are slowly making their way into the public domain and becoming more visible, they are not allowed to participate fully. Earth-beings are still stigmatised as non-modern beliefs, and hence they cannot take an active part in the public scene without disrupting politics as we know it. They are incompatible with the constitution of the modern world, which is based on the separation of nature/culture and human/non-human (Latour 1993). Hence, they are deemed, by the advocates of 'progress' – the idea that we are moving forward along a unidirectional timeline towards something 'better' based on modern science – to be a shadow from the past, or a cultural spice to give colour and flavour to enactments of markets and state power. In the next two chapters, I will see how this tension creates friction in competing understandings of 'scarcity' and 'efficiency'. The two 'solutions' that I heard time and again during my time in Colca were about making inventories of water sources and more efficient water use. These proposals implied, on the one hand, counting the number of sources, as well as measuring and registering the amount of water in them, and, on the other hand, improving the infrastructure and technology to use this water productively and avoid seepage and water loss on the way from the source to the field. While chapter 5 will discuss the concept of water efficiency, chapter 6 will discuss the issue of formalising water user rights and licences, both for irrigation water and potable water for human consumption.

5
Water Efficiency

'This is the purpose: to make the water cycle more efficient!'

(Director of water administration office in Majes, 2011)

'We engineers just see the technical aspect, but we forget about the social aspect.'

(Technical manager of *la Junta* in Colca Valley, 2011)

In 2011, the municipality of Coporaque, a district next to Chivay on the right bank of Colca River, was engaged in a project to secure the provision of safe drinking water for the village population.[1] The plan was to install a water pipe that would lead clean water from the mountain springs to an enclosed reservoir for potable water, and from there the water would flow through a system of pipes directly to the houses in the village. In addition, some of the water would be separated and used for irrigation of land in the lower parts of Coporaque. The old earthen channel was leaking, thus the aim was to have a modern and efficient water system that transported water from the source to the users without seepage. However, there were some frictions and conflicts with a couple of the landowning families in the mountain area where the pipe would be installed. I was invited to join José from the ALA, Miguel from *la Junta* and Toribio, a representative from the water users commission in Coporaque, on a walk in the mountains to inspect the springs in the area, the old canal and the planned route of the pipeline. During the inspection, it became clear that Toribio strongly supported the municipality's project, which had been planned since the 1990s. He was keen to show us that one of the springs had abundant water in order to disprove the pastoralists' complaint that there was little water in this spring and who claimed that they needed access to the water in the canal. If the water that was flowing in the open canal were to be enclosed in a pipe, however, they would lose this access. Toribio maintained that there was sufficient water coming out of this spring, but that it was 'not used well' ('*no se está dando buen uso*'). I didn't reflect upon this phrase at that moment, as it was a common way of talking about water management, especially in meetings and forums organised by the *Junta* or the ALA. At the time, I thought of 'good use' (*buen uso*) as being more or less the same as 'efficient use'. However, as I later looked back at my fieldnotes, I was puzzled by this statement. What did he mean? Was he employing the concept of efficiency, which is in fact a very powerful argument in water-related disagreements? It seemed that he was using the efficiency concept to argue that some pastoralists waste water because their way of irrigating is random and not strategically directed to enhance production.

Figure 7 Water flows in small canals made of earth and cement and the flow is guided by small gates and stones towards the fields that need irrigation. The distribution of water among peasants is overseen by the *regidor* (see chapter 3). However, this system is seen as 'inefficient' by the state authorities and many development agencies.

At the same time, he was not of the opinion that water should primarily be seen as an economic good, and he was generally concerned with maintaining the relationships with springs and other water-beings that secure the flow of water from mountains to springs.

In meetings, speeches and conversations with water engineers and managers, I often heard the notion of 'efficiency'. For example, in my interviews with the ALA director, he told me enthusiastically about his work to make the management of the watershed more integrated in order to make the water flow more efficiently. In his vision of an integrated watershed, the water would be distributed fairly among users and uses, and it would be used rationally according to the law. Therefore, he regularly sent his employees to meetings and inspections in the highlands, and he also sometimes went in person in order to have an overview of the watershed and to avoid tensions and conflicts. He concluded: 'This is the purpose: to make the water cycle more efficient!' In this chapter, I will critically discuss the notion of efficiency, and how it simultaneously overlaps with and diverges from other ways of conceptualising water use, as for instance expressed in the notion of 'good use'.

What is the difference between 'water efficiency' and 'good use' of water? I suggest that the main concern in the idea of efficiency is to put every drop of water into productive use as fast as possible, aiming for economic value generation, without letting water getting lost or seep into other unproductive uses. 'Good use', on the other hand, is a broader term that includes multiple usages, ecologies, relationalities, collectives and entities, such as peat bogs, pasture, animals, climate and earth-beings. I suggest that, to a certain degree, Toribio was implying what policy makers would call efficiency, but *not only*. Marisol de la Cadena (2019) uses the phrase 'not only' to refer to 'a plurality of things (two or more) occurring simultaneously or in a sequence' (de la Cadena 2019: 28). In that sense the notions of efficiency and good use can be understood as partially connected; overlapping and diverging at the same time. Borrowing the term 'divergence' from Stengers (2005a), de la Cadena (2019) uses it to analyse 'practices that are not the same and do not make up the same entity, yet occupy the same time-place and become with each other while continuing to be distinct' (de la Cadena 2019: 23). Thinking about how to understand and conceptualise partially connected ideas and practices is closely linked to problems of translation and what Viveiros de Castro (2004) calls 'equivocation', which is not related to imaginary ways of "seeing the world" but to the real worlds that are being seen' (Viveiros de Castro 2004: 11). Hence, the different understandings relate to different ontological assemblages, or, as in this case, different water worlds and different, yet partially connected, ontologies of water. Viveiros de Castro (2004) proposes that these equivocations can be controlled in order to learn from them. In other words, we can – and should – dwell in the space of the equivocations; not unmake them, but potentialise them. In the rest of this chapter, I will explore the notions of efficiency and good use, and discuss how they are negotiated in asymmetrical relations of power, in which relational and collective practices – accused of being 'inefficient' – are ignored and/or excluded because they are not compatible with, and disrupt the idea of 'efficiency' and 'the modern'. In the Majes-Colca watershed, the idea of 'water efficiency' – being an intrinsic part of the modernisation project – is used to promote and legitimise the implementation of new infrastructure and modern technology, which often creates new tensions and challenges for water users. In some instances, the tensions and dissonances between different water practices and water knowledges are quite strong, and hence I suggest using the word 'disencounters'. In the everyday work of water management and hydraulic engineering in Colca, however, the notions of efficiency and good use are entangled, as I will discuss in the final part of the chapter.

Efficiency: a new water culture

The concept of 'efficiency', which is closely connected to that of 'productivity', is often presented in water policy documents – both in Peru and elsewhere – as an objective ideal and as essential to achieve optimal water management (Boelens and Vos 2012). Far from being neutral, however, 'efficiency' is a central concept in the neoliberal economic theory that has guided water management in Peru since the 1990s. 'Efficiency' has also a longer history as a key concept in environmental governance, for example in the conservation movement that arose in the United States at the beginning of the 20th century, where conservation came to imply 'efficiency in the development and use of all resources' (Hays 1999: 123). Spearheaded by engineers whose goal was to master nature to produce value without any waste, the 'efficiency gospel' meant that increasing productivity and growth was more important than the preservation of landscapes (Hays 1999: 123–7). The goal of increasing economic productivity was also important for the Peruvian governments in their projects of state building, modernisation and progress throughout the 20th century. The main goal of the MIP was to achieve regional economic development by mastering the watershed and utilising water resources more rationally, efficiently and productively. According to Zamalloa's account of the official history of the area, the project was based on 'the regulation and derivation of water resources from the headwaters of the Colca and Apurimac rivers, for its rational use in irrigation of up to 57.000 hectares of new land in the pampas of Majes and Siguas' (Zamalloa 2013: 21). The abundant water in the highlands was imagined as being wasted by traditional irrigation methods in small-scale and non-competitive farming and then getting lost as it flowed into rivers and out to the sea, without contributing to the nation's development and economic growth.

This narrative of development and growth, based on the resourcification of nature, continued through the state-led developmentalist economic reforms of Velasco and into the neoliberal period. As neoliberal ideology took a strong hold in Peru in the 1990s, economic efficiency became the mantra by which everything was measured. Despite growing environmental concerns emerging together with extractivist industries, faith in economic growth and progress never waned. On the contrary, through the 1990s, the discourses on 'sustainable development' and 'ecological modernisation' grew stronger all over the world, fostering a belief that capitalist markets and economic growth are not incompatible with environmental sustainability (Adams 2009). In 1992, this view was also expressed in The Dublin Statement on Water and Sustainable Development (ICWE 1992), which listed the importance of integration, participation, women's role and formalisation of water rights, before emphasising the economic value of water and declaring it an 'economic good'. Underlying these principles, was the argument that water is a scarce resource and that 'effective management of water resources' should thus be an overarching goal. In other words, the argument for recognising the economic value of water was that a failure to do so would inevitably lead to 'wasteful and environmentally damaging uses'. The solution then appeared as a common-sensical logic: 'Managing water as an economic good is an important way of achieving efficient and equitable use, and of encouraging conservation and protection of water resources' (ICWE 1992). The Dublin declaration strongly influenced water policies all over the world, pushing for commodification and commercialisation. In Peru, however, the Fujimori government's intent to commodify water was prevented by popular protests. Therefore, the Peruvian water bureaucracy – supported by the Food and Agricultural Organization, the World Bank, and the Inter-American Development Bank – has been working hard to find other ways to make water management more 'modern', 'efficient' and 'business-like', in order to increase the agricultural productivity and the farmers ability to compete on the market (Oré and Rap 2009; French 2016).

These policies were not only influenced by the Dublin declaration, but also by integrated water resources management (IWRM), which emerged as an elaboration of the Dublin principles and became a global hegemonic framework for water governance (Franco et al. 2013). Promoted as a way to maximise economy, equity and ecosystems, IWRM has been criticised for being vague, yet this is also what makes it attractive for policy makers: it provides a lot of space for interpretation. This 'can make IWRM an apolitical cloak for processes that are deeply transformative' (Franco et al. 2013: 1664). Molle (2008) has criticised IWRM for being an attractive yet woolly consensual concept, which obscures the politics of water management and at the same time is easily captured by groups seeking to legitimise their own agendas.

In Peru, the modernising process of water management continued into the 2000s and in the National Strategy of Water Resources Management (*Estrategia Nacional de la Gestión de los Recursos Hídricos*), which was published in 2004, 'efficiency' was a key concept (Oré and Rap 2009; French 2016). Strongly influenced by the IWRM paradigm, the strategy emphasises that water is an 'economic good', and that management should be based on 'efficiency, equity and sustainability' (Perú 2004 quoted in French 2016: 70). The National Water Authority (ANA) was created in 2008, as part of the new National System of Water Resources Management, and as a key institution for ensuring efficiency (Oré and Rap 2009). In the Water Resources Law (WRL) that was promulgated in 2009, one of the fundamental principles is that of efficiency: 'the integrated management of water resources is sustained by the efficient use and conservation, encouraging the development of an efficient culture of use among the users and operators' (ANA 2010: Preliminary Title, Article III, 9th principle). The importance of efficiency in use, management and operation of infrastructure is emphasised throughout the text of the law. For example, Article 57 states that the first obligation of the holders of user rights is to 'utilise water with the greatest technical and economic efficiency'. Article 85 states that the National Water Authority can issue 'efficiency certificates' to users and operators of hydraulic infrastructures that conform to the parameters of efficiency. Since *la Junta* is defined as the operator of small-scale hydraulic infrastructure in Colca Valley, the manager and the board of *la Junta* were worried that they were being forced to run the organisation like a business and that they would be replaced by a private company if they did not succeed in meeting the standards of efficiency. Since 'efficiency certificates' also give priority for obtaining new water rights, they disproportionally favour large-scale agribusiness companies, which presumably are highly efficient, and deprive smallholders of water use rights (Boelens and Vos 2012). This is one of the reasons that Miguel in *la Junta* said that the water law is made for the coast and for 'the big' (chapter 1).

The same year that the WRL was passed, the Peruvian government received a loan from the World Bank of US $10 million to implement the 'Water Resources Management Modernization Project'. In the project appraisal document, 'efficiency' is mentioned right at the beginning as part of the rationale behind the project: 'Irrigation accounts for 80 percent of water use, however efficiency is low' (World Bank 2009: 1), and later it states that 'water should be recognized as an economic and social good to encourage rational and efficient allocation of water, discourage waste and ensure adequate water services' (World Bank 2009: 20). Among the goals, the project would contribute to curbing the growth in water demand, reducing water conflicts and 'improving Peru's resilience to climate change' (World Bank 2009: 4). The project emphasised its support of the promotion of 'a new "water culture" among decision makers, water professionals, children and the general public' (World Bank 2009: 3). The so-called 'new water culture' is also promoted by the World Bank's Water and Sanitation Programme, and it aims to teach citizens and households that they should be more efficient in their water use and avoid wasting it in daily practices (World Bank 2009; French 2016; Paerregaard et al. 2016; Schmidt 2017). The idea of a new 'water culture' implies new ways of valuing water as an economic resource that water users must learn to appreciate and take care of in efficient ways. This implies that their current practices are 'bad' and brushes over and invisibilise the plurality of practices, relationships and collectives related to water in Peru. The attempt to make the 'water culture' universal and singular is both resisted by and entangled with the multiple modes of valuing water and practising water management that exist in various places. For those engaged in communal forms of working the land and allocating water, the goal of achieving market competitiveness among individual farmers is not only counter-intuitive but impossible. Nevertheless, this remains the ideal by which farming and irrigation practices are evaluated, and 'efficiency' plays a double role as both a means and a goal in itself.

What is not recognised in the WRL and IWRM is that the goals it seeks to maximise in parallel – namely efficiency, equity and environmental sustainability – often are antagonistic, and that 'trade-offs are necessary and hard to achieve' (Molle 2008: 133). What is instead emphasised in IWRM is that these goals can be achieved if 'problem-solving can be informed by neutral and rational approaches, good science and expert knowledge' (Molle 2008: 133). This is fundamental in the ecological modernisation framework: a strong belief in rationality and neutral expertise that can inform processes of innovation, competitiveness, and technological change. In this way, ecological modernisation pursues 'rational, technical solutions to environmental problems and more efficient institutions for environmental management and control' (Adams 2009: 126). In the Majes-Colca watershed, the solutions to climate change, drought, erosion and landslides consisted mainly of more infrastructure and modern technology. However, I argue that there is no such thing as 'a neutral approach' and that promoting a solution as 'rational' would imply that other approaches are 'irrational'. What I will show in the rest of the chapter, then, is that 'efficient water use' and 'technological solutions' are embedded in unequal structures of power and different understandings of human–environmental relationships. The imposition of 'economic efficiency' and market competitiveness from above has profound implications for communal and relational water practices and worlds, and hence creates tension and dissonance.

Disencounters: technological fix and flexible design

In 2011, a modernisation of the irrigation programme – the PSI Sierra – was introduced in Colca Valley. The goal of the PSI Sierra was to achieve higher productivity and profitability in agriculture through the introduction of modern and more water-efficient irrigation technology. Through workshops, meetings and motivational talks, as well as promises of technical and financial support, the PSI engineers encouraged the farmers to shift from the traditional surface furrow irrigation (called 'gravity irrigation'; *riego por gravedad*) to modern pressurised irrigation (*riego presurizado*) such as engine-driven sprinkler and drip systems. From 1998 to 2010, the World Bank-funded Programme of Sub-sectoral

Irrigation (PSI, Programa Subsectorial de Irrigaciones) installed drip and sprinkler systems in plantations and large-scale irrigation projects on the arid coastal plains of Peru. The implementation was described as successful, and in 2010, the government approved a loan from the International Bank for Reconstruction and Development (IBRD) to finance the PSI Sierra, which would extend the programme to the Andean highlands and replicate the success there. In the presentations of PSI in pamphlets and webpages, one of the highlighted goals has been to change from a traditional agriculture to one with a higher productivity and profitability. 'Efficiency' has also been emphasised: 'improve the efficiency of the irrigation of fields, aiming to increase the intensity of land use and production of crops' (PSI 2020).

The president of *la Junta* was proud when Colca Valley was selected as one of the first areas in Peru where the PSI Sierra would start. Colca Valley was chosen because the farmers are well organised and the majority pay the tariff for the irrigation water; this was taken as evidence of commitment and responsibility. In the first phase of the programme, the aim was to convince the farmers to join the programme. This was done through so-called 'sensitisation speeches' that PSI engineers gave to all the local water users commissions, where they focused on efficiency, gains and losses. The engineers told the farmers that the water gets lost by evaporation and filtration in the traditional water channels, a claim they supported with numbers: 'with traditional irrigation you use 35 per cent of the water, and you lose 65 per cent along the way – in technified irrigation the efficiency is 70–75 per cent'. Since PSI already had defined the main problem – namely inefficient canals and irrigation systems – they also had a solution ready: the farmers who joined the programme would receive subsidised irrigation technology systems and technical support from experts. In order to join the programme, the farmers should get organised in 'PSI Entrepreneurial Management Groups', and they had to demonstrate a commitment to the programme by attending the meetings and saving money to pay their part of the installation, which was 10 per cent of the total price.

In 2013, many farmers had already formed entrepreneurial management groups, but only a few of them had managed to save the initial sum of 10 per cent. This handful of successful groups were already in the bidding process to purchase irrigation systems, and there were several irrigation technology providers competing to give the best offer. However, most groups were still struggling to save money, and some groups were already deciding to give up. All the groups were participating in different kinds of seminars and workshops, where the importance of saving water in view of the coming water scarcity was emphasised. The PSI programme was legitimised by climate change adaptation and the need for efficient water management. Since efficiency is premised on the discourse of scarcity of resources, the coming water shortage was repeated in speeches and workshops: the idea that water is a finite resource that will be more scarce because of global warming. The main tension with PSI in Colca was not that farmers disagreed with this perspective. As discussed in chapter 4, farmers observed changes in weather, seasons and water supply and their worries were confirmed by the climate change narrative. However, they did not necessarily agree that water scarcity was the one and only problem, in isolation from a wider context of problems. Most peasant farmers experience other problems that are more pressing, like smallholding and out-migration. I suggest that when the problem to be solved is singularised, in this case to a problem of 'water scarcity', the solutions are more easily found and implemented. However, these solutions tend to be short-term and quick fixes, while the long-term consequences might be devastating for small-scale farmers. As I have argued elsewhere (Stensrud 2019b), this kind of singularisation is problematic because it excludes important contextual factors such as poverty, inequality and migration.

These concerns were often communicated by farmers in meetings and workshops, but were not heard because they did not fit into the work agenda of the engineers. This miscommunication would sometimes result in meetings or groups that failed because of few attendees and little interest and engagement. The PSI engineers sometimes talked about group members who had lost interest and motivation: the farmers were described as de-motivated and disheartened (*desanimados*), and the engineers scheduled meetings and workshops to encourage them to continue. However, many farmers still left, and I suggest that it was not only because they did not have enough money to invest, but also because they were not included in the design of the programme. They did not see the same problems that the engineers saw. Where engineers clearly observed 'obvious' problems of inefficient methods due to a 'lack' of knowledge or 'ancient' traditions, most farmers did not perceive of these practices as a problem. Where the engineers enthusiastically and with good intentions presented solutions of modern science and technology, many farmers felt this as an intrusion and paternalistic imposition. The irrigation technique that is most used in Colca is called the 'gravity-method' because the water flows from the canal and over the surface of the field. The water does not flow randomly, however, but according to how the farmer guides the water into furrows, using a shovel. Most take great pride in their irrigation skills, and in every annual meeting of the water users commissions, they hold a competition: the person who directs the water most skilfully and rapidly through a field, is the winner. In 2011, the winner was a woman who was carrying her child in a blanket on her back while she was working the shovel swiftly, digging furrows and guiding the water. In gravity irrigation, the water is measured in practised time: how many hours it takes to flood a field. This time also depends on several factors, like the soil, slope, and the speed and volume of the water flow in the stream or canal. This knowledge and skill is, however, irrelevant for the PSI.

The challenges regarding the feasibility of the PSI programme in Colca Valley were various: to a large degree they related to the topographic and socio-economic conditions, but also to lack of resonance and mutual understanding. In a steep terrain characterised by agricultural terraces and tiny fields scattered across the mountain slopes, there are some obvious problems with installing engine-driven sprinkler systems, which require a certain topography and a land area of a certain size. Furthermore, the maintenance of the new irrigation systems necessitates money and technical knowledge. If a part breaks, it involves a long journey to Arequipa city or Villa El Pedregal to obtain a new part. The systems are expensive and many peasants struggle to save enough money to pay their part of 10 per cent of the installation. Although the PSI engineers ensured the participants that they would receive support from PSI for many years, most people in Colca had little reason to trust the promises made by engineers working in development programmes, since projects and programmes often stop half-way through when the finances run out.

Small-scale, creative initiatives to make alternative technologies that were cheaper and adapted to the landscapes were met with suspicion from the PSI engineers. From what I understood from the engineers' comments, such creative entrepreneurship was also admired, but could not be officially embraced by PSI. One example of this was Alfredo: a creative and resourceful man who had designed and constructed his own irrigation system on his land. Alfredo captured water from a spring in a pool and used it to irrigate with a homemade sprinkler system, which he had made by using knowledge generated from various encounters. He had attended a previous course in modern irrigation for farmers, but, as he put it, he did not believe everything the engineers told him. Instead, he combined some of what he had learned on the course with what he knew from his training as a topographer and his work experience in a mine. According to the PSI engineers, you need to have 25 metres of hydraulic altitude, but Alfredo explained that then no space would be left to plant in his 2-hectare field. Alfredo experimented with his little pool of water and asked himself what the result with 2.5 metres of altitude would be. Then he made a system of tubes of different sizes in diameter (4 inches and 2 inches), regulating switches and five sprinklers, and he made it work. When he demonstrated his system to a visiting group of farmers, we were all very impressed. However, the PSI engineer Hernán pointed to the fact that the hydraulic pressure was not as strong as it should be, and that the system was not optimal. When I interviewed Alfredo later, he said: 'You saw that it worked, but you cannot contradict the engineer, right. What would I say to him? He talks better than me, right, but it is another thing to do it in practice.'

Alfredo adapted technology, which was probably designed for other conditions, to a vertical terrain with small fields in a situation where he had no financial means to invest a lot. He also adapted the usage to the local wind currents. In the terminology of James C. Scott, he employed a form of 'mētis' – understood as 'a wide array of practical skills and acquired intelligence in responding to a constantly changing natural and human environment' (Scott 1998: 313). In contrast, the knowledge of the PSI engineers is disembedded from the particularities of local environments and transformed into general statements about efficient water usage. Based on an idea of 'neutral' expertise, aspiring to be universal, it would be what Scott calls 'techne', the opposite of the practical and dynamic mētis (Scott 1998). This formal and technical expertise was, however, not very dynamic. Alfredo's pragmatic irrigation system, on the other hand, was more like the Zimbabwe Bush Pump, as analysed by de Laet and Mol (2000), because of its 'fluidity', flexibility, adaptability and responsiveness. However, the PSI programme did not allow alternative flexible designs, even though most farms in Colca consist of tiny fields that are scattered in a steep landscape. Since replicability was built into the programme design of PSI, it could not recognise that in the varied and diverse mountain terrains of Colca, replicating a technological system that was designed for the coastal flat plains made little sense.

What I observed in Colca was an apparent mismatch between priorities, possibilities, and power to define problem issues, and I have analysed these discrepancies as 'disencounters' between PSI and the farmers (Stensrud 2019b). This concept is taken from the Spanish '*desencuentros*', which could mean failed or disappointing meetings/encounters, or disagreements. By disencounters, I mean the encounters between different modes of knowledge and practice that often lack mutual resonance and a shared understanding of what is at stake. They can also be called *failed* or *missed* encounters, because people talk past each other without encountering resonance. While encounters often tend to generate knowledge, the disencounters rather confirm different interests and exacerbate these differences. The workshops were supposed to be a space of mutual learning and dialogue, but instead I observed communication that failed to engage mutuality and understanding, as well as lack of agreement regarding what was the most pressing needs of the farmers. The PSI workshops were embedded in structures of inequality and hierarchies of knowledge, embodied both by the engineers and the farmers. In modern Peru, different practices are hierarchically organised: some practices are seen as better than others and certain forms of knowledge are perceived as more valid than others. Within the PSI programme, there was only one right answer to all questions: the need to invest in modern technology.

However, the disagreements, or disencounters, were not only about power and inequality – there were also about different understandings of local environments, technology and irrigation, as well as diverging water worlds. I will call these divergences 'ontological disencounters'. These 'disencounters' are not (only) happening between actors but between practices as well: diverging world-making practices enacting different, but partially connected, water worlds. Farmers and engineers – water users and water managers, like Alfredo, Toribio, Miguel and others – engage in different water practices that are informed by different ideas, which can be overlapping in some contexts and diverging in others. The ontological disagreements consist of different understandings of what water is and the relationships that make the water flow and keep the world in equilibrium. This does not mean that technology by itself is incompatible with 'good use' and a relational water world. Alfredo has shown us that technological devices, like sprinklers, can be flexible and fluid, and they can be part of relationships between humans, land and water, in worlds where these are interrelated beings, constituted by and with each other. As seen in chapter 3, *pago* rituals are not only made to springs, but also to canals and ponds. When the technology is embedded in ideas of 'efficiency', however, it becomes inflexible by excluding practices that are deemed 'inefficient'. In this way, it is the imposition and demand of 'efficiency', and not only the technology, which creates gaps and dissonance – or 'disencounters'

– between worlds. Nevertheless, I also observed entanglements – both conceptual and practical – of 'efficiency' and 'good use' in everyday water management. One example is the inspection in Coporaque, which was mentioned in the beginning of this chapter, but let me first say something about 'good use'.

Good use: relational fluidity

As seen in chapter 4, the 'solutions' to climate change and water scarcity promoted by the authorities in the World Water Day meeting of 2011 included the need to use water more efficiently by acquiring new knowledge and consciousness, and by investing in modern infrastructure and technology. In the same meeting, the farmers from the water users commissions mostly avoided words like efficiency and payments, and although the solutions they proposed were also related to physical infrastructure and engineering, they phrased them in terms of 'good use' (*buen uso*) of water and caring for the headwaters (*cuidar*). Their proposals focused on the need for infrastructure, and especially projects of planting trees and constructing micro-dams, called 'sowing and harvesting water'. These are ways of taking care of the headwater environment. Planting trees prevents erosion and enables the soil to store water. The micro-dams collect water when the heavy rains come in January and February and this water can be distributed in irrigation canals throughout the year. These projects were initially started by NGOs (particularly Desco Sur) in the 1990s to improve pastures and the productivity of livestock in the headwaters but in later years have been recast as adaptation to climate change. The water users emphasised the need for public investment in water harvesting, as well as funding to build and maintain other kinds of infrastructures to gather and guide water, such as ponds and canals. These kinds of small-scale hydraulic infrastructure are constructed and embedded in community life and involve relationships among water users working in *faenas* as well as offering *pagos* to the earth-beings. In chapter 3, we saw how irrigation in Colca is embedded in sociality, reciprocity, and mutual relationships with water- and earth-beings like springs, lakes and mountains. The chapter also showed how farmers organise to distribute water and maintain canals and ponds. The elected *regidor* allocates, controls and makes sure to maintain good relations with both people and earth-beings. This is a work of 'care', understood as a way of working and 'persistent tinkering' (Mol et al. 2010: 14), and it is related to what

I, in this chapter, call a 'good use' of water. In this context 'good' does not mean inherently 'good' as opposed to 'bad' or 'evil', but a balance of mutual respect coexisting with difference. In other words, making good relationships and maintaining good use of water implies negotiating with actors and entities that are different, but that depend on each other and co-constitute each other. The aim is to avoid disequilibrium, accidents and harm. Communal and relational practices, such as *faenas* and *pagos*, maintain webs of relationships and strengthen collective well-being, but they are often deemed as a hindrance to efficiency in a rational and scientific framework.

In their walks and inspections across the fields, mountains and springs, the members of the water users commissions and *la Junta* constantly evaluated the water flows, and often imagined and discussed possibilities for water harvesting, improvements of canals and ponds and potential places to build new infrastructure. Especially when I accompanied Miguel in his travels, he was always looking for possibilities for better uses of the water and potential new uses of land by redirecting the water to new places. This also happened during the inspection in Coporaque, when I was told that the municipality planned to buy land from six families in order to build a micro-dam to harvest more water. Toribio showed me where they could cultivate the land in the future if the micro-dam was built. These ideas and visualisations of how to guide the water flow and harvest the water were, I suggest, informed and influenced both by notions of efficiency and ideas of 'good use'. In addition, they were amended by pragmatic considerations about what would be practically possible and what would be acceptable by people and earth-beings. This means that to gain acceptance for a project, the authorities should enter in relationships of reciprocity and respect with the affected parties, both humans and other-than-humans. To disregard this, could lead to harmful consequences; water could dwindle, animals and humans could get sick and die.

In 2011, the villagers of Canocota, a small annex of Chivay district located close to Tuti village, were looking for ways to secure access to more irrigation water. The water they had access to came from various mountain springs and one valve in the Majes canal. However, this water was only enough to irrigate 40 per cent of the 160 hectares of land that was cultivated by 130 families. The rest of the land only got rainwater and was mostly used to cultivate plants for animal fodder. Hence, the municipal authorities, in collaboration with the water users commission, made plans for harvesting water from a mountain lake called Casaccocha. The plan was to turn the lake around (*voltearlo*), by cutting out an opening and directing the water towards their land. However, the mayor of Canocota told me that this project is very difficult and complex to carry out, for at least two reasons: First, to get the money from the regional government, you have to calculate costs and benefits, translated into monetary terms. Second, the lake Casacchocha is known to 'have powers'. The mayor told me the story of Casaccocha, which is a lake at the foot of a small rocky mountain. The story was about a conflict between two brothers, and at the end of the story, one of the brothers lost his animals. His 30 cows entered the lake and disappeared, and the only thing he could recover was a small stone with the figure of a cow, which he found on the side of the lake. The bones of the cows appeared on the other side of the mountain. The man took the stone and went to a shaman who read the coca leaves, and he said that the mountain had eaten the cows, through the lake, which belongs to him (the mountain). From that moment, people started to respect the mountain lord and his lake. Therefore, the mayor said, in order to bring this water to our village, we have to ask permission from the mountain and pay an offering. Having been on several trips up to that place, he said that every time someone in the group got sick. In this way, the mountain gives us a sign that we should first comply with the ritual, he said. In a village meeting, the mayor argued that they should make a church mass in the name of the mountain lord. And thereafter a ritual 'according to our traditions'. 'Only then can we go on with the project, and if God wills it, nothing will happen', he concluded. Sometimes, bad things do happen, however, like the tragic incident in Tuti where four members of a water users commission were killed by a mountain (see chapter 6).

Making the water flow in the highlands involves not only physical work but also relational work, both among humans and non-humans. Failing to show respect by carrying out the proper work of ritual and offerings can have fatal results. Angry mountains can disrupt the water flow and kill water users, and therefore it is important to maintain 'good' relationships and a balance of mutual respect in the web of relationships that constitute the worlds people live in. A 'good use' of water implies working for an equilibrium of respect and power. 'Efficient use', on the other hand, privileges and prioritises a singular aim for extracting and accumulating economic value. Although these two concepts seem incompatible, they are nevertheless often used interchangeably and might also overlap.

Entanglements: enclosures and leakages

I learned about the tensions surrounding the project of enclosing drinking water in a pipeline when I was invited to join Miguel from *la Junta* and José from the ALA in an inspection in the district of Coporaque in July 2011. We met Toribio, the president of the water users commission in Coporaque at 5 a.m., and we walked uphill below the starry sky, all of us chewing coca leaves to endure the hike in the cold thin air. After ascending the final steep crest, we arrived at a place with a pile of stones called *apacheta*. Toribio told me to find a stone, pass it over my body and legs, and then blow my breath (*samay*) on the stone before throwing it on top of the other stones. The stone absorbs the tiredness of your body and you can continue walking in good spirits, he explained. At 7 a.m., we arrived at the Ccantumayu irrigation canal, which takes water from the Aqente spring and brings it down to the fields. After a rest where we shared bread, apples and coca leaves, we continued to the water spring called Ccallancca at an altitude of 4,271 metres. Miguel had not brought his measurement equipment (*aforador*), but by watching the water, he calculated the water flow rate (*caudal*) to be 3 litres per second. I asked about the origin of the water and Miguel said that it probably came from the snowcapped Mt Mismi in Tuti district, from where rain- and meltwater flows in underground channels and appears in springs.[2] Toribio selected three coca leaves to make a *k'intu* (bouquet of coca leaves), and after blowing his *samay* on it, he 'paid' it to the spring by putting it under a stone. Miguel, José and I did the same thing; this was both an act of respect to the spring, acknowledging it as a living being, and also to ensure continued supply of water.

Afterwards, we continued walking until we arrived at the Llanchahui spring at 4,325 metres, and here too we sat down to pay *k'intu* offerings to the spring. Miguel and Toribio agreed that the spring is a woman, and Miguel reminded us all that we must not speak bad words, or the spring could make bad things happen to us. José and Miguel calculated the water flow in the Llanchahui spring to be approximately 10 litres per second. Then, they filled a plastic bottle of water, drank and praised the good flavour: 'This is pure water!' They fantasised and joked about how they could sell bottled water from this spring and make a fortune, because it tasted much better than the bottled water of the Coca Cola-owned brand 'San Luis' that is sold in Arequipa city and to tourists in Colca Valley. Although this was indeed meant as a joke at this moment, it was also a painful reminder of the constant threat of commodification of water. José said that if people from the city came up to the highlands to see these springs, which are called the 'water eyes' (*ojos de agua*), they would appreciate water more: 'Now, they don't know and they don't appreciate; they don't value [water] [*no valoran*]'. To value water can imply a respect for water sources, a willingness to take care of the headwater environment and the relationships enabling water to flow. However, it can also mean a willingness to pay the cost of maintaining the sources, as well as the ponds, canals and pipes. The tension between the two different yet overlapping meanings of value – the economic versus the moral value (Graeber 2001) – is constantly present and negotiated in water discourses and practices (see also Ballestero 2019b). Similarly, the concepts of 'good use', implying practices of care and relationality, and 'efficient use', which in contrast rests on an understanding that the economic value of water is most important, often converge in the same conversation or in the same argument. This entanglement can sometimes seem a bit confusing because people often think they are talking about the same thing when they are also referring to diverging understandings of what water is and where it comes from. In other cases, people might participate in the same world-making practices in which they acknowledge and respect the power of the sentient landscape, but they disagree on how to achieve fair water distribution and how to approach conflicts.

To collect the water from the Llanchahui spring, the municipality had constructed a well (*poza*) beneath the spring. From the well, a 6-inch pipe takes the water several kilometres downhill, and at one point, the pipeline divides into two pipes: one takes 3 lps of water for human consumption in the village, and the other conducts 5 lps of water for irrigation of land below the village, where there is little water available for the farmers. Toribio explained: 'There is a conflict going on between using water for human consumption in the village and agricultural use.' When José and Miguel inspected the pipe division later that day, they recommended that a better gauging device should be installed: instead of a float valve, they should have a tubemeter (*tubímetro*) or flowmeter (*flujometro*) to ensure that the correct amount of water flowed into each pipe. 'A meter is always necessary to avoid conflicts', José insisted. However, this was not the only conflict in Coporaque; there were also tensions between the municipality and the herders in the highlands. This conflict was not only about the distribution of quantities of water, but about access to water flows: whether the water flow should be enclosed and controlled in pipes or be able to seep out to flow freely in the landscape. The pipeline that ran from the well was built into the old crumbling irrigation canal. During the inspection, an alpaca farmer who lived nearby came to talk to us about a complaint he had sent to the *Junta*. He claimed that because they had enclosed the water from the Llanchahui spring in a water pipe, his cushion bog pastures (*bofedal*) had dried. Earlier, when they used the old canal, water would always seep out, but now there was nothing to irrigate the cushion bogs where his animals grazed. Therefore, he wished to formalise his allocated amount of water from the Ccallancca spring. To formalise means that he would have to apply the National Water Authority for a formal licence for a use right for a specific amount of water measured in litres per second (see chapter 6). Miguel and José listened carefully and said that they would look into the case.

A moment later, the mayor of Coporaque came to meet us, accompanied by the engineer leading the project. The mayor pointed out that the water was running freely from the spring to the well, and they would like to enclose the water higher up. The engineer explained that they wanted to collect the water closer to the spring to avoid contamination from the defecating animals. This is after all for human consumption and should be as clean as possible. Could they just do it, then? the mayor asked. José pointed out that the construction did not have authorisation from the state and that the municipality should apply for a formalisation of the construction of the well and the pipeline. The papers should be sent to the ALA, but before they could give the authorisation, the ALA had to check that the project did not affect third parties. The mayor insisted that the issue had been discussed in a collective meeting (*asamblea*) and that 'the people have decided; it is not the decision of one person'. 'But if a hundred people decide to take water from one person, is that okay?', José replied rhetorically. José continued to explain that they should first present the project documentation to the *Junta* and the water users commission, who would express their opinions, and then the ALA would make a final decision. Miguel said that they should read the papers carefully and consider the people affected by the project, since they already had received one complaint from a pastoralist, and a woman had complained directly to the ALA. One person complaining is enough to create a conflict, he said: 'we should find a solution so that there will be water for everyone'. Then, he continued thoughtfully: 'We engineers just see the technical aspect, but we forget about the social aspect.'

In this case, the district municipality aims for efficiency, while the state and the *Junta* are the ones advocating a careful consideration of all the affected parties and relationalities. In the project description the municipality states that they will collect the water directly from the spring, and that among the six land-owning families all agree except one woman who wants to have 1 lps for her pastures. After descending the mountain, the woman who was opposing the project waited for us at the entrance to the village. She insisted on giving us a bottle of *chicha* (maize brew) and wanted to give her version of the story. She complained that when she had gone to José's office, he had rejected her because she had not brought any documents. Now when she had our attention, she talked non-stop in Quechua as we were approaching the village plaza. What I understood from her speech was that she was afraid of losing the water that nourishes her *bofedal* pasture; the pipeline would make it dry. José and Miguel asked her why she had not made this claim earlier? They told her to file a complaint and claim her right to water with documents, with the receipts of the irrigation water tariffs paid to the *Junta*, and the title deeds of her property. She said that she did not have a title deed, but she could provide other documents to substantiate her ownership. This was not the first time I saw people having problems due to lack of documents. By forcing users to substantiate their claims to water rights and descriptions of good use through formal and legal documents, many uses, purposes and relations of water are excluded simply because there are no documents, or they are deemed invalid. In this way, undocumented uses – which are often deemed 'inefficient' – are not seen in the paperwork of the water administration. Idealistic state officials and bureaucrats may want to take all aspects into account and make decisions based on ideas of fairness and equity, but when complaints and claims are not made in the 'correct' format, they cannot be taken into account.

Toribio clearly doubted the woman's motives and afterwards he expressed his suspicion that she was planning to profit from the water. He claimed that the 1 hectare of land she referred to formally belonged to her brother and he argued that she was not producing anything. When Toribio, earlier in the inspection, insisted that there was sufficient water in the Llanchahui spring, arguing that it was not 'used well', it seems clear that he was referring to notions of efficiency and productivity. He seemed to suggest that since the woman was not using the water to produce, she did not deserve it. This insinuation did not take the surrounding landscape, flora and fauna into consideration. Miguel, on the other hand, worried about what would happen if they enclosed all the water from this spring; how would it affect the surrounding ecology and the animals? 'This water is their source of life!', he said. The enclosure would also affect the micro-climate, he argued, because open water regulates the temperature and has the function of a cooler. In the daily work, practices and conversations of farmers, engineers, ALA bureaucrats and *Junta* managers, the ideas of efficient and good use seep into each other and mix, just as the different meanings of the concept of valuation do. Water efficiency is to bring water from a source to productive use without loss, yet such 'loss' might become 'good use' to others. This depends on the eyes that see, on people's perspective and interests. When some pastoralists opposed the project, the aim was not to protect a pristine landscape of peat bogs, but to be involved in the design of that landscape, which is fundamental to make their livelihoods worthwhile (Li 2008). In public planning, however, only formalised water rights and user licences count as valid, and water use has to be documented and registered with proper documents (deeds and receipts) in order to be counted as a part of the hydrological cycle. Unpaid and unregistered uses can be 'good' to the user, but this doesn't matter to the state if it is not formalised (see chapter 6).

If water is defined to fulfil a single purpose only, in this case provision of potable water for domestic use (and in other cases irrigation for agribusiness), leakage is seen as a problem that hinders an efficient fulfilment of that purpose. An engineer's view of the system from the outside would almost always frame leakage as a problem of inefficiency. Following the flow of the water would tell us, however, that the water seeping out is not lost, but keeping the highland *bofedales* alive and flourishing. From the point of view of the people in the highlands, then, seepage is seen as good for the irrigation of pastures (Verzijl 2020). An integrated water management should take these flows and uses into account. However, it is clear that some uses and purposes are more integrated than others, and these other uses might be either invisibilised, not seen, or not thought of as useful, resourceful, productive, and thus not part of an efficient watershed where water flows efficiently through the hydrological cycle. Although relations with earth-beings and world-making practices are not necessarily contradictory to 'water efficiency', they do not flow well with the official ideas of 'efficient and rational water use'. When saying the water is not used well, it seems that there is an overflow of meaning, or a slippage between 'efficiency' and 'good use' of water: the meanings seem to seep into each other, they mix and flow together, while sometimes they diverge. The main point here is that the divergence is not between persons, but practices and ideas that sometimes overlap and flow together and sometimes go in different directions. While Toribio valued good relationships among people, land and water, which I see as inherent in the 'good uses' of water, he also supported the enclosure of water, which would separate the water from the land and would benefit some and harm others.

Conclusion

In the WRL, the 'new water culture' is defined as 'generating consciousness and attitudes that support the good use and valuation of water' (ANA 2010: principle 3). Although the wording of the law is quite ambiguous and open for interpretation, it is clear that in the context of the government's priorities, what is called 'good use' is the same as 'efficient use' and value means 'economic value'. In Peru's project of building a modern state, the introduction of modern technology and new infrastructure has played a key role in avoiding unproductive use and water loss and utilising all available resources to create economic growth. As seen in the case from Coporaque, however, the notions of good use and efficiency are entangled in everyday politics of water, and they converge and diverge when it comes to understanding enclosures and leakages, inclusion and exclusion. Hence, 'good use' can imply 'efficient use', but *not only*; it can also refer to ecological and ontological inclusiveness and respectful relationships towards the sentient landscape.

This chapter has also shown how the unequal relationships, tensions and conflicts that are caused by the Majes canal are no less complex when we zoom into one specific spring, canal or *bofedal* in Colca. In Coporaque, the new pipes recast relations between those who are able to tap into the flow and those who see the flow diverted away from their pastures (cf. Barnes 2012). Furthermore, the dominance of the efficiency concept makes other water concepts and water practices less visible to the public eye. The benefits of leaking canals and free water flow, the skills involved in guiding and teaching the water to flow in furrows, the importance of mutual respect and equilibrium in relationships, are examples of practices that are invisibilised. The resourcification of water, the standardisation of measurement, the registration of water sources and the formalisation of user rights all contribute to the Peruvian state's modernisation project, in which the ideal of 'efficiency' is key. One of the premises of this concept is the narrative of scarcity, which will be discussed in the next chapter in relation to formalisation and legibility.

6

Legible and Illegible Water

In the 2011 World Water Day meeting in Chivay, the proposed 'solutions' to climate change and water scarcity not only included efficient water use, but also payments of tariffs and licences for user rights.[1] As the representative of the government (*el gobernador*) put it, paying the licence fee to the state would ensure the farmers had the right to use water 'almost like proprietors'. Although the WRL does not allow private ownership of water, the right to use water needs to be formalised either in the form of a licence, a permission or an authorisation. The 'user licence' – referred to as *la licencia* – is the most permanent and the most relevant for farmers in Majes and Colca. The WRL stipulates that all uses of water in Peru, including agricultural, industrial, mining, and population usage (drinking water), as well as the management of waste water, need to be formalised (ANA 2010). With the creation of the new National System of Water Resources Management in 2008, the regulation of all kinds of water and all kinds of uses – not only agricultural use, but also industrial and populational use – was centralised in the ANA. In this chapter, I suggest that the formalisation of water user rights creates a form of legibility (Scott 1998), which means making water use visible for the state. Giving the state an overview over all registered uses and users enables the state to achieve order and control over water sources, uses and users.

However, I argue that we not only need to look into what is made visible and for whom, but also what is made invisible in the processes of formalisation. What is excluded from a narrow vision of legibility, where water is reduced to a finite economic resource? I suggest that social inequalities are created among humans, where those who cannot produce documents and make their case lose and are denied water access. Also the relationships among humans and non-humans – land, water, beings – are severed as they are reduced to a singular contractual relationship between users and the state. I propose that while 'efficiency' justifies physical enclosures in pipes, 'legibility' justifies and enables abstract enclosures in documents. Hence, the project of making water use legible makes other water practices illegible, since they do not fit in the forms and registers of the state. They nevertheless sometimes appear in different encounters. For many people in Colca, they are partially connected in everyday water life. Legible and illegible water use are as entangled as the 'efficient' and 'good' uses discussed in chapter 5.

Figure 8 To apply for a water user licence, it is necessary to have all the documents in order, like the title deed of your land and personal identity papers. These papers, which often have been obtained through long and difficult processes, are carefully guarded in people's homes.

This chapter will discuss the tensions involved in formalising water user rights, focusing on the introduction of water use licences for potable water use in the highland municipalities of Caylloma province. These licences for population use were legitimised by the need to secure water for the future to protect against climate change, water scarcity, or the intrusion of mines, tourist hotels or other market actors. Most local municipalities were highly sceptical and resistant, however, and perceived it as another step towards commodification of water. The formalisation of water user rights is connected to the formalisation of property rights, and the chapter will also discuss the challenges related to land titles and access to potable water in the desert surrounding the irrigated lands in Majes. First, I will discuss the notion of 'scarcity', which underlies and legitimises the policies of efficiency and legibility.

Water scarcity and legibility

As described in chapters 4 and 5, the story of global warming in Colca Valley mainly translates into water-related problems and uncertainty. Various actors – state institutions, NGOs, and water user organisations – often talk about 'water scarcity' as if it were an undisputed fact that there is insufficient water supply that will affect everyone equally. However, several scholars have shown that the concept of 'water scarcity' is socially constructed in political and institutional processes. In other words, 'scarcity' does not only refer to physical absence of water, but of a lack of economic resources or political power to access water (Swyngedouw 2004, 2009; Mehta 2007; Budds 2008; Urteaga-Crovetto 2016). Furthermore, the concept of 'water scarcity' has often been used to mobilise different economic and political interests and 'solutions' (Budds 2008); stories of scarcity have been used to justify controversial infrastructure projects, such as large dams (Mehta 2007), and to legitimise particular forms of governance (Hellberg 2020). In Peru, Urteaga-Crovetto (2016) has argued that discourses of water scarcity have created conditions of exclusion, and that by rendering the calculation of water supply as a technical matter, the appropriation of water is depoliticised. In Colca Valley, the notion of 'water scarcity' is used to argue the need to implement regulations and projects: formalisation of user rights, registration of water sources and water use, new infrastructure and more efficient irrigation technology. I suggest that these policies are different forms of enclosures, which are not only physical enclosures in dams and pipes, as seen in chapter 5, but which can also be conceptual and abstract. In other words, to formalise the rights to use water in state-issued licences is a way of enclosing water use in documents. These policies of enclosures are justified by a neoliberal narrative of scarcity, which represents water problems in terms of competition over a finite economic resource, which is very different from earlier responses to challenges related to aridity.

Colca has always been semi-arid and depended upon irrigation and collaboration between people to construct and maintain irrigation systems, canals and terraces. There is also a long history of conflicts over access to water in Colca Valley, and there are particular conflicts that have been going on for a long time, for example between Chivay and Yanque Anansaya, and between Coporaque and Yanque Urinsaya. Many conflicts started when the population, land and water resources were reorganised under colonial rule in the second half of the 16th century. When the Spanish viceroy Francisco de Toledo imposed the '*reducciones*' in the 1570s, the indigenous population were forced to settle in centralised villages where they were more easily controlled (Benavides 1998). When the administrative districts were created after independence in 1821, the boundaries were defined without considering the traditional uses of water sources and canals, creating conflicts between Yanque and Coporaque and also between other districts in Colca (Benavides 1998; see also Brandshaug 2020). After formal independence from the colonial power, water remained a private matter, and landowners controlled the water sources within their properties. The nationalisation of water in 1969 through Velasco's General Water Law was followed by a need to regulate water access through public administration based on irrigation districts. Since the 1990s, neoliberal ideology has impacted water legislation and regulations, entailing the fostering of individual property rights, the treatment of water as an economic resource, and prioritisation of economic growth. The neoliberal narrative of scarcity imposes a sense of competition instead of collaboration between entities, groups, individual farmers and communities, and also between different uses: agricultural use (irrigation water), domestic use (potable water) and industrial use (mining, agribusiness, tourism). A logic of competition, justified by perceived scarcity, will often generate a need to formalise assets, which in turn can create two intrinsically interconnected effects: legibility and control on the one hand, and commodification and marketisation on the other. Climate change exacerbates an already existing concern with water uncertainty and strengthens the narrative of scarcity, and the fear that if you do not formalise your exclusive right to use a certain amount of water from a particular source, someone else will take it. New ways of registering water use happen together with capitalisation of agriculture and neoliberal management of water and land, and formalisation of user rights can be seen as a form of 'proxy privatisation', in the sense that water is organised and managed in ways that approximate and can ultimately lead to private property and commodification (Osborne 2015). While neoliberal ideology favours less state intervention, several scholars have shown how so-called free markets need state involvement and regulations to work (Polanyi 1944; Brenner et al. 2010; Weiss 2012). Hence, instead of focusing on deregulation, neoliberalisation should rather be seen as 'regulatory restructuring' or modes of governance 'to impose, extend or consolidate marketized, commodified forms of social life' (Brenner et al. 2010: 330).

The Peruvian economist Hernando de Soto, leader of the Institute for Liberty and Democracy (Instituto Libertad y Democracia), had considerable influence on economic policies in Peru in the 1980s and 1990s, and his ideas on the formalisation of assets as a way for poor countries to achieve capitalist development have been influential all over the global South and within the World Bank. De Soto addressed the need for making legal systems simpler and universal: 'a good legal property system obtains and organizes knowledge about recorded assets in forms we can control' (De Soto 2000: 218). Second, he proposed the formal titling of property to activate the potential value in an asset and to enable it to 'perform functions that generate capital' (De Soto 2000: 221). Applying these ideas of formalisation and property to water would imply abstracting water from the web of relationships in which it is entangled; in other words, it implies a simplification and singularisation that reduces water to an abstract and standardised resource. According to Scott's (1998) argument of state control and legibility, the simplification of water makes it easier for bureaucracies to measure, register, control and manipulate water use. This bureaucratic logic of legibility is practically synonymous with a commercial logic, meaning that both markets and states are dependent on legibility (Scott 1998). Legibility is indeed central in de Soto's ideas: he has argued that 'representational systems' of property 'help us manipulate and order the complexities of the world in a manner that we can all understand' (2000: 220). However, this indicates a view of the world as an even playing field, where peasants, mines and agribusiness companies would be treated as equal players in a global competition to access resources, extract value and generate capital.

Formalising water user rights in Colca Valley

After the water users had been paying both the potable water tariff and the irrigation tariff for some years and were becoming used to this arrangement (see chapter 3), a new regime of formalisation and licences for water user rights was introduced in 2006, when the formalisation programme Profodua (Programa de Formalización de Derecho de Uso de Agua) started its work in Colca valley. This programme was part of the World Bank-funded Water Resources Management Modernization Project. Through this programme, most farmers whose formal land titles were in order, obtained licences as part of large groups called 'irrigation blocks' (*bloques de riego*). However, according to Miriam Seemann (2016), who studied this process of formalisation in Yanque, these were in fact individual rights, attached to personal names, ID-number, identification of land plots and personal water volumes. Therefore, many water users were excluded from obtaining a licence for water use right because they lacked the required documentation: land property title, water tariff payment receipts, or ID-cards. Local customs for how to define users and allow access were not recognised in this process (Seemann 2016).

Those who did not receive a licence through Profodua, have to apply on an individual basis for the right to use a specific amount of water (measured in litres per second) from a specific source. This application, like other paperwork regarding the uses of and conflicts over water, has to be handed in to the ALA office. The licence holder also needs to pay an annual fee for the licence entitling them to the right to use water. In return, the ANA promises to protect these individual rights to use water. However, registration and control require a simplification of nature to make it more susceptible to measurement, calculation and manipulation. Hence, the multiplicity of water practices and relationships is singularised and reduced to an economic resource. According to Seemann and Boelens (2014), the introduction of licences in Yanque caused increased individualism and weakened communal water management. Since licences are directly linked to property titles, new social inequalities were created because the market value of land with attached licences increased. While it was presented as a way of ensuring water security, the process was depoliticised and thus the increase in state control and market mechanisms was made invisible (Seeman and Boelens 2014). I suggest that, in addition to increased individualism, marketisation and inequality, formalisation of rights also alters the relationships between people, water, land and other-than-human beings by reducing these relationships to contractual agreements between users and the state regarding water-as-economic-resource.

As described in chapter 1, in 2011, José was sent to Chivay to represent the ALA in Colca Valley two days a week. The first task assigned to him was to inform all the municipalities in Colca Valley about the WRL, which was then still referred to as 'the new law', and particularly to instruct them about the obligation to formalise the municipalities' rights to provide their populations with drinking water, and also to formalise their waste water treatment. According to the WRL, all municipalities must have treatment plants for waste water, and have to apply for licences for the right to dispose of treated waste water. To make his work in Colca easier,

José made a deal with his godfather's son-in-law, who worked for a rural development agency with an office in Chivay. The agreement meant that he could borrow his friend's rented room once a week and borrow his motorbike, so that he could make visits to different districts. José was also in charge of coordinating the visit of another ALA employee, Cesar, who carried out the inspections and measurements, and did paperwork for formalisation. José planned to visit all the municipalities in Colca to inform them about the licences and coordinate the inspection, and he invited me to accompany him to do the first unannounced visits in June 2011.

Autonomy versus control and commodification

We set out on the motorbike on a Monday around 10 a.m., and first we went to Canocota, which is an annex of Chivay district. The offices in the municipal building were closed, however, and the whole town was deserted except for an alpaca wandering around the plaza. Since all the inhabitants, including the mayor, are farmers, they were probably working in their fields. We continued to the village of Tuti, where we found the mayor and two council members in the mayor's office of the municipality. José gave them a printed copy of the WRL and informed them about *la licencia*, explaining that they should formalise their user right to potable water and pay an annual fee to the state. Since this was considered to be an area of extreme poverty, he assured them that the fee would be no more than 200 *soles*. He informed them that a technician from the ALA, Cesar, would come to inspect the point of water intake and to measure the water flow. He also informed them about the obligation to make a treatment plant and formalise the dumping of waste water, and that the municipalities that did not do this before a certain deadline, would be fined.

Hearing this, the mayor and the council members got very upset. The mayor explained that the villagers of Tuti have done all the work to construct the infrastructure for drinking water by themselves, and that the provision of drinking water is organised by an 'Administrative Committee of Sanitary Services' called CASS (Comité de Administración de Servicios de Saneamiento) with members elected by the community. The households in Tuti do not pay for the drinking water, and the mayor rejected the idea that they now should pay the licence fee. 'It starts at 200 *soles*, and afterwards it will be increasing', he predicted. The district's monthly budget was only 28,000 *soles*, the mayor explained: 'There is no room in our budget. The state should take care of this. We are living in extreme poverty, and this would mean more expenses.' The mayor could not understand why the state would force a poor district to pay for the user right to water, and even worse, that the ALA threatened them with fines instead of offering support to treat waste water properly: 'It is illogical!' José said that they could apply for support to do these kinds of projects, but this annoyed the men even more, since it is very expensive to develop a project application: it has to be done by an engineer which can cost 1,000–2,000 *soles*. One reason for this reaction to José's visit could be a structural feeling of injustice in poor rural districts that are marginalised and 'abandoned' by the state. When the state finally arrives, the purpose is to interfere, to control, to charge taxes and hand out fines. Another reason would be that the inhabitants of Tuti have done all the work of obtaining access to this drinking water, and they are currently doing all the work of maintenance and distribution. Hence, they feel ownership not only of the water sources in their district, but also of the reservoir, the pipes and their system of management and distribution.

Later that day, I talked to the governor of Tuti,[2] an elderly man who confirmed the sense of ownership, autonomy and resistance against external actors trying to intervene and control their water. He remembered well how the local authorities worked to obtain potable water 30 years earlier. In the 1980s, the community agreed to capture water from a spring in the mountains and install pipes to the village, 'at our own cost', the governor proudly told me. They also applied for funding from NGOs in order to buy pipes and other materials. In communal work parties, the villagers built a small reservoir in order to capture the water from the spring. 'The communal work was like *ayni-minka*; one for all and all for one', the governor said. *Ayni* and *minka* are Quechua concepts for labour exchange based on mutual reciprocity (Allen 1988; Mayer 2002). In the beginning, people carried water in buckets from public pumps in the plaza to their houses. Little by little, they installed pipes to every house in the village. Then, Sedapar, the public company in charge of providing potable water in Arequipa city and Chivay, tried to intervene and take over the management in Tuti. However, the people rose up and did not allow this company to enter the district. 'The water is our own', the governor explained, and 'if we give it to Sedapar, they will make us pay every month.' Today, the potable water is administered by the CASS committee, and one person is in charge of the cleaning of the reservoir, chlorination and controlling the amounts of water that is used. Instead of paying monthly fees, every household pays 15 *soles* a year to CASS.

A couple of weeks after José's visit, I accompanied Cesar on his inspection in Tuti. This time, the mayor was not present. Instead, Cesar and I met with the vice-mayor, a council member, the president of CASS, the treasurer of the municipality, the vice-president of the water users commission, and the district governor. The council member and the CASS president were women, and the rest were men. Cesar started by explaining that water for human consumption was given priority in the new law on water resources, and that the municipality must apply for a licence to have the right to use the water that they capture from the spring for domestic usage. The licence application, he said, should specify the exact amount that they are using and the amount that they expect to use in the future, with a 20-year projection of population growth. The listeners were sceptical, and the council member talked about their disappointing experience with the formalisation of user rights licences for irrigation water. First, the engineers from the Profodua programme had told the farmers that the procedure would not cost anything, but those who did not obtain their licences in the first round, now had to pay a fee when filing the application. Therefore, people feel deceived and call it a 'business', she explained. The treasurer asked how the CASS could apply for an exemption or a minimum payment, and Cesar replied that they could just talk with the officials in the ALA and, since this was a poor highland area, it could be considered for a minimum payment. The president of the CASS, a woman in her thirties, stated 'We have to bring this proposal to the people, and they have to accept it or reject it. If not, they will ask why we have done this without consulting the people.' The governor agreed: 'We have to decide this in a meeting; if not, the people will rise and send the authority away on a donkey.' The governor was especially worried that this process would 'open the way for Sedapar'.

'I come here to talk, not to impose', Cesar insisted, and they proceeded with the inspection, walking uphill to the 'capture point', where a water flow rate of approximately 3 lps went into a pipe from the spring to the reservoir, and the rest entered an irrigation canal. Cesar was surprised that this small amount of water was sufficient for 700 families, and they confirmed that they did not use much water during the day, when most were out working in their fields. The conversation continued by the reservoir, under a sign that read 'Water is life. Do not waste it.' Cesar explained that they should apply for a licence covering 3 lps, in addition to a future projection that considered population growth. He suggested that they apply for 5 lps, and he recommended that they install a measuring valve in order to pay for the amount that they actually use and not for the amount written in the licence. If they have a licence for 5 lps, but the valve shows that they only used 3 lps, then they would only pay for 3 lps. However, if they do not measure and report this, they would be charged for 5 lps. The CASS president explained that things were a bit more complicated: since the households only use water during the day (mostly in the morning and afternoon), the water is diverted to an irrigation pond during the night. Cesar responded that they could calculate their consumption by 12 hours a day instead of 24 in order to pay less. They were not happy with this solution, however, commenting that this would create more control, less flexibility and more conflicts. According to the council member, this would start a war between the municipality and agriculture, and she pointed out that every afternoon there was an overflow of water from the reservoir that went into another irrigation canal. 'We do not waste anything, we make use of everything', she said. Once again, Cesar suggested that they install a gauge in the reservoir. Here, we could pause for a bit to think about what is meant by 'not wasting' in this context. Did the council member refer to what the WRL and 'new water culture' refer to as 'efficient use', or did she rather imply what I, in chapter 5, called 'good use', in the sense of sufficiency, collaboration and inclusion. In other words, that they allocate sufficient water for potable use, and when the households do not need more water, they give to agriculture, where it is needed to irrigate the fields. Of course, since most families in in Tuti are also farmers, this seems practical, and in line with Princen's (2005) argument that 'sufficiency' (or 'seeking enough') is about doing well; about good work and good governance, and it is contrary to modernity's dominant principle of 'efficiency'. What the logic of efficiency does is build up the need for technological devices, like water gauges, which evoke a sense of control and distrust, and as the council member indicated, it would impose a competition between irrigation water and potable water, which does not make any sense for the farmers in villages like Tuti.

Cesar talked as if the quantitative amount was the crux of the problem, and emphasised that according to his calculations, the minimal fee of 200 *soles* for the licence, divided among the 700 families in Tuti, resulted in only 28 *céntimos* per family per year. For the community leaders, however, much more was at stake. I suggest that the conflict revolved around the qualitative change in how to govern water: the measurements and licences introduced by the state agencies meant more external control and the villagers feared that this would escalate and open the way for private companies and commodification of water. The group of leaders were not calmed down by Cesar's calculation, and kept asking for details. For example, would this money cover the chlorination and maintenance of the infrastructure? Cesar explained that no, that would be another payment. Cesar also informed them that in order to apply for a licence, they would have to pay a fee of 183 *soles* for the 'right to procedure', and they would also have to pay 300 *soles* for the 'right to inspection'. The vice-president of the water users commission stated that he disagreed with paying this money. He compared it with the tariff that all farmers pay for the irrigation water; the major part of this tariff is returned to the commission so that they can spend it on maintenance of canals and other things. However, all the money for the licence payment would go to the state and not be used for the benefit of Tuti. He pointed to the heart of the matter when he emphatically said that 'This is the work of the people, we have built it in communal work (*faena comunal*)'. The president of CASS commented that she had heard that in other villages, the farmers have refused to pay for the licences for irrigation water use. 'They come here and they do not say the whole truth', she complained. She lamented that people who wanted to be courteous and correct ended up by obeying the state and paying more and more. The governor supported her and told Cesar that there is a 'lack of trust' and people resist payments. Cesar did his best to convince them that they could trust him and that the ANA and ALA had their best interests in mind. He repeatedly emphasised that they should think of their children, because the water sources are drying up little by little because of climate change. Therefore, they should protect their rights in case other actors like mining companies or tourist hotels applied for a formal right to that water.

It became quite clear during the inspection and conversation that a formalisation process is not a simple assertion of rights to access water. It was embedded in, and legitimised by, a discourse of scarcity and competition, followed by demands for 'efficiency', which produced an image of actors fighting to access a finite resource. In addition, formalisation brings with it a whole range of associated material and social effects, such as valves, measuring technologies and control mechanisms, which also indicates a lack of mutuality and trust and collective responsibility. These material gauging devices support an idea that socio-environmental problems can be fixed by modern science and technology.

Mountains, reciprocity, respect and ownership

The next municipality that José and I visited after Tuti was Sibayo, which is higher up and next to Callalli. Here, he presented a shorter and less confrontational version of the information about user licences and made arrangements for Cesar's inspection. When I arrived with Cesar two weeks later, we met with the municipal manager and one council member, who was also serving as secretary of the water users commission. They told us that they were worried because of the declining water supplies: the glaciers and the snow had disappeared from the mountaintops and many springs were dry. They took us to the point of capture of potable water: after a 30-minute car drive, we walked for 20 minutes to get to the spring, located at an altitude of 4,381 metres. They explained that when the water supply in this spring diminishes in November and December, they take water from another spring located 600 metres away. The two springs belong to an *apu* who receives *pagos* from the people in the village twice a year; every August and February. In collective work, the villagers installed a pipe connecting the two springs and a 20-km pipeline from the main spring to the reservoir. There, the water is chlorinated before being distributed to all the households in the village. The municipality organised this work around 20 years ago, and today, the households do not pay any money for potable water.

After the inspection, Cesar explained the process of formalisation of water user rights as stipulated by the new law, and about payments for the *licencia*. He said, 'The purpose is not to sanction or create problems. We must talk and find solutions.' The council member and the manager asked whether it was possible to pump water from the Colca River in order to have more water. They were concerned with the dwindling supplies and future scarcity. However, Cesar explained that the water in Colca River 'already has an owner'. This water comes from the Condoroma dam, which is located upstream in the neighbouring district of Callalli, and is destined for the Majes canal, which starts downstream in the water intake (*bocatoma*) in Tuti. The final destination of this 'regulated water' is the irrigated pampa of Majes. Although Cesar was open to a dialogue to help the water users in Sibayo, their suggestion about taking water from the river passing their village was out the question. As representative of the ALA, he also represented the state, which gives priority to agribusiness and export-oriented economic growth. Cesar's goal was to the contrary to formalise – and enclose in a licence – the use of water that was given by the *apu* to the people of Sibayo. This goal was explicitly legitimised by the narrative of scarcity due to climate change and drought. However, what was not openly discussed in this meeting in Sibayo was the question of how the public employees from the ALA could talk about water scarcity when there was enough water in Colca to irrigate 15,000 hectares of desert in Majes. The water destined for Majes could not be touched; not only because it was enclosed in the canal, but also because it was enclosed in the registered user licences of the MIP.

There are many interpretations of what the formalisation of user rights implies: either as an insurance and support, or as a strategy to commodify and privatise water. The diverging views on the consequences of formalisations reflect different relationships with and experiences of the state: those who have experienced the state as an employer and protector of rights can easily see the formalisation of rights as insurance for the future. On the other hand, those who – based on previous experiences – have reasons to distrust state officials and professional engineers, and those who have experienced the state as a colonising power and/or as a distant and elusive entity, will be inclined to see formalisation as yet another attempt to exploit and mislead them. The WRL, which is legitimised by global climate change and the threat of water scarcity, transfers responsibilities from the state to private *Juntas* on the one hand and emphasises formalisation and control on the other. Although more work is given to private user associations, the state imposes more regulations and payments. This creates mistrust among water users, who refuse to be monitored and exploited. Peasant farmers in Peru generally have extensive experience of deception and abuse, which makes it very difficult to trust state officials. Most peasant and indigenous communities and small municipalities prefer to manage their resources in their own way.

When ALA officials say that the licence will protect people against the abuses of private mining companies, it is a strong argument. However, many farmers in Colca find it hard to trust that the licence is a guarantee when they also see that the government gives priority to multinational corporations like agribusiness and mines. Most farmers in Colca seem to have a general scepticism regarding tariffs, fees and taxes, and many express fear that the payments will increase and that formalisation is the beginning of privatisation – in the sense of enclosure and commodification – of water. What formalisation does is change and sever relations between institutions, people, mountains and springs. By formalising and enhancing the state–citizen/user relation, it simultaneously severs the relations between people, springs, mountains, ponds and canals.

These relationships are invisible in the formal documents of licences and ownership, and they are seldom mentioned in meetings with officials or negotiations between state and citizens, as in the inspection in Tuti. One of the reasons would be that people generally do not wish to be perceived as 'indigenous', a social category loaded with the historically produced stigma of being 'backward' and representing the opposite of progress. In internal meetings, however, the beings in the surrounding landscape are taken into consideration. If they are not, the outcome might be tragic, even deadly. Towards the end of my first period of fieldwork in Colca, on Monday morning 3 October 2011, four persons died in Tuti, when they were crushed by huge rocks falling from a mountain. They were members of the water users commission and were going to do repair work on a water canal when the mountain killed them. I was told that this mountain (*cerro*) had always been known to be particularly powerful and dangerous. People were afraid to pass there at night because the mountain is known to be demonic and may lure you inside by opening up and show you a nice market with beautiful things. When the farmers made the irrigation canal many years ago, they had made a good offering: I was told that they had given the mountain a human foetus. That meant, however, that the mountain got used to the taste of humans and craved for more. But this time, the water users commission had been careless. They should have made a new powerful offering before starting working on the improvement of the canal. In fact, the vice-president of the water users commission had pointed this out at their meeting on Sunday night. But since it was late and they did not have the right ingredients, they decided to postpone the offering. This was indeed an act of carelessness and disrespect. The next morning, the vice-president was leading the group along the canal, and he and three others were crushed by big rocks. People said that they were eaten by the mountain. The whole village was terrified, in shock and grief, as they arranged a wake ceremony and buried them the day after.

As shown in chapter 4, I learned a lot about the characteristics and relationships to mountains through everyday conversations with friends. After the burial in Tuti, my *compadres* in Chivay invited me for tea, and they talked about the accident and the mountain. I learnt that the name of the mountain was Layqa Layqa, which means '*brujo brujo*', or 'Sorcerer' (witch/wizard); it is known to be a dangerous mountain, and it has many stories. At night you can see lights, and sometimes a big door opens up and it calls on you to enter, but if you enter you will never return, I was told. 'The mountain needs blood, he always wanted people, four persons.' My *comadre* had heard that when the police came to take away the dead people, stones started to fall. When the police withdrew, it calmed down. The police officers walked in again, and 'the mountain started to throw stones'. So, they had to make a *pago* in order to take out the dead. They brought a *curandero* to make the *pago*, and the mountain finally calmed down. This was a disconcerting reminder of the power of the mountains who also sustain the people with water. Mountains control who gets access to water and the canals. Access is given or denied based on relations of reciprocity and respect. Mountains are not impersonal and neutral, on the contrary they have personhood and different personalities, and can be highly volatile and unpredictable. What is certain is that according to the logic of relationality, it does not matter whether you have a documented licence from the state if you have not paid the proper respect and *pago* to the mountain and other earth-beings.

After a long process, the municipalities of Tuti, Sibayo and the majority of the districts in Colca Valley, got their formal licences for potable water user rights in order approximately four years after José and Cesar's first visits. José explained the initial conflict as a problem of communication and lack of information. I suggest that the problem is about much more than this, however. The key question for many people in Colca Valley seems to be not about formal rights or not, but having control over the surroundings and the design of the land they live in, and to have control over their lives and future. Who decides how they organise the distribution of water – the source of life – is essential, and most prefer to make their decisions collectively in communal meetings. What I learned in Colca was also that the other-than-human beings are also taken into consideration when making these decisions (see chapter 5). The mountains were the ones keeping and giving water to humans, and could therefore be seen as the true owners of water (see chapter 7). Officially, however, the formal owners of the water flowing from the Condoroma dam, through Colca River and into the Majes canal is the pampa of Majes, represented by Autodema. However, there are many people in Majes who do not have access to this water.

Land titles, legibility and potable water in Majes

In Majes, far away from the water eyes in the highlands, the population is increasing rapidly as new people move in every day in search of work, business and land. Many of these people have moved from highland communities in an attempt to flee poverty and get closer to the opportunities that modern life has to offer. However, most soon realise that access to jobs, housing and basic services, such as water, is limited, and the struggle to survive continues, although in different ways. In 2014, the number of inhabitants was roughly estimated to be somewhere between 100,000 and 120,000. This population is spreading out in the surrounding desert, where there is no infrastructure for the provision of water and electricity. The majority make a living as land labourers, often on day-to-day contracts, or work in factories, mechanical workshops or in the service sector. Many are self-employed as taxi drivers or food-and-drink vendors in the streets, in the marketplace or in small restaurants. The dream that many of these working poor are pursuing is not only a stable income but also a piece of land in order to build a house of their own. Earlier, the state distributed land lots at subsidised prices, but today many of these lots are sold for large sums. In 2014, buyers paid between US $20,000 and $30,000 for a lot. The prices of both farms and housing lots in regulated areas that are connected to the water grid have increased tremendously, and most migrants from the highlands cannot afford them. Instead, many families in search of a house of their own 'invade' a piece of empty land, where they build houses of straw mats, and claim ownership. These invasions are often done collectively by groups of hundreds or thousands of people searching for a place to live and/or to run a business, and this is not an uncommon strategy in Peru, where millions of people have escaped poverty in the rural highlands and moved to the urban coastline where they occupy 'empty' desert land in the outskirt of cities like Lima and Arequipa (Ødegaard 2019).

In 2004, a desert area of 6,200 hectares, destined for urban expansion, was transferred from Autodema to the municipality of Majes. A part of this land was already divided into lots that had been sold to private owners before the transfer, and the rest was supposedly municipal property. However, the land that was not already occupied by squatters was soon invaded. When I talked to the sub-director of the Municipal Office of Formalisation in 2014, she told me that they had land invasions every day. The largest part of the 'urban expansion' area is the Ciudad Majes, in which module A and B is already divided into independent individual lots which are registered in the Public Registry with title deeds. The modules C, D, E, F and G are still in a process of 'formalisation', which means that title deeds for the properties have not yet been issued. In March 2014, the sub-director said that they had 20,000 case files in the formalisation office, and these files represent properties in different phases of the process. Whether the owners have bought the property, or occupied it, they must formalise and register the property. According to the law, a person who has lived on a piece of land for a certain amount of time can claim 'possession' and apply for the right to buy the land and get a formal title deed. A decree from 2012 stated that persons who had lived on a lot since before 25 November 2010 are allowed to stay. This meant that the majority of the squatters living in Ciudad Majes in 2014 could enter the formalisation process. They had to provide evidence of having lived there from before this date, and each family was not allowed to claim ownership for more than one lot. Among the 20,000 cases, there were many who already had paid for their properties, and some had contracts, while others have yet to present documentation to support their case.

Squatting is often done collectively by so-called 'invasion groups', who occupy desert land in and around Ciudad Majes (Stensrud 2018). These squatter groups are often led by people who have previous experience in grassroots organisation and squatting, and they are joined by recently arrived migrants and people who have lived for a while in Majes, renting small rooms and working in the informal economy by taking odd jobs for farmers, or in shops or construction firms. However, some of the leaders of these squatter groups have been accused of becoming land traffickers and of profiting from desperate people wanting to buy a cheap property in a market that is difficult to navigate. For example, I heard about properties that had been sold to several people by a cynical dealer. Others found that the property they had bought, had been occupied by a squatter before they had managed to build a house there. I heard many examples of such illegal transactions, conflicts, evictions and violent encounters between owners, squatter groups and the police. Although the 30 lawyers employed at the Municipal Office of Formalisation were working hard to achieve an overview, order and control, the housing situation in Majes was often described as chaotic and corrupt. The sub-director of the office also complained about politicians in election campaigns who tell people to take possession of land, promising them that they will 'fix' the problem if they get elected.

The municipality is also responsible for providing basic infrastructure and services, such as electricity, water and sewage, to the urban population. These projects are costly and take time, however, and many of the landowners with property title deeds in order choose to live in other places while they wait for these services. On the other hand, according to the sub-director, the municipality cannot install infrastructure in areas without people living there; there should be an existing population to receive the services. From the people who had no choice other than to live in the desert, I heard the other side of the story: they had been waiting for water and electricity for many years and were getting impatient. In most neighbourhoods, people have organised in housing associations as a collective strategy to formalise ownership, obtain title deeds, and eventually get access to water pipes, electricity, roads and other infrastructure. Meanwhile, families buy potable water from trucks that come once a week, or they boil water from the irrigation canals.

In 2014, I met Lucía, a 38-year-old woman who was married to the leader of one of the housing associations. She lived in the desert, without any water and electricity in the house, with her husband, their 8-month-old baby and two children from her first marriage. She was born into an Aymara-speaking peasant family in the highlands of Puno, and as a 7-year-old, she was sent to Arequipa city, where her aunt arranged work for her. For the next ten years, she worked as a domestic servant for several middle-class families and experienced different degrees of exploitation and abuse. At the age of 19 she met a man who was also from Puno; she got pregnant, they married and moved to Villa El Pedregal. She told me that she endured 14 years of married life with this man who was controlling and abusive; he would not let her have a job and she mostly stayed at home in the room they rented, taking care of their four children. After some years, she managed to convince him that she had the right to an education, and she studied hairdressing. When she finally left him, she started working as a shop assistant, and later she found work as a hairdresser in a hair salon. There, she met her second husband, Alfredo, who was also from Puno, and they married in 2013. Alfredo worked as a night watchman, in addition to occasionally driving a pirate taxi. While Alfredo's first wife stayed with their children in the house they had built in one of the new neighbourhoods in the desert, he moved in with Lucía in a rented room in Villa El Pedregal. They soon decided to build a house of their own on a land lot in the desert that Lucía had acquired when the state was handing out subsidised lots and that she had been paying for little by little. They built the house together, one room at a time, and today they live there with their baby son and Lucía's children from her first marriage. There are no roads, water pipes or electricity in the area. At night, they light candles so that the children can do their homework for school. Once a week, a truck brings water, which they store in plastic containers. They must use this water very carefully so that it lasts for the whole week. In other settlements, people take water from irrigation canals, although it is known that this water is contaminated and not safe to drink. For lack of an alternative, however, many boil the water and use it anyway.

However, only a few of the property owners actually live there, because of the lack of infrastructure, and surrounding Lucía's house there are vast areas of desert land. At one point, a group of squatters tried to invade the area, which they saw as 'empty', and the property owners had to defend themselves. After this, the people who owned property there decided to organise in a neighbourhood association, and they elected Alfredo as their leader. The purpose of the association is to defend their land, and to obtain access to electricity and water. They also wish to have a marketplace and a primary school. They have meetings once a month on Sunday mornings, since most of the neighbourhood's residents are agricultural workers and Sunday is their only day off. Alfredo was trying to convince more people to build their houses, to show that this land has owners and to put pressure on the municipality to give them roads, pipes and cables. He was constantly knocking on doors in the municipality to obtain electricity and water for the neighbourhood. Lucía supported him: 'We should make an effort; if one doesn't insist, nothing happens.'

Access to land, housing, safe water, electricity, and roads is not taken for granted by people like Lucía and Alfredo, who know that they will gain nothing by just waiting for help. Instead, they work hard, organise, and insist – based on legal possession and title deeds – on their right to services. 'Everything that I have, I have achieved it by myself,' Lucía said. Shortly before I met her in 2014, she started to run her own hair salon business. She rented a space, got a credit loan from a bank to buy equipment, and she planned to pay it back in two years. Hence, she had gained economic and social mobility by her own work and effort, despite her lack of formal education and the other hindrances that life had offered her. Instead of becoming a peasant, a domestic worker, or a subdued housewife, she had worked hard to gain skills, work experience, and finally her own house and business. Land and water are connected in different ways in Colca and in Majes, for the state bureaucracy and for peasant communities. From the state's legal perspective, people need to have land titles to be proper water users with a licensed user right to water, while in highland communities, relationships to land and water are also maintained through nourishment and reciprocity. People living in Majes are dependent upon the municipality to get access to water, and they need to formalise their property rights to land before they can claim water. The constant struggles and negotiations to connect to the water flow and to be integrated in the grid testifies to the increasing sense of water uncertainty in Majes; the mounting fear of becoming disconnected because of the crumbling canal, earthquakes and climate change.

Conclusion

In both Colca and Majes, the state aims to achieve legibility and control over property relations and the use of water and land. However, since the socio-material landscapes are different, so are the goals and means of the state. In Colca Valley and the Caylloma highlands, the state authorities know how the land is distributed in registered and formalised properties, although they do not know of all the informal uses and agreements. What they want to know more about is the locations and water flow rates in all the different water sources, as well as the different uses, canals, pipes and ways of organising distribution. When something looks chaotic and unorderly from the outside, the state strives for order and legibility. In Majes, on the other hand, the state authorities have detailed information about the water flows, since the Majes canal and the grid of canals and pipes is highly regulated. However, the invasions and possessions of land are happening in unorganised, unorderly and chaotic ways, at least from the state's perspective. Hence, the authorities' priority is to achieve legibility, order and control of the land properties and inhabitants, before establishing the infrastructure for potable water.

Defining and governing a watershed necessitates legibility, simplification, registration, and mapping of sources and water flow rates, water uses and water users. The argument is that the state will help water users to defend their rights if they have formalised and paid for their licences. This does not mean that people think that having a documented licence will ensure you water in times of drought, but as long as you have the paperwork, you can make claims and demands that are legible and legitimately recognised by the state. Chapter 7 will look into how the logic of registering water sources and uses is adopted by people in the headwaters to claim their right to access water and land in Majes.

7
Owning Water

> There is no private property of water.
>
> (Article 2 of the Water Resources Law)

> The state [...] promotes and safeguards the respect for the conditions granting water security to the investment related to its use, whether it is public, private or in cooperation.
>
> (Article 4 of the Water Resources Law)

> 'We are the owners of the water!'
>
> (Leader of the water users commission in Callalli)

After years of climate change, drought and earthquakes, most farmers in Majes have become more aware of their dependency on the headwaters.[1] In addition to the concerns about water supply, the future price of water is also a cause of constant worry among farmers. The second phase of the irrigation project – Majes-Siguas II – has been planned for many years and is expected to be implemented in the near future. Majes-Siguas II is promoted as a modern project that will create progress, employment and development for the region. Nevertheless, there are still tensions and unresolved issues concerning control, ownership and payments. A foreign concessionaire – the Spanish-owned Angostura-Siguas consortium – will finance and construct the infrastructure, and large-scale agribusiness companies will be able to buy large areas of land. During the past two decades, an agro-export boom, dominated by corporations, has led to new hydrosocial territories, water scarcity and social inequality in various coastal areas of Peru (Damonte et al. 2016; Damonte and Boelens 2019). The key question for many in Arequipa is whether small-scale farmers will be able to survive, or if the future is reserved for transnational corporations? At the same time, the pastoralists around the headwaters are those who are most severely affected by global warming, water uncertainty and dispossession due to the construction of the dams, tunnels and canals to transport water to the desert. There are still deep structural inequalities between the highlands – marked by centuries of marginalisation, poverty, racial discrimination and exclusion – and Majes and the rest of the urban coast, which has been privileged with financial investments, government support, infrastructure and economic growth. The highland population is protesting, but also making demands for compensation and the right to access water and land. The pastoral farmers in Callalli – the district where the Condoroma dam was built 40 years ago – proclaim themselves rightful owners of the water that originates from the mountains in their territories, and claim the right to be compensated for the water that is sent to Majes. In this chapter, I will look more closely at different claims for ownership to water. I will specifically discuss two forms of investment, based on finance and nurture, and I ask: in what ways can investments of finance or nurture grant rights to access and control the water flow? I will further explore what forms of ownership – and what kind of water – are being enacted by financial investments as opposed to nurturing ones.

Around the world, water is usually seen as naturally belonging to 'the commons', while both scholars and activists are concerned with the over-

Figure 9 A group of people from the highland district of Callalli watering the trees they have planted on an area of desert land in Majes. They were claiming the right to irrigate and cultivate this land based on their asserted ownership of the water from Callalli that gives life to Majes. Since there was no infrastructure on this land, they had to buy water in a tank and rent a car to water the trees.

hanging threat of transforming water into a commodity. Hence, water is often seen to oscillate between public and private ownership: as either part of the commons or a commodity. This is a constant tension, and activists, politicians and public employees negotiate the status of water in political struggles and in everyday practices (Ballestero 2019b). The Peruvian Water Resources Law teeters on a thin line when it comes to the question of ownership; the law is ambiguous at best, and contradictory at worst. While the law acknowledges water as public property, it also emphasises the economic value of water and encourages private investment in hydraulic infrastructure. As seen in previous chapters, the introduction of tariffs and formalisation of user rights are seen as ways of enabling the commodification of water. Threats to weaken local autonomy and free access to water are conceptualised as commodification and privatisation attempts. I suggest, however, that water does not rest easily within the dichotomy of commons versus commodity (Paerregaard and Andersen 2019). On the contrary, water tends to overflow and disrupt dichotomous categories like public–private, nature–culture, living–non-living, passive object–active subject. Inspired by Brightman, Fausto and Grotti (2016) and Blaser and de la Cadena (2017), I conceive of ownership as an ongoing process, always in the making, and the process of making the commons – the 'commoning' – consists of practices of nurturing and nourishing relationships. I will argue that the farmers' practices in highland Caylloma produce specific forms of ownership: processual, dynamic and conditional forms of ownership emerge from collective investments of labour, practices of nurture and reciprocity in social relationships, including human–environment relations. In turn, these forms of ownership are combined with notions of economic value and made into specific claims to land and water. In the following sections, I will first discuss concepts of ownership, property and the commons, before analysing how these concepts are enacted in negotiations over access, control and autonomy at different altitudes in the Majes-Colca watershed.

Ownership, property and the (un)commons

The notion of individualised private property was a key factor in the rise and spread of global capitalism and colonisation. In the 17th century, European theories of property, such as the philosopher Locke's ideas of appropriation through labour, were used to justify the colonisation of America and the dispossession of indigenous people (Arneil 1996).[2] Both

Marx (1976 [1867]) and Polanyi (1944) demonstrated how previously established forms of property relations, embedded in social formations, were destroyed by capitalism. This implied that short-term gain overshadowed public aspects, as well as moral and long-term values (Hann 1998). Marx (1976 [1867]) discussed how large areas of farm- and pastureland that used to belong to 'the commons' in 18th-century England were enclosed as private property. Today, the commodification and enclosure of communal land and water has caused destruction and conflicts in many places of the world. Water grabbing has been defined as a situation where powerful actors are able to take control of, or reallocate for their own benefit, water resources already used by local communities or that feed aquatic ecosystems on which their livelihoods are based (Mehta et al. 2012: 197). In line with the arguments presented in this book, however, processes of enclosure do not just involve grabbing water as 'resource' but can also imply a politics of nature and diverging conceptualisations of the ontology of water. Consequentially, there is also a need to scrutinise the meaning of 'ownership'.

There are no universally accepted definitions of ownership and property, and social conflicts related to natural resources often hinge on conflicting notions of ownership. Social anthropologists have defined property relations as social relations between people with respect to things, and argue that property must be understood in their historically specific socio-material contexts, rather than through narrow and legal notions such as 'rights' and 'claims' (Hann 1998; Verdery 1998, 2003). Busse and Strang (2011) use the wider term 'ownership' to discuss 'a set of processes through which people assert and contest rights rather than a static bundle or structure of rights' (Busse and Strang 2011: 4). In Colca Valley, different hydrosocial and ontological relationships give rise to different notions of ownership and rights, which leads to tensions in encounters between state representatives, district municipalities and peasant communities (see chapters 5 and 6). The distinctions are, however, more complex that just a conflict between individual and collective, or private versus public. Karen Bakker (2010) shows how policy debate tends to rely on the assumption that the distinction between public and private equates with that between governmental and non-governmental. Conventionally, the latter category is held to be synonymous with market activity for profit. However, simple public–private dualisms break down when confronted with the complexity of water supply provision in the global South (Bakker 2010: 27), especially in poor urban areas (see for example Andersen 2014; Anand

2017). Property rights may be absent, informal, or customary, and governments have never provided universal public services. Hence, unregulated alternatives appear, and people organise to provide themselves with the water-supply services that their governments are unable or unwilling to provide, as seen in chapter 6. In agreement with Bakker's observations, all of these are '"private" (in the sense of nongovernmental) strategies for providing services for and by members of the "public"' (Bakker 2010: 29). For example, water can be officially public, yet subjected to commodification. On the other hand, water can be 'privately' controlled by a collectivity or a community. In Colca Valley, water emerges from other ontological compositions, and is conceived as a vital force given by living mountains, yet at the same time used for consumption and production.

The commons refers to resources that are shared by many people and that are traditionally managed as collective or common property (Robbins 2012: 51). The popular 'Tragedy of the Commons' theory was written by Garrett Hardin (1968), who based it on rational choice theory, arguing that over-exploitation and degradation were the inevitable outcome of 'the commons', because 'as a rational being, each herdsman seeks to maximise his gain'. His argument was based on the idea that humans ultimately wish to seek their own benefit and therefore take as much as possible from collective resources, eventually leading to ecological crisis. This theory has been heavily criticised, however, and research has widely demonstrated how the commons is governed by implicit and explicit rules that regulate access and use, and reduce the risk of depletion of the resources (Robbins 2012: 53). Economist Elinor Ostrom (1990) famously criticised Hardin's theory based on institutional studies of communal management around the world, and she identified a list of principles – among them 'rules tailored to local conditions' and 'autonomy' – for a successful management of the commons.

Commodities have been critically analysed as objects that are abstracted from their socio-material contexts, standardised and made exchangeable and alienable for capitalist (disembedded) markets (Polanyi 1944; Castree 2003; Osborne 2015). However, in addition to scrutinising the concept of 'commodity', we should also examine the meaning of the 'commons' and the 'common good', since both notions rest on an ontology where humans are set apart from 'nature', either as exploiters or custodians. Blaser and de la Cadena (2017) note that there seems to be a paradoxical conceptual convergence between extractivist governments' justifications for the enclosure of commons and the justifications of environmental and social justice movements for a defence of the commons. The convergence consists in that the justifications are based on an ontological discontinuity between humans and non-humans. Hence, Blaser and de la Cadena (2017) propose to use the concept of the 'uncommons' to disrupt the idea of the common world as a shared ground and to accommodate for other-than-humans.[3] Brightman et al. (2016) have similarly discussed alternative regimes of ownership in Amazonia, where objects can have subjectivity and agency, and ownership as relations between persons and things is intrinsically bound up with processes of nurture. I find these lines of thinking helpful to understand how relationships of reciprocity among humans and other-than-human beings in Colca Valley and the highlands of Caylloma are constituted and maintained through nurture and nourishment, and that these world compositions are also investments in the land and water. These investments create forms of ownership and give rise to new claims to water and land. Before looking into investments of nourishment and nurture, however, I will discuss investments through financial capital and what kinds of hydrosocial relations, water and ownership are enacted by these.

Financial investment: the re-colonisation of land and water

Since its inception, the Special Project Majes-Siguas was conceived as an irrigation project in two phases: the first phase consisted of the building of the Condoroma dam, the Majes canal and the irrigation of the pampa of Majes, while the second phase would include the construction of the Angostura dam and the irrigation of 38,500 hectares in the neighbouring pampa of Siguas. In 2006, the second phase was launched through a public procurement call as a US $550 million project called 'Majes-Siguas II'. The concession was awarded to the transnational private consortium Angostura-Siguas, comprised of the Spanish firm Cobra and the Peruvian firm Cosapi. In 2018, however, after technical challenges and political pressure during the repercussions of a large-scale corruption scandal, Cosapi withdrew and sold its shares to Cobra, making the consortium owned solely by a Spanish firm (Comercio 2018; Ullberg 2019). Since the contract was signed in 2010, twelve addendums have been added, and the project has been delayed for various reasons, such as the opposition of and demands from the highland population. In 2009, farmers in the highland province of Espinar, in Cusco region, started to protest against the Angostura dam, contending that it would leave them with less water. Espinar receives water from the headwaters of the Apurímac river basin, which are the same sources that will feed Angostura. In 2011, the constitutional court halted the project and ordered a new environmental impact assessment and water balance report. After the new report, which was based on quantitative measurements of water resources, concluded that there was enough water, the court allowed the project to proceed as planned in 2013. However, in 2015, the environmental flow in the Apurimac River that should be guaranteed by the Majes-Siguas II project was increased from 0.5 m^3/s to 2.4 m^3/s (Vilca Begazo 2020). This was considered a win for Espinar, and created new challenges for the Majes-Siguas II project.

The Majes-Siguas II project is organised as a public–private partnership, in which the Peruvian government and the private consortium will share the investments. These kinds of partnerships are encouraged by the 2009 Water Resources Law and its regulations. Paragraph 37.2 of the regulations states that private entities can be operators of public hydraulic infrastructure of 'new projects that they have financed with their own resources or with the participation of the state so that they can recuperate their investments within a term set by the state'. This has also been called a build-operate-transfer model, which means that a private actor is responsible for financing, constructing and operating hydraulic infrastructure for public water supply; 'In return, the concessionaire has the right to generate revenue from the facility for a specific period of time until the facility is transferred to the grantor (normally the state)' (Ullberg 2019: 509–10). The fact that the new infrastructure would be administered by the private consortium created a lot of concern among the farmers in Majes during my stay there in 2014. What they most feared was increased water tariffs, which they perceived as a form of privatisation.

On 6 February 2014, I accompanied two of the ALA employees to watch the formal inauguration ceremony of Majes-Siguas II. A crowd of a few hundred people gathered in front of the stage, which was set up for the occasion in the middle of the desert of Siguas, and from the supportive applause it seemed that the majority welcomed the start of the project. I was later told that the inauguration was not organised in the highlands out of fear for protesters. In an impassioned speech, president Ollanta Humala promised a modern export-oriented agriculture where large-scale agribusiness corporations would spur economic growth and create employment:

> all the productive forces in Arequipa should dive into Majes-Siguas II, to make a modern agriculture, an agriculture that can be exported and

> that generates 200,000 work places, because it is estimated that Majes-Siguas II will generate this. And it will benefit 300,000 families who will live off our agriculture, of our export agriculture.[4]

Humala went on to talk rhetorically about what he called the 'democratisation' of water use, and he promised that 'the water belongs to the people and I will not privatise it', a statement that received much applause. At first sight, this promise seemed to be contradictory in view of the concession given to the private consortium and the privileges given to large-scale corporations. However, it soon became clear that he was referring to the water users organisations, the Juntas de Usuarios (see chapters 1 and 3), which had grown since the 1990s, when they gained more autonomy and responsibility as private operators of hydraulic infrastructure. Since they have been managing the water tariffs paid by the farmers, some of the *Juntas* have been criticised for lack of transparency and concentration of power in small groups of leaders. In 2014, the government presented a law proposal – the so called Ley Zamudio, named after the senator who proposed it – that would modify the water administration and the election process of the leaders of the water users. The aim, as it was expressed by the government, was to make water management, and especially the *Juntas*, more democratic and transparent. However, most *Juntas* perceived the proposed changes as an attack on their autonomy. Furthermore, there is clearly a difference between the small *Juntas* that represent small-scale peasants in the highlands and the richer and more powerful *Juntas* along the coastline, which is dominated by large-scale export-oriented plantations and agribusiness farms.

The *Junta* in Majes (Junta de Usuarios Pampa de Majes) insisted that they were working for the benefit of the farmers, most of whom are smallholders with their 5-hectare farms. The *Junta*'s leader told me in an interview that he was sceptical about the benefits of Majes-Siguas II for farmers:

> With Majes-Siguas II it will be hard for the small farmers to get access to land. It will not benefit us. If it fosters more jobs, it would be good. But it will harm us because we will have to pay the same for the water as the big firms; the tariff will increase.

The *Junta* and the smallholders in Majes anticipate that big corporations, which are able to pay more for the water, will buy most of the land in

Siguas. While the land in the first phase was sold in units of 5 hectares at subsidised prices, the 38,500 hectares of new farmland in Siguas will be sold in large units of 200, 500 and 1,000 hectares in order to attract big capital and ensure that large-scale export-oriented agribusiness will create economic growth. Hence, there will not be any opportunities for the children of farmers to buy land, and people fear the dominance of transnational large-scale agribusiness.

On 12 March 2014, hundreds of farmers gathered outside Majes and blocked the Panamericana highway in a protest called an 'agrarian strike' against the proposed law. Many of the farmers, however, carried signs that were not referring to the Ley Zamudio. Instead, their messages were against the Majes-Siguas II project and said no to the large estates (*latifundios*). Apparently, this protest was about much more than a change in the laws regulating the *Juntas*. Some of the farmers explained to me how they feared that the land would again be dominated by large estates, as in the times before the 1969 land reform. Since the consortium Angostura-Siguas won the concession to construct the infrastructure of the second phase, they will administer the canal for 20 years, and the farmers in Majes and Colca worry that they will increase the water tariff to recover their investments. 'We call this privatisation,' farmers repeatedly said. No matter how strongly the government argues that the water will still be public property, the farmers know that the operator that administers the infrastructure will control the water flow.

Three years later, in 2017, the consortium suggested a change in the plans for the irrigation system in the Siguas plains from a gravity-fed open canal system (as in Majes) to a more efficient pressurised pipes system, arguing that more water-efficient technologies are necessary because of the threat of evaporation due to climate change and the granting of water to highland communities in Espinar. This change is described in the thirteenth addendum to the contract with Angostura-Siguas and, at the time of writing, it was still much discussed, since it implied a cost increase of US $104 million that the regional government of Arequipa would have to bear. Disagreements and discussions concerning whether to sign this addendum or not have led to further delays (*El Buho* 2020a, 2020b; Orihuela 2020; Ullberg 2019). In addition, the process of clearing the land where the dam and the tunnel are to be built has taken much longer than expected due to legal problems of land ownership. The project has been halted several times by social protests in the highland areas where the new dam, canals and tunnels will be built. The inhabitants demand employment and compensation for the lost land and the negative impact on their livelihoods (Ullberg 2019: 510). For example, in 2017, when digging the opening of the tunnel near the community of Tarucamarca in Tisco district, the company built storage facilities, munition dumps and camps without compensating the peasants for using their land, as promised (Orihuela 2020). Miguel, from *la Junta* in Colca, once commented that this is not a new kind of behaviour; MACON behaved in the same way during the construction of the first phase in the 1970s. Later, Autodema has always 'entered the highlands as if it were their house, and without respect; they do what they want, and they have never asked permission from *la Junta* in Colca'. Since people in the highlands are pastoralists and not farmers, they have traditionally not been organised in water users commissions. Therefore, when Autodema has financed and built small and medium-sized dams in the districts of Tisco, Sibayo and Callalli, they have not asked permission. On the contrary, they have intended to operate them and take the water directly to the Majes canal. Miguel found this utterly disrespectful, but he also admonished the people in the highlands of 'sleeping' when they should be organising and uniting forces. Towards the end of my fieldwork, however, the district municipalities and some newly formed water users commissions in the highlands were starting to form a united front to defend the water in the highlands. We see that allowing private financialisation of hydraulic infrastructure enables increased control by big corporate capital, which provokes reactions and protests among peasants, smallholders and working poor. Their biggest fear is that water – which their lives and livelihoods depend on – will be transformed into a commodity and that private companies will take control over the water flow to make profit.

With the intrusion and expansion of mining concessions, this is already happening. Encouraged by the WRL, which allows private companies to intervene and invest in water management and infrastructure (del Castillo 2011), the mining company Cerro Verde – the most powerful corporation in Arequipa region – has, in partnership with the electric company EGASA, invested in several dams in the region: the Pillones dam, the Bamputañe dam and the Challhuanca dam. The mine has also financed a drinking water treatment plant and partially financed several water towers in the city of Arequipa (Andersen 2014). This is problematic because mining companies have direct interests in acquiring access to large amounts of water for their extractive operations. Cerro Verde's copper mine uses huge quantities of water and, according to the law, they are legally entitled to as long as they pay the ANA for the user right licence. However, they do not pay tariffs to the *Junta* and do not pay compensation to peasant communities.

Watershed politics I: measuring and harvesting water

When the Condoroma dam was built in the district of Callalli, the landowners received new land in Majes as compensation for the land they lost to the dam. However, nobody thought of claiming anything for the water that was sent to Majes. In contrast to the districts located along the Majes canal in Colca Valley, Callalli has not increased its supply of water, and does not receive any compensation for the water that is channelled down to Majes. The 2,500 inhabitants in Callalli (called *callallinos*), like the people in the rest of the headwaters above the altitude of 4,000 metres, are among the poorest in the region, and they suffer from the impact of 'double exposure' to economic globalisation and climate change (O'Brien and Leichenko 2000). Most households struggle to make a living on alpaca pastoralism, by selling the wool and meat to wholesalers for a low price.[5] Another challenge is that land properties are divided among heirs, and although many migrate to the city of Arequipa in search of jobs, it is becoming harder for those who stay to sustain the alpacas and a livelihood. In addition, the people in the headwaters are the first to experience the consequences of global warming in the Andes: the permanent snow and glaciers, which have functioned as natural water reservoirs, have disappeared, affecting the water supply, the earth, plants and animals. The springs dry out, and the *bofedales* – which are wet cushion bogs used as pastures for alpacas – also become dry. The rain is often irregular and starts late, and when it finally comes, it is torrential and causes erosion of the soil (Stensrud 2015). Farmers complained that the water goes straight to the river and out to the ocean, taking the soil with it. Furthermore, the incidence of deep frost periods and heavy snowfall are more common than before and harder to anticipate. In 2011, temperatures hit a record low, and 35 per cent of the districts' baby alpacas (*crías*) – 2,400 animals in total – died of the intense cold. The majority of families were affected, and since alpaca is their main source of income, the municipality asked the regional government for support (*RPP Noticias* 2011). Since 2011, the local authorities have declared a state of emergency in the high parts of Caylloma province almost every year. This situation made people in Callalli realise that they needed to organise in a water users commission, and in 2011, I met Víctor, the first leader of the newly formed commission. He told me about how he perceived the recent environmental changes:

> The situation in Callalli is very difficult because ten years ago there was a lot of snow, glaciers on the mountains. Today you don't see that. There are no snowfields, they have practically disappeared. So what happens is that when there used to be snow, there were water mattresses where each mountain deposited water. So the springs were maintained all year. Today there are no snowfields, and thus there are no water cushions deposited under the mountains, within the *apus* [the mountain-lords] as I consider them to be. [...] Sometimes it rains a lot, in January, February, but it rains as if it were raining on a mirror or on a rock or on cement or something like that. It is raining, but it runs directly to the streams and watersheds and those waters go directly to the Pacific Ocean.

When Victor and the other pastoralists in Callalli decided to organise in a water users commission, they asked the *Junta* of Colca Valley for support, and Miguel provided both moral and technical support and guidance. First of all, in order to be formally recognised by the ALA, they should formalise their water user rights. This requirement went hand in hand with the municipality of Callalli's promise to finance a project to make a complete inventory of all water resources in the district in order to document them, protect them and make claims for compensation. I accompanied Miguel from the *Junta* and José from the ALA to a meeting in the municipal hall of Callalli in July 2011. Victor welcomed us and said that the aim of the meeting was to learn about the organisation and rules of the *Junta* and commission, and to learn how to carry out measurements of water. He would also select a few of the young men who would be employed to do the work of measurement and registration. There were many persons interested in this job, and the meeting hall soon filled up. When it was time to start, Victor closed the doors, and said 'time is time', indicating that people who did not make it on time did not deserve to get employed.

Miguel started by talking about the work of the *Junta* and the importance of taking care of the water and to be organised. He emphasised how mining companies are polluting the water in the highlands with toxic waste 'while we are asleep', and that there should be sensors in the river to monitor and stop this pollution. Then, he went on to talk about different methods for measuring water flows. He focused on two methods that did not require expensive or unavailable technology: 'the volumetric method' and the 'floating method'. For the first method, they needed a bucket (of a size between 4 and 20 litres) and a stopwatch. For the second they needed a small floating object (like a cork), a measuring tape and a stopwatch. They also needed a notebook, a pencil, and a GPS. After the theoretical introduction, the selected young men went out in the field to practise. During the next month, they went out to every corner of the district to register every water source with name and GPS location, and the recorded litres per second. As seen in chapter 6, measuring water is a way of achieving legibility and is often employed by the state to register and control resources (Scott 1998). When the local authorities in Callalli take the initiative to measure and document the water sources in their territories, it can be understood as a way of taking control into their own hands and of creating a sense of predictability. Water flows that are measured and documented become 'facts' that can be used in negotiations of claims. Their motivation seem similar to the arguments presented by the ALA engineers who justified the need to formalise water user rights: the need to protect the water resources against intrusions of private mining companies and to be able to have information about changes in the water sources due to climate change. In the case of Callalli, however, they are taking the lead and taking control over the measurement performed in their territory.

The members of the new commission in Callalli also knew that, according to the WRL, water is primarily seen as an economic resource, and therefore counting water implies counting money. After 2009, the political discourse of the authorities in Caylloma province incorporated water as a main theme, and the provincial mayor often talked about water as 'our wealth'. Hence, measurements enable and strengthen claims to compensation and for financial support of tree planting projects ('water sowing') and the construction of water-related infrastructure, particularly micro-dams ('water harvesting'). During my stay in 2011, nearly all the farmers, politicians and leaders of water users commissions in Caylloma talked about the importance of harvesting water in order to meet future water scarcity. The micro-dams collect water when the heavy rains come in January and February and thus protect the soil against erosion and enable a more even distribution of water in irrigation canals throughout the year. The municipality of Callalli had several projects to build micro-dams in 2011, and it applied for financial support from other institutions, like the regional government, and the *Junta* in Majes, justifying the claim in terms of climate change and its effects on the water supply, the *bofedales* and the rearing of llamas and alpacas.

The farmers in Majes, represented by the *Junta*, have committed themselves to support these projects in Callalli because they directly benefit from the water that originates there. The *callallinos* claim that the Majes farmers are morally obligated to reciprocate and to contribute to the necessary infrastructure. The transfer of money from the pampa to the highlands began in 2010, after almost 30 years of channelling water to the pampa, and it is presented as the result of a struggle and a victory for the poor highlands. Victor, who had taken the lead in getting the *callallinos* organised, took much of the credit for the victory:

> We have gotten this with a pure fight because *they* consume *our* resources.... I am a fighting man; I like to make things clear. I went to Pedregal and called a meeting where I made it clear that they should support the highlands with the construction of water harvests and that I would close the dam so that their lands would dry up. At first they wanted to attack me, but with the passage of time we have come to an agreement that they should contribute.

By threatening to stop the water, the point was made that Majes is entirely dependent on the goodwill of the highlands. According to those who had worked with water management for many years, like Miguel, there have 'always' been tensions between the high and low parts of the watershed. These tensions were based on inequalities in economic development and political influence, but also on racial discrimination. People in the highlands are seen as more indigenous and, according to the racialised geographical and social hierarchies in Peru, they are thus also seen as more uneducated, poor and 'uncivilised' (de la Cadena 2000).

Victor was a politically engaged man in his forties, who called himself a 'fighting man' (*hombre de lucha*). He was known for his radical views and passionate speeches in which he advocated the defence of their water resources against mining and agribusiness companies. He was given several nicknames after other leaders of indigenous movements, who had become famous because of violent protests and conflict with the police. He was for example called 'Pizango' after the leader of AIDESEP, the indigenous organisation in the Amazon who defied the government's free trade policies in 2009, and 'Aduviri' after the leader of the anti-mining protests in Puno in 2011. These nicknames were given in a mixture of joking, admiring and warning tones: social protests are criminalised in Peru and both Alberto Pizango and Walter Aduviri[6] have been arrested. The García government made social protests and strikes illegal through the modifications of legislative decree no. 982 in July 2007. This decree opened up aggravated penalties for persons participating in social protests and strikes by labelling them 'extortionists'; and it provided exemption for police and military agents who used firearms against protesters causing death and injuries. Two years later, the world witnessed and condemned the Bagua massacre of 5 June 2009, where indigenous activists protesting the new legislation giving concessions to multinational oil and mining companies in the Amazonian forest, as well as police officers, were killed in a violent encounter.

Victor was not afraid of confrontations, and therefore he was respected. However, his demands were not radical, and he was not trying to stop a transnational mining company, as they did in Puno. On the contrary, all of the watershed, and especially Majes, would benefit from the water harvest: 'Now the watershed and the cushion bogs and the rivers will continue to be alive and continue to maintain the water resources, because if there is no water in the high parts the people in the lower parts will practically die.' This struggle is driven by a desire to have a role in the designing of the landscapes and worlds where people live and make their livelihoods (Paredes and Li 2019), and, as we will see even more clearly in the next section, the struggle went beyond the headwaters and included the vertical connections of the watershed.

Watershed politics II: nurturing and claiming water and land

I met Victor again in February 2014, but this time in Majes, where he was coordinating a collective land claim on behalf of 300 families from Callalli. They had started to organise in 2012, and had submitted a formal application to Autodema in which they claimed the property rights to 400 hectares of arid land in Majes, as well as infrastructure and water to irrigate and produce on this land. The group argued that people from Callalli – known as *callallinos* – have the right to land and water in Majes, because the water that enables export agriculture and economic growth in Majes originates in their district. Hence, the water – and, by extension, the fertility of the land – also belong to the headwaters in Callalli where it originates. Thereby, they argue that they are the 'real' owners of water. In an interview, Víctor eagerly explained:

> We, as proprietors of the water, as owners of the water, owners of the earth, owners as *arequipeños* and as *cayllominos* – who we are because these lands belong to Caylloma – we have taken this democratic and legal option in order to be able to take on this project with the regional government.

Víctor had agreed to meet me on a Sunday morning near a bus stop in Villa El Pedregal, where he had arrived together with a group of people who had never been to Majes before. They had taken the bus from Callalli at 11 p.m. on Saturday night, and arrived at Arequipa at 3.30 a.m. From there, they had taken the first minibus to Majes at 5 a.m. When I met them, they had just eaten breakfast and had bought some plants at a market. They were joined by more *callallinos* who live in Arequipa, and together we went in a car to see the area that they were taking into possession. We stopped by an intersection in the road, where there was a petrol station and a shop. It was in the middle of the desert, and the only thing I could barely see in the distance was the fence surrounding the private agribusiness plantation of the Pampa Baja Group. Victor went into the shop to order a tank of water, and we went to the land area, which was marked by a stone that said 'Private Property of Autodema – Villa Callalli'. Victor explained that while they were waiting for a formal recognition from Autodema and title deeds from the municipality of Majes, they were taking turns to care for the land. They had organised in smaller groups of 15–20 persons, and every Sunday a group would travel to the property where they planted trees along the boundaries. That was the reason people were carrying plants. I followed them along the border to check the trees that had already been planted. Some were dead and had to be replaced, and then they planted 20 more trees along a straight line. The shop owner had sent a truck with the water tank, and they used a hose to water all the trees well. The irony that they had to pay for water that came all the way from Callalli in order to nourish the land that they claimed access to based on their ownership of the same water, was disturbingly clear. The work of planting trees and nourishing them with the water was a way of appropriating the land; by nourishing their relationship to the land, they created a sense of possession and ownership. In the process, they also re-established the connections between the land and the water and between Majes and Callalli, and strengthened the bonds among the families who stood in this fight together. After they had finished planting the trees under a burning sun, the group went to the shop to sit in the shadow, drink and talk about the next steps forward.

Victor explained to me why their claim was just and legitimate. After the Condoroma dam and the Majes canal had been built, the peasant communities along the canal in Colca Valley got access to more water and some districts like Cabanaconde extended their cultivated lands. Callalli and the other headwater districts, however, have not received any benefits from the dam and the irrigation project. Victor said that the MIP was supposed to be integrating the high, middle and low part of the watershed. However, only the middle part – Colca Valley – had been included, while the high parts had been abandoned and forgotten. Conveying a profound feeling of structural inequality and injustice between Callalli and Majes, he said that this claim is part of what he called 'the social vindication of the highlands'. Victor and the other *callallinos* were inspired by the protesters in Espinar, whom they admired and called their 'brothers' (*hermanos*). Although the population in Espinar did not manage to stop Majes-Siguas II, they won a concession: compensation in the form of financial support for infrastructure and other projects in their province. By calling the *espinarenses* their brothers and sisters, they made them allies in spite of the general discourse in Arequipa that portrayed Espinar as the 'enemy' due to the fact that they tried to stop Majes-Siguas II and thereby cancel all the jobs, economic growth and progress that most people in Arequipa were anticipating.

The *callallinos* have seen that their water has enabled the MIP and is creating economic growth in Majes, and they want their part of the growth and to be included in the region's development plans. Hence, the *callallinos* take the WRL very seriously, using the legal principles of the water's economic value to justify their right to compensation in the form of land and access to water in Majes. In one of the Sunday meetings that the Callalli group had on their claimed land, Víctor told the others what he had said when he met one of the engineers working for Autodema:

> I said to his face: 'Why do you drive around in the 4×4 Toyota Hilux van? Because of your abilities? No! Because of my water!' Why does the security guard in Autodema earn 2,500 *soles*? Why? Because Autodema produces something? Autodema does not produce anything! Just because of the water do they earn like that! They employ 300 employees. What should be our proposal? That 50 per cent of the

> workers in Autodema should be our people! But [we get] nothing [...] Because we are not well organised.

The injustice is deeply felt, and is rooted in centuries of structural exclusion by which the indigenous population in the highlands have been marginalised. The colonial legacies of social stratification and racism is expressed in everyday life, in workplaces, in politics and in the streets. The Sunday morning when I accompanied the group from Callalli to their desired land, I heard someone yell stereotypical insults about Puno from a car that drove by. Victor and the others were clearly annoyed by this; not only because they are not from Puno, but because *puneños* – like all *serranos* (highlanders) – are being racially stigmatised in the coastal cities. I heard people in Chivay, Arequipa and Majes – including people whom I considered to be friends – talk about *puneños* in a variety of ways based on stereotypical traits associated with Puno: from expressing admiration and envy for their hard work and entrepreneurship, to complaining about how they reproduce 'like rabbits' and are 'everywhere'. In social hierarchies in Peru, ideas of ethnicity and race are intrinsically mixed with class and level of education, where the term 'mestizo' is used to describe educated, urban, and 'modern', while being indigenous is stigmatised as equivalent to being poor and uneducated (de la Cadena 2000). This means that classifications in terms of 'racial' identities – as indigenous or mestizo – are fluid and dynamic ways of categorising and discriminating against each other. Furthermore, this everyday racial politics takes place in a racialised geography, where the rainforest and the highlands are associated with poverty and indigeneity, while the coast is associated with urban modernity, political and economic power, and white elites who look towards Europe. In the Arequipa region, a person is generally considered to be more indigenous and poorer, the higher up he or she lives. Hence, when Quechua-speaking pastoralists from a district located at an altitude of 4,000 metres claim the right to take part in the economic growth of a modern irrigation project near the coast, from which they have been excluded for nearly four decades, it can be said quite clearly that this claim for compensation is also a claim for justice – not only water justice, but a claim to be seen as worthy of being accounted for. In this way, this claim for water echoes the environmental justice movement, which in Latin America is also called 'ecologism of the poor', and which addresses conflicts about unequal access to nature's services and resources and connects economic and ecological distribution to political power (Martínez Alier 1992).

Víctor clearly saw this land claim as a way to fight for justice and, in the meetings that were held after planting trees, he used to say that if they did not get this project through, they would make 'a water war', with clear references to previous water-related conflicts in Latin America, like the famous 2000 water war in Cochabamba, Bolivia, where the population shut down the city as a way to protest against the privatisation of drinking water (Schultz 2008). Despite the revolutionary rhetoric, however, the claim was not very radical. Many peasants and workers in Peru, and especially in the highlands, are critical of neoliberalism and extractivism, and tend to vote for politicians who promise nationalisation, distribution and inclusion. This land claim, however, was not in opposition to the government, and not aiming to stop the neoliberal and extractivist policies. Rather, the *callallinos* wished to be recognised as being part of the watershed and as having the right to participate in the design of the water flows by nourishing and cultivating land and water. They wanted to have a part of the benefits from the MIP, but according to their own terms. Víctor said it clearly: 'We have not come to beg for charity from anyone; on the contrary we come to contribute, we want to invest here.' What they are asking for is legitimate access to invest, work and produce. The vice-mayor of Callalli told me that the rearing of alpacas in Callalli and the cultivation of fodder in Majes are complementary activities; when there is scarcity of water and grass in the highlands, they can send fodder from Majes. Most of the people in the group did not wish to move permanently to Majes, but to have enough land and water to sustain their alpacas and families. In this way, the project is also about practising the vertical way of organising production across several ecological niches of different altitudes as has been done for centuries. Social and economic life in the Andes have traditionally been organised vertically, which means that several ecological zones at different altitudes belong to the same community (Fonseca 1972; Murra 2002). This changed with the forced resettlement of the indigenous population in the colonial period and the establishment of administrative districts in 1800s (see chapter 6). However, some of the extensive families in Caylloma still have houses at different altitudes; those who have alpaca herds in the high mountain areas (*la puna*) have *estancias* – small farmsteads with huts made of stones and straw roof – where they stay when they watch the alpaca herd, and some also have cultivated fields lower in the valley, and a main house in one of the villages. In addition, many strive to construct a house in the provincial capital Chivay, and/or in one of the migrant neighbourhoods surrounding Arequipa city, where they have access to work and income in the urban informal economy. In 2011, a group of families from Colca organised an invasion of an empty desert area close to the road from Arequipa to Chivay. They divided the land into plots, where each family made a construction of straw mats as a way of taking possession of the land, and they applied for legal property deeds. Other families have joined similar squatter groups in Majes (see chapter 6).

However, there is another dimension to the claim that goes beyond vertical livelihood strategies, environmental justice and political ecology, because it was based on a way of thinking of ownership that is very different from the way property is established according to the state and the market. I suggest that the claim to ownership of water emerged from a particular way of being in the world and being connected with the surroundings. Hence, the claim emerged from world-making practices and human–non-human relationships that opened up disagreements on the definition of water and the world itself. These relationships and life projects are hidden from public speeches, formal paperwork and title deeds, but can be observed in everyday practices and ritual work in the communities of Colca Valley and highland Caylloma.

Conclusion: nourishing investments and conditional ownership

What does it mean 'to own'? Water cannot be owned in the same way as land, yet the sources can be controlled, and the flow can be enclosed and channelled to specific uses and users. The water flow rates can be enclosed in formalised licences of user rights and registered by the state, thus reducing the ownership to a relation between the state and the user.

In this chapter, I have proposed that financing and nurturing are two different forms of investment that enact different modes of ownership and constitute diverging versions of water. While monetary investment enacts ownership as mastery and water as commodity, nourishing investment enacts ownership as mutual and conditional, from which water emerges with the other beings and entities that co-constitute collectives and webs of relationships. The land claim from Callalli was articulated through different notions of ownership that emerge from particular ontological compositions in which land, water and people are co-constituted by mutual care and nurturing. This does not just mean that the water and people belong together but that they are made together. Hence, I suggest rethinking water ownership in terms of nurture and conditionality, which emerge from webs of mutual and co-constitutive relationships that are being severed by processes of enclosure and commodification.

The *apus*, who are the powerful mountain-lords – also called *tirakuna* (Allen 1998) and earth-beings (de la Cadena 2015) – are the guardians and protectors of land, animals and people in the Andes (Gose 1994; Gelles 2000; Allen 1998). As such, they are also owners of water and alpacas, and they give fertility and wealth to those who live in their lands. By letting the water flow over the land, giving life to humans, plants and alpacas, the *apus* nourish and nurture the web of life and beings in their territories. In turn, humans need to reciprocate by giving food and drink in the form of *pagos* and *t'inkas*. I suggest that feeding and nourishing the *apus* through *pagos* and *t'inkas* is a form of investment that gives humans the right to design the landscape and guide water to their fields, pastures and households. Following from this, I argue that the claim of water ownership emerges from the notion that water is conditionally given to humans by the *apus* who guard the territories that they overlook. I say conditionally, because the gift of water is not permanent and cannot be taken for granted. As shown in chapters 3 and 4, the relationships of reciprocity and guardianship have to be reaffirmed each year through *pagos* and other ritual work. The mountain-lords can be vengeful and dangerous when they are disrespected or have not received offerings (see chapter 6). Hence, living well in Colca Valley and Caylloma highlands implies taking part in intricate and affective relationships between humans and mountains, earth and water. Relationships to land and water need to be nurtured and nourished in order to ensure water supply and the fertility of land and animals. Through these actions, humans are endowed with the right to use the water emanating from the land. Since the mountain-lords are the keepers of water, which they offer to the humans through springs, the water is seen as belonging to the territories where it is born and where humans also are born and raised. The relationships between humans, land, water and mountains are maintained though sharing food and drink (Paredes and Li 2019; Salas 2019).

This is translated as 'ownership', but it is a mode of ownership that is processual and dynamic, and based on care, nurture and reciprocity. This ownership is not attached to individuals, but the collectives of humans and non-humans who mutually constitute each other in places like Callalli. I propose that water, land, mountains and people are inherently interconnected and part of the mutual composition of place, as in the concept of 'being in-*ayllu*', which means that 'persons are not from a place; they are the place that relationally emerges through them' (de la Cadena 2015: 102). Practices of nurture, then, are co-constitutive – persons become *with* a place, and this also implies an obligation. De la Cadena explains that what have been described as relations of reciprocity in Andean ethnographies are not relations *between* entities, but relationships 'from where entities emerge, it makes them, they grow from it' (de la Cadena 2015: 103). Following this line of thinking, I suggest that water, earth-beings, and people constitute Callalli (and other places in Caylloma) together as they mutually nurture each other into being; they become *with* each other. Ownership is in Quechua often expressed with the suffix '-*yuq*', meaning 'with'. Being with water, then, would mean being an owner of water, which would also imply an obligation to nurture and take care of the water. As described in chapter 3, the leader in Yanque Urinsaya explained the interdependency of farmers and water by saying that 'everyone participates in the collective work, because the water obliges us.' Hence, the water mother (Yakumama) not only reciprocates with vitality and fertility because she receives care and nourishment but also obliges humans to participate in the relationships in which they all co-constitute each other.

Practices of nurture are also those that enact processes of 'commoning', making water flow through *pagos*, sharing of food and drink, and collective work parties. All the water users need to work and earn the right to use water by working in communal *faenas* and paying tariffs. People also have to participate in giving *pagos* to mountains and water sources to earn the right to use water. This is not a kind of romantic stewardship nor is it about preserving the purity of water and nature. On the contrary, it is about using water responsibly and carefully. People in Colca invest time and work in making territory where land, water, humans, animals, mountains, and infrastructure are connected in a relational web. From this territorial web emerges a form of ownership that exceeds the dichotomies of private versus public, individual versus collective, as well as the possessing subject versus the possessed object (cf. Brightman et al. 2016; Stensrud 2019d). Nourishing and guiding the water flow can also be understood in terms of 'ontological design' (Escobar 2018) and 'design on the land' (Paredes and Li 2019), which are concepts that emphasise the dynamic interaction between humans and the environment. By not trying to master the earth-beings, they design the land and water flows with them, through mutual relationships. Hence, the land claim of the *callallinos* can also be understood as an attempt to participate in the design of the watershed – and to become a recognised, acknowledged and respected part of the watershed. I suggest, then, that when people from the headwaters protest against the uneven distribution of resources, they are also demanding to be heard according to their own notions of ownership and investment, which are embedded in particular ontological relationships. In other words, people wish to live their lives by their own designs. In that sense, the land claim is indeed a political act, according to Rancière's (1999) definition of politics as that of breaking with the configuration whereby parts are defined and making a place for 'the part of those who have no part' (Rancière 1999: 30).

In 2020, I heard from interlocutors in Caylloma that the land claim in Villa Callalli had been abandoned, at least temporarily. However, it seems that the claim from Callalli had been included in a larger claim organised by and for the whole province of Caylloma for 3,000 hectares from Majes-Siguas II. The current mayor of Caylloma province, who was elected in October 2018, had water justice on his agenda from the first day, with his main slogan being 'United by/for the water' (*Unidos por el agua*).

Conclusion: Water Multiplicity

> 'It seems like the nature got annoyed. Like a sign, a message: that Majes depends on the highlands.'
>
> (Miguel, technical manager of *la Junta* in Colca Valley)

By following the water as it flows through the landscapes; through underground streams, mountain springs, cushion bogs and deserts; through canals, gates, pipes, valves and gauging devices; through documents, receipts and licences; and through stories, concepts and practices, we not only learn about its diverse directions, uses and meanings, but also where it stops, divides, hides, diverges and cause tensions and disagreements. One of the engineers who worked for the PSI – the World Bank-funded state programme for the modernisation of irrigation technology – had studied sociology at the university and was exceptionally interested in the socio-cultural aspects of irrigation. When he learned that I was an anthropologist, the first thing he told me was this: 'We have two different perspectives in this watershed: the Andean cosmovision and the Water Resources Law that talks about legislation and tariffs, and these two views collide.' Since the European conquest and colonisation of the Americas, people and practices have been divided into two opposing categories in Peru: the 'indigenous', associated with primitiveness and backwardness, and the 'modern', associated with Europe, scientific rationality and the future. Both indigeneity and modernity were invented by colonisation and reproduced through the 'coloniality of power', by which hierarchies based on ideas of 'race' and class maintain global inequalities (Quijano 2000). Coloniality of power is inherently linked to extractivism and global capitalism; as a discourse and practice, coloniality simultaneously preaches the natural inferiority of subjects and the colonisation of nature, which marks certain subjects as dispensable and nature as pure raw material for the production of goods in the international market (Maldonado-Torres 2007: 135). In the dominant discourse of modernisation and progress of contemporary Peru, indigenous practices are often ridiculed and seen as 'ancient' customs that should be eradicated because they are hindering progress and economic growth. One striking example is when President

García – the president who promulgated the WRL in 2009, publicly stated on national television that we 'must defeat the absurd pantheistic ideologies [...] these primitive forms of religion where they say "do not touch that mountain"' (*Los Andes* 2011). During the García government (2006–11), 193 people were killed in socio-environmental conflicts, most of which were related to protests against extractivist industries (Huacasi 2019).

This book has not entered into the violent conflicts that have erupted in Peru during the past two decades – often related to mining concessions and toxic pollution of land and water – but rather has scrutinised everyday practices of water users, managers, engineers and bureaucrats, and how policies are implemented through meetings, inspections, and negotiations of control, care, power and respect. In these meetings and inspections, diverging concepts and practices are entangled, and these entanglements can sometimes be a cause of confusion, misunderstandings and 'uncontrolled equivocations', in which ontological difference is not recognised (Viveiros de Castro 2004). In order to capture and understand this ontological multiplicity, one of my aims in this book has been to show that instead of analysing the politics of a watershed as two colliding perspectives on one world – one singular watershed and one universal reality – a more open-minded and fertile approach would be to look for how different water-related practices enact worlds that are both diverging and partially connected.

In their daily work of processing applications, granting licences, regulating water flows and supervising users commissions, bureaucrats and engineers in the public water administration, continuously make conceptual and practical separations – what Latour (1992) called 'work of purification' – between what is considered to be modern/efficient/legible and what is deemed 'ancestral'/inefficient/illegible. These separations tend to align with the distinctions of the one-world world versus the heterogeneous worldings of the pluriverse (Blaser and de la Cadena 2018). The latter tends to be placed in the category of 'indigenous culture' or 'indigenous religion', and thus excluded from political decisions. These entanglements and separations in everyday work and life might not be fully visible for everyone, however. What you see depends on what you are looking for and, for ethnographic researchers, it depends on the mode of immersion and on the scale of attention, which is not a matter of big versus small, but of different points of perception (Hastrup 2013b). By shifting focus from the global (capitalism, climate change) to micro-practices in water users commissions, households and offering rituals and back again, I have aimed to show how the local and the global are always 'enfolded in each other' and that empirical complexity remains potentially the same at any scale (Hastrup 2013b: 148).

In the offices of the local water administration (ALA) in Villa El Pedregal, the relational and collective practices were not visible other than as problems of backwardness and inefficiency that should be fixed. Although ALA employees encountered these practices in their inspections and meetings with water users, they did not include them in their reports, where all water-related practices were translated into terms of measurements and production. In my interviews with the ALA director, he patiently explained the technical details of water measuring, the allocation of water user rights and the changes brought by the Water Resources Law of 2009. While this information often appeared as quite technical and 'dry', from time to time, he became very passionate when talking about his visions for the watershed. One day, when we were sitting in his office, the director explained how everything in the watershed was interconnected, and that the lower parts depended on the headwaters, where micro-dams, filtra-

Figure 10 Canals of different sizes are crisscrossing the steep landscape of Colca Valley, guiding water from the mountain springs to the cultivated fields. Since canals are vital for farming, they are often the source of disputes, but they are also maintained and cared for in collective ritual practices and entangled in human-nonhuman relations.

tion ditches, reforestation, and the management of pastures and *bofedales* are all chained together. This was the reason why water users in the arid pampa of Majes were collaborating in the funding of water harvesting in micro-dams in the headwaters, which had become more urgent because of climate change, he said. He continued to explain that the harvested water would be distributed during the whole year through small canals that would improve the quality of highland pastures. 'When the pasture quality improves, the income from animals will also improve for the pastoralists, who have given their manual labour to build the micro-dams. This is a symbiosis – everyone wins!', the director claimed enthusiastically.

However, as this book has shown, based on the experience of encounters and conversations with water users in the headwaters and Colca Valley, the benefits from water harvesting and other infrastructural projects in the 'integrated watershed management' are highly unevenly and unequally distributed. While Majes is growing due to a booming economy, entrepreneurial activity and population growth, the provincial capital Chivay and the other villages upriver in the Majes-Colca watershed experience declining agriculture, decreasing water supplies and out-migration of young people. The pastoral farmers in the headwaters are the first to experience the consequences of climate change and the last to gain access to the benefits from mega-projects of 'development' like the MIP and Majes-Siguas II. There are clearly tensions between the highlands (*parte alta*) of the watershed, represented by the official province capital Chivay, and the lowlands (*parte baja*), represented by Majes, the richest district of Caylloma province. Since mining revenues (*canon minero*) are distributed according to population in each province, Majes receives a much bigger share of this money than the highland districts where most mines are located, and where the land, water and people are directly affected by the impact of mining. In the past decade, politicians in the high parts of Caylloma have put forth demands for a 'water canon' (*canon hídrico*) to be paid by those actors downriver that profit from the water (especially the MIP and the mining company Cerro Verde) to the districts in the headwaters. This is an attempt to achieve water justice based on the principle of reciprocity (see also Stensrud 2016e).

In 2012, there were heated discussions about why Chivay should continue to be the capital of the Caylloma province, and the population of Majes wanted to separate from Caylloma to become a province apart. A couple of days after this had been publicly stated, the Majes canal broke because of an earthquake in Achoma district in Colca Valley. When the water did not arrive in Majes, it caused a sense of crisis and made explicit the vulnerability of the place. Miguel, the manager of the *Junta* of Colca, suggested: 'It seems like nature got annoyed. Like a sign, a message: that Majes depends on the highlands.' In modern discourse, such explanations are not possible; they are ridiculed, ignored, or at best patronised or 'tolerated' as culturally peculiar or silly jokes. Miguel was very much aware that, from a scientific perspective, there is no nature with sentience and intentional agency, and he showed this in our conversation through moderating his statement by saying 'it seems like'. As an engineer working with water management, he participates in the world of science, but he also participates in practices that make other worlds emerge: for example, he is cautious when approaching particular springs because they have life and powers. This shows the complexity of contemporary life in the Andes, where 'indigenous' and 'modern' worlds are not separate units but emerging realities and always overlapping (de la Cadena 2015).

I propose that approaches to water – both academic, practical and political – should take pluriversal entanglements seriously and learn how to coexist and live together with difference. Article 2 of the WRL states:

> The water constitutes the patrimony of the nation. [...] It is a good of public use and its administration can only be granted and exerted in harmony with the common good, the environmental protection and the nation's interests. There is not private property of water. (ANA 2010)

But what is the common good? What is the environment that needs protection, and what are the interests of the nation? Such questions are at the core of current water conflicts and are ambiguously tackled in national water policies; while the WRL aims to ensure equity and respect for indigenous communities' rights, the government's overall priority is large-scale investments to promote industries and economic growth for the 'common good' of the majority of citizens. It is very difficult, not to say impossible, to achieve just distribution of rights to access water for all, ensuring equity, fairness and respect for different livelihoods while at the same time giving preference to market-oriented agriculture and urban human consumption. On a regional and national scale, profit-enhancing industries such as mining, tourism and large-scale agribusiness are given priority. This is a dilemma that is constantly negotiated by the employees in public water administration, who are guided by the WRL, which is criticised for being ambiguous and open to interpretation. The law states that both economic and ecological concerns should be taken into account, in addition to the rights of indigenous communities, yet it is the principles of efficient and rational use and productivity which mark the bottom line. It is often left to the bureaucrats' own judgement, influenced by the wider political agenda, to assess which of the values should be given most weight in each case.

Although the law refers to the 'common good', it also establishes policies that enable commodification without recognising the contradictions between the commons and commodities. At the same time, private property is negated, but the diversity of modes of 'owning', for example through practices of nurture, are invisibilised. Multiple forms of being, practices and enactments of water are singularised and simplified into contractual relationships with only one purpose: to produce and create economic value. In this process, people are transformed into 'users', and earth and water are reduced to 'resources'. Enclosures and singularisations are both conceptual and material; water flows in streams and open earthen canals are physically enclosed in pipes and legally enclosed in formalised licences of user rights. I suggest that to fully understand the processes of enclosures, commodification and formalisation, scholars should not take for granted what water is, but acknowledge that water can have many natures (Bonelli et al. 2016), and that these realities are enacted in the different practices that make the water flow.

Guiding the water involves investments and work of different kinds: giving *pagos* to mountains and coca leaves to springs as part of relations of reciprocity; sharing food and drink; financing, constructing and maintaining infrastructure; cleaning canals; making projects and applications; organising distribution; opening and closing gates; holding meetings and inspections; regulating valves; writing documents and protesting and making demands. Sometimes water flows through leakages and seepages and, if it is enclosed, it can be necessary to make holes with dynamite, as a group of peasants did in Cabanaconde in 1983. The waters in the Majes-Colca watershed are made to flow by an assemblage of partially connected practices and devices; rituals, measurements, nourishments, canals, pipes, leakages and seepages, and farmers' irrigation organisations. Water users associations in Colca invest time and work in making territory where land, water, humans, mountains and infrastructure are connected in a relational web. From this territorial web emerge forms of ownership that transcend the dichotomies of private versus public, individual versus collective, commodity versus commons, as well as the possessing subject versus the possessed object. Ownership in the Colca Valley is conditional and based on reciprocity: a group of people cannot take ownership for granted, even if they occupy the land or territory where water sources are located. Ownership is granted through the reaffirmation of reciprocity and nurture in relations between humans and non-human beings like *apus*.

I suggest that opposition and disagreements often are generated in encounters where different notions of 'nature' and ownership are included without explicitly acknowledging the differences. Therefore, critical scholars, activists and leaders should try to 'slow down' reasoning and to provoke the kind of thinking that would allow a *cosmopolitics*, which in Stengers' (2005b) use, is *not* the same as the Kantian term cosmopolitanism, which refers to a 'good common world' for all humans. On the contrary, Stengers' idea is to 'slow down the construction of this common world, to create a space for hesitation regarding what it means to say "good"' (Stengers 2005b: 995). What Stengers refers to as 'cosmos', then, is *not* a common ground but what she refers to as 'the unknown constituted by multiple, divergent worlds' (Stengers 2005b: 995). In that sense, the cosmopolitical proposal has nothing to do with decisions that 'put everyone into agreement' (2005b: 1003). By this token, de la Cadena (2010) has analysed the involvement of *apus* in Andean mining conflicts as a form of 'indigenous cosmopolitics'. Making world-making practices and earth-beings visible in public is close to what Rancière sees as the *political*, which 'consists in re-figuring space, that is in what is to be done, to be seen and to be named in it' (Rancière 2010: 37). When ontological multiplicities and disagreements are brought into the public eye, this allows for pluriversal politics to unfold (Blaser 2009; de la Cadena 2010).

Acknowledging both multiplicities and processes of singularisation is part of a pluriversal politics aiming for inclusiveness and justice. Protecting water from commodification may need other singularisations, like water as 'life' or a 'vital force', which also reduce water to singular forms. One example is the main slogan of the current mayor of Caylloma province, who was elected in 2018. The slogan '*Unidos por el Agua*', I suggest, does not only mean 'united *for* the water', implying that people should unite to defend and protect water as a common cause against depletion, but also that people are being united *by* the water, because the water obliges humans to unite and participate in world-making projects. As people all over the world are confronted with urgent environmental challenges that are global in scale, as policy makers, activists and scholars are debating how to respond to the global threat of climate change and how to live in the Anthropocene (Crutzen and Stoermer 2000), the need to slow down is greater than ever. I would like to follow Verran's (2013) proposal that, instead of translating difference into sameness, and thus explaining other knowledges away, we could rather be 'doing difference together' (Verran 2013). Hence, difference and diversity should not be avoided as obstacles to an idea of progress and improvement, but rather be opportunities to engage in the creation of better worlds within a multiple and heterogeneous cosmos.

Notes

Introduction: Water and Watershed Politics

1. The general term 'water users associations' is used when discussing water organisations in general terms. These organisations include the *Juntas* or boards, the commissions (*comisiones de usuarios*) and also the smaller committees.
2. In Egypt, Jessica Barnes (2014) shows how state engineers constantly negotiate with farmers organised in water users associations about the provision of irrigation water for the land along the Nile. In Mumbai, Nikhil Anand (2017) describes the hydraulic system as a social network that is controlled by a variety of residents, engineers and administrators who move water in the city.
3. The Dublin Statement on Water and Sustainable Environment came out of the International Conference on Water and the Environment held in Dublin in 1992. The four guiding principles of the 1992 Dublin statement are: (1) Fresh water is a finite and vulnerable resource, essential to sustain life, development and the environment, (2) Water development and management should be based on a participatory approach, involving users, planners and policy-makers at all levels, (3) Women play a central part in the provision, management and safeguarding of water, (4) Water has an economic value in all its competing uses and should be recognised as an economic good (ICWE 1992).
4. La ley de recursos hídricos (ANA 2010): Preliminar Title, Article 3, Principles 1, 2, 5, 9.
5. For more information on the IWRM see the UN webpage: https://www.un.org/waterforlifedecade/iwrm.shtml
6. Majes is the name of the arid pampa between the river valley of Majes and the river valley of Siguas, and it is also the name of the irrigation project in this pampa and the name of the irrigation canal leading water from the Colca River. Majes is further the name of the new district that was created in 1999 as part of Caylloma Province in Arequipa Region.
7. According to the National Population Census, Caylloma province had a population of 73,718 in 2007, and 86,771 in 2017. Of these, 26,663 lived in the highland districts, while the registered population in the lowland Majes District, comprising the MIP, was 60,108 persons (INEI 2018). According to the latest Agricultural Census, there were 16,588 farm units in Caylloma province in 2012, a number which included both the pastoralist farms in the high mountains, the peasant farms in the valley and the newer farms in the MIP. The Agricultural Census also counted the number of alpacas in Caylloma province to be 323,127 (INEI 2013).

8. In 2011, I carried out more than 40 formal interviews with local authorities, leaders of water users' associations and state officials, in addition to informal interviews with engineers, farmers and villagers. In November 2013, I returned to Colca and from January to April 2014, I lived in Majes, where I conducted 25 formal interviews with leaders of farmers' organisations, water users' associations, local politicians, state officials, agronomists, hydraulic engineers, and farmers, in addition to numerous informal conversations during meetings and visits to farms and workplaces. All personal names of interlocutors in this book are pseudonyms.

1 *Engineering Water Flows*

1. Parts of chapter 1 have previously been published in 'The social embeddedness of hydraulic engineers in the regulation of water and infrastructure in Peru', *Environment and Planning C: Politics and Space* 37(7): 1235–1251, 2019.
2. However, many other parts of the arid Peruvian coastline have been irrigated, farmed, populated and urbanised since pre-Columbian times. Hydraulic engineering has a long history in Peru, where water is abundant in most parts of the highlands (*la sierra*) and scarce in most parts of the coastal plain (*la costa*). In northern Peru, the Moche (AD 100–800) and Chimú (AD 700–1470) civilisations were based on intricate systems of canals and wells. Chan Chan, the capital city of the Chimú Empire, is testimony to the fact that ancient hydraulic engineering and a dynamic urban life already existed in the middle of the desert (Moseley and Day 1982). In southern Peru, the Nazca civilisation (100 BC–AD 800) is known for the *puquio* system: a technology for tapping and filtering groundwater in a system of wells, reservoirs and canals, both for irrigation and domestic use (Schreiber and Lancho Rojas 2003).
3. The *chinchilikos* seem to be very similar to the *muki* described in ethnographies from the central Andes; see, for example, Salazar-Soler (1987).
4. The godparents sponsor parts of the celebration/ceremony and afterwards act as 'moral guardians', giving advice and support.
5. Source: https://lta.reuters.com/article/idLTASIEA3008M20140401, accessed 7 June 2018.

2 *Colonising the Desert*

1. Parts of chapter 2 have previously been published in 'Safe milk and risky quinoa: the lottery and precarity of farming in Peru', *FOCAAL Journal of Global and Historical Anthropology* 83: 72–84, 2019.
2. Peru has maintained strong connections with Israel for decades, in trade and cooperation in developing projects, especially related to modernisation of agriculture, water management and technology, especially drip irrigation. In 2011, it was calculated that 67 per cent of irrigation technology used in Peru (i.e. 'modern' equipment) comes from Israel (Andina 2011).
3. There are four population centres in Majes: Santa Maria de La Colina, Villa El Pedregal, San Juan del Alto and Juan Velasco Alvarado.

4. See chapter 4 for an explanation of the *t'inka*. The bond between *padrinos* and car owners (as between *padrinos* and parents in the baptism of a child) should be sealed by drinking alcohol together. In this case I was excused since I was pregnant.
5. For a more thorough discussion of *ayni* and other forms of reciprocity in the rural Andean highlands, see among others Allen (1988), Gose (1994), Mayer (2002) and Salas (2019).
6. The war between the Shining Path guerrilla and the armed forces, in which 69,000 people were killed, created thousands of refugees from the highlands, mainly to Lima, during the 1980s.
7. The fact that he was an engineer with a practical and technical approach, driving around in a tractor during the campaign, was probably appealing to many poor farmers. He was also a fresh alternative to the established political parties and the known presidential candidates from the white elite. His efforts to build roads and provide electricity in rural areas are still applauded by parts of the population.
8. See: http://www.pampabaja.com/eng/main.php, accessed 6 September 2016.
9. Fujimori, who is son of Japanese immigrants, is colloquially called 'el Chino' by most Peruvians, who tend to call any person with a physical 'Asian' appearance 'Chinese' (*chino/a*). This tendency can be seen as a product of the history of global migration whereby 'coolies' were employed throughout the global South (including Peru) as cheap slave-like labour on plantations and railroads in the last part of the 19th century and the first part of the 20th. This is also part of the process of interlocking coloniality/modernity that provides the backdrop to current structural and casual racism in Peru.
10. Fujimori was later convicted of corruption and human rights violations – crimes that were still debated during my fieldwork – and this may have influenced farmers' account of that period.

3 Water Payments

1. Parts of chapters 3 and 4 have previously been published in 'Climate change, water practices and relational worlds in the Andes', *Ethnos: Journal of Anthropology* 81(1), 2016.
2. Communities in the Andes are traditionally organised dually in upper and lower parts. *Hanan* or *Anan* means 'upper' in Quechua; *Hurin* or *Urin* means 'lower', and *saya* means 'part'. The third part has probably been added more recently. *Ccapa* means 'rich' or 'powerful'.
3. The anthropologists Valderrama and Escalante (1988: 109) translated *iranta* as 'food for the gods'. According to the Quechua–Spanish dictionary of Academia Mayor (2005), the verb *irantay* means to fill a special container with grease for the *pago* to Pachamama. According to Adelaar (2004: 278), a translation from Aymara would be 'to introduce small objects'.
4. *T'inka* and *ch'alla* are often used as synonyms in daily speech. However, according to some of my interlocutors, the two words describe slightly different practices: *t'inka* is used to describe the act of sprinkling drops of alcohol in

the air or on objects, invoking the earth-beings, and it is often performed for new things that are bought, so that they will last longer. *Ch'alla* is used more generally to describe the practice of pouring drops of beer on the earth (and on the floor or on things) or emptying whole glasses of beer by throwing them on the ground.

5. In some places of the Andes, water is seen as male, for example as semen that gives fertility to the female earth. Similarly, mountains can be both female and male.

4 Water Uncertainties and Disasters

1. CIP is a research-for-development organisation that is part of CGIAR (https://cipotato.org/). For more information about La Única, see: https://cipotato.org/blog/unica-a-potato-for-farmers-around-the-world/
2. Yareta (*Azorella compacta*) is an evergreen perennial plant in the *Apiaceae* family that grow in the Andean highlands. Since it has traditionally been used as fuel and because of its slow growth, it is in danger of extinction in many places.

5 Water Efficiency

1. Excerpts of chapter 5 have previously been published in '"You cannot contradict the engineer": disencounters of modern technology, climate change and power in the Peruvian Andes', *Critique of Anthropology* 39(4), 2019.
2. Farmers in several districts use the water originating in Mismi; not only in Tuti and Coporaque, but also farmers in Yanque Urinsaya bring water from Mismi in a 25 km canal that goes through Coporaque district to Yanque, a district with few water sources of its own.

6 Legible and Illegible Water

1. Excerpts from chapter 6 have previously been published in 'The formalisation of water use and conditional ownership in Colca Valley, Peru', *Water Alternatives* 12(2), 2019.
2. The governor (*gobernador*) of the district works as the representative of the central government. The role of the governors ensures that the state is present all over the country, as part of Peru's decentralisation policies. As we see in this case, however, governors of districts in Colca Valley are also part of their communities and often act on behalf of the people. In other words, in practice, and presumably in many parts of the rural highlands, the district governors often seem to have a mediating role between the central government and the people.

7 Owning Water

1. Excerpts from chapter 7 have previously been published in 'Water as resource and being: water extractivism and life projects in Peru', in *Indigenous Life-making Projects and Politics of Extractivism in South America: Ethnographic*

Approaches, edited by Juan Javier Rivera Andía and Cecilie Vindal Ødegaard, Palgrave Macmillan, pp. 143–64, 2019.

2. In the 'Age of Enlightenment', the English philosopher John Locke (1632–1704) theorised the establishment of property as appropriation through labour: for example that cultivation of land justifies ownership over it (Busse and Strang 2011: 3). Locke imagined a world with plenty of unused land for 'industrious and rational' men: 'labour, in the beginning, gave a right of property, wherever any one was pleased to employ it upon what was common, which remained a long while the far greatest part, and is yet more than mankind makes use of' (Locke 2002: 20–21). The 18th-century philosophers such as Hume, Rousseau and Kant, on the other hand, argued that property should be based on prior possession or occupation, rather than labour (Busse and Strang 2011: 3).
3. The making of an uncommons is 'the negotiated coming together of heterogeneous worlds (and their practices) as they strive for what makes each of them be what they are, which is also not without others' (Blaser and de la Cadena 2018: 4).
4. I have found no information regarding the details of these numbers, or the calculations on which they are based.
5. Although the market prices fluctuate, I was told in 2011 that in one year you could sell the wool from one alpaca for approximately 27 *soles* (from three shearings), which is only US $10. The same year, the meat price of one alpaca was 180 *soles* (US $66). Pastoralists in Callalli said that the prices had improved after they established collection centres (*centros de acopio*) instead of selling individually to intermediary traders.
6. Adiviri's indigeneity was questioned because he had a university degree as a lawyer. This shows that in Peru, educational differences legitimise social and racialised hierarchies, in which indigeneity is associated with illiteracy and poverty, while higher education enables social mobility and even 'social whiteness' (de la Cadena 2000: 8–10). Therefore, it is difficult for a person with a university degree to still be acknowledged as 'indigenous' in Peru.

Bibliography

Academia Mayor de la Lengua Quechua. 2005. *Diccionario Quechua – Español – Quechua*. 2nd edn. Cusco: Gobierno Regional.

Adams, W.M. 2009. *Green Development. Environment and Sustainability in a Developing World*. London: Routledge.

Adelaar, W.F.H. 2004. *The Languages of the Andes*. Cambridge: Cambridge University Press.

Adger, W. Neil, Irene Lorenzoni and Karen L. O'Brien (eds). 2009. *Adapting to Climate Change: Thresholds, Values, Governance*. Cambridge: Cambridge University Press.

Allen, Catherine J. 1988. *The Hold Life Has: Coca and Cultural Identity in an Andean Community*. Washington, DC: Smithsonian Institution Press.

Allen, Catherine J. 1997. When pebbles move mountains: iconicity and symbolism in Quechua ritual. In *Creating Context in Andean Cultures*, edited by R. Howard-Malverde. New York: Oxford University Press.

Altamirano, Teófilo. 1983. Migración y estrategias de supervivencia de origen rural entre los campesinos de la ciudad. *Anthropologica del Departamento de Ciencias Sociales* 1(1): 127–158.

ANA (Autoridad Nacional del Agua) 2010. *Ley de recursos hídricos y su reglamento. Ley No. 29338*. Lima: Ministerio de Agricultura.

Anand, Nikhil. 2017. *Hydraulic City: Water and the Infrastructure of Citizenship in Mumbai*. Durham, NC: Duke University Press.

Andersen, Astrid O. 2014. *'Water Is Life': An Ethnography of Urban Ecology and Water Politics in Arequipa, Peru*. PhD thesis, Faculty of Social Sciences, University of Copenhagen.

Andina. 2011. El 67% de la tecnología de riego que se usa en Perú proviene de Israel, *Andina Agencia Peruana de Noticias*, 2 May: https://andina.pe/agencia/noticia-el-67-de-tecnologia-riego-se-usa-peru-proviene-israel-356458.aspx, accessed 25 January 2021.

Arneil, Barbara. 1996. *John Locke and America: The Defence of English Colonialism*. Clarendon: Oxford University Press.

Bakker, Karen. 2010. *Privatizing Water: Governance Failure and the World's Urban Water Crisis*. Ithaca, NY: Cornell University Press.

Bakker, Karen. 2015. Neoliberalization of nature. In *The Routledge Handbook of Political Ecology*, edited by T. Perreault, G. Bridge, J. McCarthy. London: Routledge, pp. 446–457.

Ballestero, Andrea. 2019a. The anthropology of water. *Annual Review of Anthropology* 48: 405–421.

Ballestero, Andrea. 2019b. *A Future History of Water*. Durham, NC: Duke University Press.

Barnes, Jessica. 2012. Pumping possibility: agricultural expansion through desert reclamation in Egypt. *Social Studies of Science* 42(4): 517–538.

Barnes, Jessica. 2014. *Cultivating the Nile: The Everyday Politics of Eater in Egypt.* Durham, NC: Duke University Press.

Barnes, Jessica and Samer Alatout. 2012. Water worlds: introduction to the special issue of Social Studies of Science. *Social Studies of Science*, 42(4): 483-8.

Barry, Andrew. 2001. *Political Machines: Governing a Technological Society.* London: The Athlone Press.

Bates, B.C., Z.W. Kundzewicz, S. Wu and J.P. Palutikof (eds). 2008. *Climate Change and Water.* Technical Paper of the Intergovernmental Panel on Climate Change, IPCC Secretariat, Geneva, 210 pp.

Bear, Laura, Karen Ho, Anna Tsing and Sylvia Yanagisako. 2015. 'Gens: a feminist manifesto for the study of capitalism', fieldsights – theorising the contemporary. *Cultural Anthropology Online*, 30 March.

Benavides, María A. 1998. Las batallas de Chachayllo: la lucha por el agua de riego en el valle del Colca (Arequipa, Perú). *Espacio y Desarrollo* 10: 75–93.

Blaser, Mario. 2016. Is another cosmopolitics possible? *Cultural Anthropology* 31(4): 545–570.

Blaser, Mario. 2019. On the properly political (disposition for the Anthropocene). *Anthropological Theory* 19(1): 74–94.

Blaser, Mario and Marisol de la Cadena. 2017. The uncommons: an introduction. *Anthropologica* 59(2): 185–193.

Blaser, Mario, and Marisol de la Cadena. 2018. Introduction. Pluriverse: proposals for a world of many worlds. In *A World of Many Worlds*, edited by Marisol de la Cadena and Mario Blaser. Durham, NC: Duke University Press, pp. 1–22.

Boelens, Rutgerd. 2009. The politics of disciplining water rights. *Development and Change* 40(2): 307–331.

Boelens, Rutgerd. 2015. *Water, Power and Identity: The Cultural Politics of Water in the Andes.* London: Routledge.

Boelens, Rutgerd and Jeroen Vos. 2012. The danger of naturalizing water policy concepts: water productivity and efficiency discourses from field irrigation to virtual water trade. *Agricultural Water Management* 108: 16–26.

Boelens, Rutgerd, Jaime Hoogesteger and Jean Carlo Rodriguez de Francisco. 2014. Commoditizing water territories: the clash between Andean water rights cultures and payment for environmental services policies. *Capitalism Nature Socialism* 25(3): 84–102.

Bolin, Inge. 2009.The glaciers of the Andes are melting: indigenous and anthropological knowledge merge in restoring water resources. In *Anthropology and Climate Change: From Encounters to Actions*, edited by Susan A. Crate and Mark Nuttall. Walnut Creek, CA: Left Coast Press, pp. 228–239.

Bonelli, Cristobal, Denisse Roca-Servat and Mourik Bueno de Mesquita. 2016. The many natures of water in Latin-American neo-extractivist conflicts. *Alternautas* 3(2): 81–92.

Brandshaug, Malene. 2020. *Liquid Landscapes: Human–Water Interactions and Water Scarcity in Yanque, Peru.* PhD thesis, School of Global Studies, University of Gothenburg, Sweden.

Brenner, Neil, Jamie Peck and Nik Theodore. 2010. After neoliberalization?, *Globalizations* 7(3): 327–345.

Brightman, M., C. Fausto and V. Grotti. 2016. Introduction: Altering ownership in Amazonia. In *Ownership and Nurture: Studies in Native Amazonian Property Relations*, edited by M. Brightman. C. Fausto and V. Grotti. New York: Berghahn Books, pp. 1–35.

Budds, Jessica. 2008. Whose scarcity? The hydrosocial cycle and the changing waterscape of La Ligua river basin, Chile. In *Contentious Geographies: Environmental Knowledge, Meaning, Scale*, edited by Michael K. Goodman, Maxwell T. Boykoff and Kyle T. Evered. Ashgate Studies in Environmental Policy and Practice. Farnham, Surrey, UK: Ashgate, pp. 59–68.

Budds, Jessica and Leonith Hinojosa. 2012. Restructuring and rescaling water governance in mining contexts: The co-production of waterscapes in Peru. *Water Alternatives* 5(1): 119–137.

Budds, Jessica, Jamie Linton and Rachael McDonnell. 2014. The hydrosocial cycle. *Geoforum* 57: 167–9.

Busse, M. and V. Strang. 2011. Introduction. In *Ownership and Appropriation*, edited by V. Strang and M. Busse (eds). Oxford: Berg, pp. 1–19.

Cant, Anna. 2012. 'Land for those who work it': a visual analysis of agrarian reform posters in Velasco's Peru. *Journal of Latin American Studies* 44: 1–37.

Carey, Mark. 2008. The politics of place: inhabiting and defending glacier hazard zones in Peru's Cordillera Blanca. In *Darkening Peaks: Glacier Retreat, Science, and Society*, edited by Ben Orlove, Ellen Wiegandt and Brian H. Luckmann. Berkeley: University of California Press, pp. 229–240.

Carey, Mark. 2010. *In the Shadow of Melting Glaciers: Climate Change and Andean Society*. New York: Oxford University Press.

Carrithers, M., M. Candea, K. Sykes, M. Holbraad and S. Venkatesan. 2010. Ontology is just another word for culture: motion tabled at the 2008 meeting of the Group for Debates in Anthropological Theory, University of Manchester. *Critique of Anthropology* 30(2): 152–200.

Castree, Noel. 2003. Commodifying what nature? *Progress in Human Geography* 27(3): 273–297.

Cepek, Michael L. 2016. There might be blood: oil, humility, and the cosmopolitics of a Cofán petro-being. *American Ethnologist* 43(4): 623–635.

Cereceda, Verónica. 2006. Mito e imagines andinas del infierno. In *Mitologías Amerindias*, edited by Alejandro Ortiz Rescaniere. Madrid: Editorial Trotta.

CIP (Colegio de Ingenieros del Perú). 2013. Ambicioso y esperado proyecto multipropósito Majes-Siguas II. *Ingeniería Nacional: Revista Oficial del Colegio de Ingenieros del Perú, Consejo Nacional* 3(12): 40–42.

Crate, Susan A. 2011. Climate and culture: anthropology in the era of contemporary climate change. *Annual Review of Anthropology* 40: 175–194.

Crate, Susan A. and Mark Nuttall (eds). 2009. *Anthropology and Climate Change: From Encounters to Actions*. Walnut Creek, CA: Left Coast Press.

Collier, David. 1978. *Barriadas y élites: de Odría a Velasco*. Lima: IEP.

Crabtree, John. 2002. The impact of neo-liberal economics on Peruvian peasant agriculture in the 1990s. *Journal of Peasant Studies* 29(3–4): 131–161.

Cruikshank, Julie. 2005. *Do Glaciers Listen? Local Knowledge, Colonial Encounters, and Social Imagination*. Vancouver: University of British Columbia Press.

Crutzen, Paul J. and Eugene F. Stoermer. 2000. The 'Anthropocene'. *IGBP Newsletter* 41: 17–18.

Cupe Burga, Javier (ed.). 2001. *Programa de fortalecimiento de organizaciones de usuarios: Legislacion para Juntas de Usuarios y Comisiones de Regantes, JNUDRP (Junta Nacional de Usuarios de los Distritos de Riego del Perú) y PSI (Proyecto Subsectorial del Irrigacion)*. Lima: Rolling Impresores SA.

Damonte, G. and R. Boelens. 2019. Hydrosocial territories, agro-export and water scarcity: capitalist territorial transformations and water governance in Peru's coastal valleys. *Water International* 44(2): 206–223.

Damonte, G., I. Gonzales and J. Lahud. 2016. La construcción del poder hídrico: agroexportadores y escasez de agua subterránea en el valle de Ica y las pampas de Villacurí. *Anthropológica* 34(37): 87–114.

Defensoría del Pueblo. 2015. *Conflictos sociales y recursos hídricos*. Seria Informes de Adjuntía – Informe No. 001-2015-DP/APCSG. Lima: Defensoría del Pueblo.

de la Cadena, Marisol. 2000. *Indigenous Mestizos: The Politics of Race and Culture in Cuzco, 1919–1991*. Durham, NC: Duke University Press.

de la Cadena, Marisol. 2010. Indigenous cosmopolitics in the Andes: conceptual reflections beyond 'politics'. *Cultural Anthropology* 25(2): 334–370.

de la Cadena, Marisol. 2014. The politics of modern politics meets ethnographies of excess through ontological openings. *Fieldsights – Theorizing the Contemporary, Cultural Anthropology Online*, 13 January: http://www.culanth.org/fieldsights/471-the-politics-of-modern-politics-meets-ethnographies-of-excess-through-ontological-openings.

de la Cadena, Marisol. 2015. *Earth-beings: Ecologies of Practice across Andean Worlds*. Durham, NC: Duke University Press.

de la Cadena, Marisol. 2019. Earth-beings: Andean indigenous religion, but not only. In *World Multiple: The Quotidian Politics of Knowing and Generating Entangled Worlds*, edited by Keiichi Omura, Grant Jun Otsuki, Shiho Satsuka and Atsuro Morita. London: Routledge.

de Laet, Marianne and Annemarie Mol. 2000. The Zimbabwe bush pump: mechanics of a fluid technology. *Social Studies of Science*, 30 (2): 225–263.

del Castillo, Laureano. 1994. Lo bueno, lo malo y lo feo de la legislación de aguas. *Debate Agrario* 18: 1–20.

del Castillo, Laureano. 2011. Ley de recursos hídricos: necesaria pero no suficiente. *Debate Agrario* 45: 91–118.

Deleuze, Gilles and Félix Guattari. 2004 [1980]. *A Thousand Plateaus: Capitalism and Schizophrenia*. London: Continuum.

Delli Priscoli, Jerome. 2013. Keynote Address: Clothing the IWRM emperor by using collaborative modelling for decision support. *Journal of the American Water Resources Association* 49(3): 609–613.

Denevan, W.M. 2001. *Cultivated Landscapes of Native Amazonia and the Andes*. Oxford: Oxford University Press.

de Soto, Hernando. 2000. *The Mystery of Capital: Why Capitalism Triumphs in the West and Fails Everywhere Else*. New York: Basic Books.

Earls, John and Irene Silverblatt. 1978. La realidad física y social en la cosmología andina. In *Actes du XLII Congrès International des Américanistes*, Paris, vol. 4, pp. 299–325.

Edwards, Paul N. 2003. Infrastructure and modernity: force, time and social organization in the history of sociotechnical systems. In *Modernity and Technology*, edited by Thomas J. Misa, Philip Brey and Andrew Feenberg. Cambridge, MA: MIT Press.

El Buho. 2020a. Majes Siguas II: Polémica en Consejo Regional por la adenda 13. 18 February: https://elbuho.pe/2020/02/majes-siguas-ii-consejo-regional-pone-a-discusion-la-adenda-13/, accessed 18 October 2020.

El Buho. 2020b. Majes Siguas II: Las razones del gobernador para defender la adenda 13. 9 September: https://elbuho.pe/2020/09/majes-siguas-ii-las-razones-del-gobernador-para-defender-la-adenda-13/, accessed 18 October 2020.

El Buho. 2013. Provincia de Caylloma es declarada en emergencia, 2 March: https://elbuho.pe/2013/03/provincia-de-caylloma-es-declarada-en-emergencia/, accessed 10 January 2019.

El Comercio. 2018. Cosapi se retira de Majes-Siguas II tras completar venta de acciones, 24 July 2018, https://elcomercio.pe/economia/peru/cosapi-completa-venta-acciones-sale-majes-siguas-ii-noticia-539316-noticia/?ref=ecr, accessed 18 October 2020.

Escobar, Arturo. 2007. Worlds and knowledges otherwise. *Cultural Studies* 21(2–3): 179–210.

Escobar, Arturo. 2018. *Designs for the Pluriverse: Radical Interdependence, Autonomy, and the Making of Worlds*. Durham, NC: Duke University Press.

Fernández Juárez, Gerardo. 2013. El 'Tío' está sordo: los mineros bolivianos y el patrimonio cultural inmaterial. *Revista de Antropología Iberoamericana* 8(3): 303–322.

Fonseca Martel, Cesar. 1972. La economía 'vertical' y la economía de mercado en las comunidades alteñas del Perú. In *Visita de la Provincia de León de Huánuco en 1562*, vol. 2, edited by John V. Murra and Ortiz de Zúñiga. Huánuco, Peru: Universidad Nacional Hermilio Valdizán de Huánuco.

Franco, Jennifer, Lyla Mehta and Gert Jan Veldwisch. 2013. The global politics of water grabbing. *Third World Quarterly* 34(9): 1651–1675.

French, Adam. 2016. ¿Una nueva cultura del agua? Inercia institucional y gestión tecnocrática de los recursos hídricos en el Perú. *Anthropologica* 37: 61–86.

Gal, Susan. 2016. Scale-making: comparison and perspective as ideological projects. In *Scale: Discourse and Dimensions of Social Life*, edited by E.S. Carr and M. Lempert. Oakland: University of California Press, pp. 91–111.

García Pérez, Alan. 2007. El síndrome del perro del hortelano. *El Comercio*, 28 October: https://indigenasdelperu.files.wordpress.com/2015/09/26539211-alan-garcia-perez-y-el-perro-del-hortelano.pdf, accessed October 2020.

Gelles, Paul H. 2000. *Water and Power in Highland Peru: The Cultural Politics of Irrigation and Development*. New Brunswick, NJ: Rutgers University Press.

Gloria SA. 2016. Exportaciones. From: http://www.grupogloria.com/gloria EXPORTACIONES.html, accessed 19 October 2016.

Gose, Peter. 1994. *Deathly Waters and Hungry Mountains: Agrarian Ritual and Class Formation in an Andean Town*. Toronto: University of Toronto Press.

Graeber, David. 2001. *Toward an Anthropological Theory of Value: The False Coin of Our Own Dreams*. New York: Palgrave.

Guevara, Armando Gil (ed.). 2008. *Derechos y conflictos de agua en el Perú*. Lima: Departamento Académico de Derecho de la Pontificia Universidad.

Guillet, David. 1992. *Covering Ground: Communal Water Management and the State in the Peruvian Andes*. Ann Arbor: University of Michigan Press.

Guillet, David and William P. Mitchell (eds). 1994. *Irrigation at High Altitudes: The Social Organization of Water Control Systems in the Andes*. Washington, DC: Society for Latin American Anthropology.

Gupta, Akhil. 2012. *Red Tape: Bureaucracy, Structural Violence, and Poverty in India*. Durham, NC: Duke University Press.

Guyer, Jane I. 2004. *Marginal Gains: Monetary Transactions in Atlantic Africa*. Chicago: University of Chicago Press.

Hann, Chris M. (ed.). 1998. *Property Relations: Renewing the Anthropological Tradition*. Cambridge: Cambridge University Press.

Haraway, Donna. 1991. *Simians, Cyborgs, and Women: The Reinvention of Nature*. New York: Routledge.

Hardin, Garrett. 1968. The tragedy of the commons. *Science* 162: 1243–1248.

Harvey, David. 2005. *Spaces of Neoliberalization: Towards a Theory of Uneven Geographical Development: Hettner Lecture 2004*. Stuttgart: Franz Steiner Verlag.

Harvey, Penny and Hannah Knox. 2012. The enchantments of infrastructure. *Mobilities* 7(4): 521–536.

Harvey, Penny and Hannah Knox. 2015. *Roads: An Anthropology of Infrastructure and Expertise*. Ithaca, NY: Cornell University Press.

Hastrup, Kirsten. 2009. *The Question of Resilience: Social Responses to Climate Change*. Copenhagen: Royal Danish Academy of Sciences and Letters.

Hastrup, Kirsten. 2013a. Anthropological contributions to the study of the climate: past, present, future. *WIREs Climate Change* 4: 269–281.

Hastrup, Kirsten. 2013b. Scales of attention in fieldwork: global connections and local concerns in the Arctic. *Ethnography* 14(2): 145–164.

Hastrup, Kirsten and Frida Hastrup. 2016. *Waterworlds: Anthropology in Fluid Environments*. New York: Berghahn Books.

Hays, Samuel P. 1999 [1959]. *Conservation and the Gospel of Efficiency: The Progressive Conservation Movement 1890–1920*. Pittsburgh: University of Pittsburgh Press.

Hellberg, Sofie. 2020. Scarcity as a means of governing: challenging neoliberal hydromentality in the context of the South African drought. *Nature and Space* 3(1): 186–206.

Hogue, Emily J. and Pilar Rau. 2008. Troubled water: ethnodevelopment, natural resource commodification, and neoliberalism in Andean Peru. *Urban Anthropology and Studies of Cultural Systems and World Economic Development* 37(3/4): 283–327.

Hommes, Lena and Rutgerd Boelens. 2018. From natural flow to 'working river': hydropower development, modernity and socio-territorial transformations in Lima's Rímac watershed. *Journal of Historical Geography* 62: 85–95.

Howe, Cymene et al. 2016. Paradoxical infrastructures: ruins, retrofit, and risk. *Science, Technology, & Human Values* 41(3): 547–565.

Huacasi, Wilber. 2019. Van 299 fallecidos por los conflictos sociales en los últimos cuatro gobiernos, *La República*, 19 August: https://larepublica.pe/politica/2019/08/19/conflictos-sociales-van-299-fallecidos-en-los-ultimos-cuatro-gobiernos-toledo-alan-gacia-humala-ppk/, accessed 2 November 2020.

Hunefeldt, Christine. 1997. The rural landscape and changing political awareness: enterprises, agrarian producers, and peasant communities, 1969–1994. In *The Peruvian Labyrinth: Polity, Society, Economy*, edited by Maxwell A. Cameron and Philip Mauceri. University Park, PA: Pennsylvania State University Press, pp. 107–133.

ICWE. 1992. *The Dublin Statement on Water and Sustainable Development*, Report of the International Conference on Water and the Environment, Dublin, 26–31 January: https://www.ircwash.org/sites/default/files/71-ICWE92-9739.pdf, accessed 31 October 2020.

INEI. 2013. *IV Censo Nacional Agropecuario: El Nuevo Rostro del Campo. Resultados preliminares a nivel provincial*. Lima: Instituto Nacional de Estadística e Informática and Ministerio de Agricultura.

INEI. 2018. *Resultados definitivos de los Censos Nacionales 2017, Arequipa, XII de poblacion, VII de vivienda y III de comunidades indígenas*. Lima: Instituto Nacional de Estadística e Informática.

Jensen, Casper Bruun and Atsuro Morita. 2017. Infrastructures as ontological experiments. *Ethnos* 82(4): 615–626.

Klarén, Peter F. 2000. *Peru: Society and Nationhood in the Andes*. New York: Oxford University Press.

Kohn, Eduardo. 2013. *How Forests Think: Toward an Anthropology beyond the Human*. Berkeley: University of California Press.

Krohn-Hansen, Christian and Knut G. Nustad (eds). 2005. *State Formation: Anthropological Perspectives*. London: Pluto Press.

Lacroix, P., A. Dehecq and E. Taipe. 2020. Irrigation-triggered landslides in a Peruvian desert caused by modern intensive farming. *Nature Geoscience* 13: 56–60: https://doi.org/10.1038/s41561-019-0500-x.

Larkin, Brian. 2013. The politics and poetics of infrastructure. *Annual Review of Anthropology* 42: 327–343.

Latour, Bruno. 1993. *We Have Never Been Modern*. Cambridge, MA: Harvard University Press.

Latour, Bruno. 2004. Whose cosmos, which cosmopolitics? Comments on the peace terms of Ulrich Beck. *Common Knowledge* 10(3): 450–462.

Law, John. 2004. *After Method: Mess in Social Science Research*. London: Routledge.

Leduc, Timothy B. 2011. *Climate, Culture, Change: Inuit and Western Dialogues with a Warming North*. Ottawa: University of Ottawa Press.

Li, Fabiana. 2008. Negotiating livelihoods: women, mining, and water resources in Peru. *Canadian Woman Studies* 27(1): 97–102.

Li, Fabiana. 2013. Contesting equivalences. controversias over water and mining in Peru and Chile. In *The Social Life of Water*, edited by John Richard Wagner. New York: Berghahn.

Li, Fabiana. 2015. *Unearthing Conflict: Corporate Mining, Activism, and Expertise in Peru*. Durham, NC: Duke University Press.

Linton, J. 2010. *What Is Water? The History of a Modern Abstraction*. Vancouver: University of British Columbia Press.

Locke, John. 2002. *The Second Treatise of Government, and A Letter Concerning Toleration*. Mineola, NY: Dover Publications.

Los Andes. 2011. Ignorancia de García Pérez califica de absurdas creencias andinas. Video, 17 June: http://www.losandes.com.pe/Nacional/20110617/51373.html, accessed 5 May 2017.

Lynch, B.D. 2012. Vulnerabilities, competition and rights in a context of climate change toward equitable water governance in Peru's Rio Santa Valley. *Global Environmental Change*, 22: 364–373.

Maldonado-Torres, Nelson. 2007. On the coloniality of being. *Cultural Studies* 21(2–3): 240–270.

Mariátegui, José Carlos. 2001 [1928]. *Siete ensayos de interpretación de la realidad peruana*. Lima: Empresa Editora Amauta.

Martínez Alier, Joan. 1992. *De la economía ecológica al ecologismo popular*. Barcelona: Icaria.

Marx, Karl. 1976 [1867]. *Capital*, vol. 1. New York: Penguin Books.

Maurer, Bill. 2006. The anthropology of money. *Annual Review of Anthropology* 35: 15–36.

Mayer, Enrique. 2002. *The Articulated Peasant: Household Economies in the Andes*. Boulder, CO: Westview Press.

Mayer, Enrique. 2009. *Ugly Stories of the Peruvian Agrarian Reform*. Durham, NC: Duke University Press.

McDonell, Emma. 2018. The Quinoa boom goes bust in the Andes. NACLA, 12 March: https://nacla.org/news/2018/03/12/quinoa-boom-goes-bust-andes, accessed 14 February 2020.

Mehta, Lyla. 2007. Whose scarcity? Whose property? The case of water in western India. *Land Use Policy* 24: 654–663.

Mehta, Lyla, Gert Jan Weldwisch and Jennifer Franco. 2012. Introduction to the special issue: Water grabbing? Focus on the (re)appropriation of finite water resources. *Water Alternatives* 5(2): 193–207.

Mehta, L., S. Movik, A. Bolding, A. Derman and E. Manzungu. 2016. Introduction to the special issue – Flows and practices: the politics of integrated water resources management (IWRM) in southern Africa. *Water Alternatives* 9(3): 389–411.

Mignolo, Walter D. 2000. Local histories/global designs: coloniality, subaltern knowledges, and border thinking. Princeton, NJ: Princeton University Press.

Mitchell, Timothy. 1991. The limits of the state: beyond statist approaches and their critics. *American Political Science Review* 85(1): 77–96.

Mol, A. 2002. *The Body Multiple: Ontology in Medical Practice*. Durham, NC: Duke University Press.

Mol, Annemarie, Ingunn Moser and Jeannette Pols. 2010. *Care in Practice: On Tinkering in Clinics, Homes and Farms*. Bielefield: Transcript-Verlag.

Molle, Francois. 2008. Nirvana concepts, narratives and policy models: insights from the water sector. *Water Alternatives* 1(1): 131–156.

Moseley, M.E. and K.C. Day. 1982. *Chan Chan: Andean Desert City*. School of American Research Advanced Seminar Series. Albuquerque: University of New Mexico Press.

Mosse, David. 2005. *Cultivating Development: An Ethnography of Aid Policy and Practice*. London: Pluto Press.

Mrázek, R. 2002. *Engineers of Happy Land: Technology and Nationalism in a Colony*. Princeton, NJ: Princeton University Press.

Mukhtarov, Farhad. 2014. Rethinking the travel of ideas: policy translation in the water sector. *Policy and Politics* 42(1): 71–88.

Murra, John V. 2002. *El mundo andino: población, medio ambiente y economía*. Lima: IEP/Pontificia Universidad Católica del Perú.

Narotzky, Susana. 2016. Where have all the peasants gone? *Annual Review of Anthropology* 45: 301–318.

Nash, June. 1979. *We Eat the Mines and the Mines Eat Us: Dependency and Exploitation in Bolivian Tin Mines*. New York: Columbia University Press.

O'Brien, K. and R. Leichenko. 2000. Double exposure: assessing the impacts of climate change within the context of economic globalization. *Global Environmental Change* 10: 221–232.

Ødegaard, Cecilie V. 2010. *Mobility, Markets and Indigenous Socialities: Contemporary Migration in the Peruvian Andes*. Farnham, Surrey: Ashgate Publishing.

Ødegaard, Cecilie V. 2019. Within and beyond the law: The ethics of collective action in urban markets, Peru. *History and Anthropology*, 26 September: doi: 10.1080/02757206.2019.1669590.

Oré, María Teresa and Edwin Rap. 2009. Políticas neoliberales de agua en el Perú: antecedentes y entretelones de la ley de recursos hídricos. *Debates en Sociología* 34: 32–66.

Oré, María Teresa, Laureano del Castillo, Saskia Van Orsel and Jeroen Vos. 2009. *El agua, ante nuevos desafíos: actores e iniciativas en Ecuador, Perú y Bolivia*, Agua y Sociedad series. Lima: Instituto de Estudios Peruanos.

Orihuela, Roberth. 2020. Majes Siguas II: otros US $48 millones para reactivar proyecto en Arequipa, *La República*, 6 March: https://larepublica.pe/sociedad/2020/03/06/majes-siguas-ii-otros-us-48-millones-para-reactivar-proyecto-en-arequipa-lrsd/)/, accessed 19 October 2020.

Orlove, Ben. 2009. The past, the present and some possible futures of adaptation. In *Adapting to Climate Change: Thresholds, Values, Governance*, edited by W. Neil Adger, Irene Lorenzoni and Karen O'Brien. Cambridge: Cambridge University Press.

Orlove, Ben and Steven C. Caton. 2010. Water sustainability: anthropological approaches and prospects. *Annual Review of Anthropology* 39(1): 401–15.

Orlove, Ben, Ellen Wiegandt and Brian H. Luckman (eds). 2008. *Darkening Peaks: Glacier Retreat, Science, and Society*. Berkeley, Los Angeles, and London: University of California Press.

Osborne, Tracey. 2015. Tradeoffs in carbon commodification: A political ecology of commonproperty forest governance. *Geoforum* 67: 64–77.

Ostrom, Elinor. 1990. *Governing the Commons: The Evolution of Institutions for Collective Action*. Cambridge: Cambridge University Press.

Paerregaard, Karsten. 1994. Why fight over water? Power, conflict and irrigation in an Andean village. In *Irrigation at High Altitudes: The Social Organization of Water Control Systems in the Andes*, edited by David Guillet and William Mitchell. Washington, DC: Society for Latin American Anthropology, pp. 189–202.

Paerregaard, Karsten. 1997. *Linking Separate Worlds: Urban Migrants and Rural Lives in Peru*. Oxford: Berg.

Paerregaard, Karsten. 2013. Governing water in the Andean community of Cabanaconde, Peru: from resistance to opposition and to cooperation (and back again?). *Mountain Research and Development* 33(3): 207–214.

Paerregaard, Karsten. 2018. The climate–development nexus: using climate voices to prepare adaptation initiatives in the Peruvian Andes. *Climate and Development* 10(4): 360–368.

Paerregaard, Karsten and Astrid O. Andersen. 2019. Moving beyond the commons/commodity dichotomy: the socio-political complexity of Peru's water crisis. *Water Alternatives* 12(2): 459–469.

Paerregaard, K., A.B. Stensrud and A.O. Andersen. 2016. Water citizenship: negotiating water rights and contesting water culture in the Peruvian Andes. *Latin American Research Review* 51(1): 198–217.

Paredes Peñafiel, Adriana Paola and Fabiana Li. 2019. Nourishing relations: controversy over the Conga mining project in northern Peru. *Ethnos* 84(2): 301–322.

Pastor, Manuel and Carol Wise. 1992. Peruvian economic policy in the 1980s: from orthodoxy to heterodoxy and back. *Latin American Research Review* 27(2): 83–117.

Perú 21. 2011. TITLE, 18 March, p. 7.

Perú 21. 2017. El 50% de los conflictos de los últimos 10 años en Perú fueron por el agua, 1 July: https://peru21.pe/lima/50-conflictos-ultimos-10-anos-peru-agua-85039-noticia/?ref=p21r, accessed 1 February 2020.

Phillips, Katherine and Liz Roberts. 2019. Introduction: a new era for human–water relationships. In *Water, Creativity and Meaning: Multidisciplinary Understandings of Human–Water Relationships*, edited by K. Phillips and L. Roberts. New York: Routledge.

Pinker, A. and P. Harvey. 2015. Negotiating uncertainty. neo-liberal statecraft in contemporary Peru. *Social Analysis* 59(4): 15–31.

Polanyi, Karl. 2001 [1944]. *The Great Transformation: The Political and Economic Origins of Our Time*. Boston, MA: Beacon Press.

Princen, Thomas. 2005. *The Logic of Sufficiency*. Cambridge, MA: MIT Press.

PSI. 2020. *¿Qué hacemos?* Programa subsectorial de irrigaciones, Ministerio de Agricultura y Riego: https://www.gob.pe/4310-programa-subsectorial-de-irrigaciones-que-hacemos, accessed 7 September 2020.

Quijano, Aníbal. 2000. Coloniality of power, Eurocentrism, and Latin America. *Nepantla: Views from South* 1(3): 533–580.

Rancière, J. 1999. *Disagreement: Politics and Philosophy*. Minneapolis, MN: University of Minnesota Press.

Rancière, J. 2010. *Dissensus: On Politics and Aesthetics*. London: Bloomsbury.

Randle, Sayd and Jessica Barnes. 2018. Liquid futures: water management systems and anticipated environments. *WIREs Water* 5(2).

Rap, Edwin and Maria Teresa Oré. 2017. Engineering masculinities: how higher education genders the water profession in Peru. *Engineering Studies* 9(2): 95–119.

Rasmussen, Mattias Borg. 2014. Dry technologies and community bureaucracies. In *Living with Environmental Change: Waterworlds*, edited by K. Hastrup and C. Rubow. London: Earthscan, Routledge.

Rasmussen, Mattias Borg. 2015. *Andean Waterways: Resource Politics in Highland Peru*. Seattle, WA: University of Washington Press.

Rénique, José Luís. 1991. *Los sueños de la sierra. Cusco en el siglo XX*. Lima: CEPES.

Rivera Cusicanqui, Silvia. 2012. Ch'ixinakax utxiwa: a reflection on the practices and discourses of decolonization. *South Atlantic Quarterly* 111(1): 95–109.

Robbins, P. 2012. *Political Ecology: A Critical Introduction*, 2nd edn. Chichester: Wiley-Blackwell.

RPP Noticias. 2011. Arequipa: Callalli registra 35% de muertes de crías de camélidos, 8 June: https://rpp.pe/peru/actualidad/arequipa-callalli-registra-35-de-muertes-de-crias-de-camelidos-noticia-373691, accessed 20 October 2020.

RPP Noticias. 2012. Arequipa: declaran en emergencia la provincia de Caylloma por lluvias, 13 February: https://rpp.pe/peru/actualidad/arequipa-declaran-en-emergencia-la-provincia-de-caylloma-por-lluvias-noticia-450725, accessed 10 January 2019.

RPP Noticias. 2013. Arequipa: declaran en emergencia provincia de Caylloma, 1 March: https://rpp.pe/peru/actualidad/arequipa-declaran-en-emergencia-provincia-de-caylloma-noticia-572158, accessed 10 January 2019.

RPP Noticias. 2014. Arequipa: sequía y heladas dejan pérdidas por 14 millones en Caylloma, 18 February: http://rpp.pe/peru/actualidad/arequipa-sequia-y-heladas-dejan-perdidas-por-14-millones-en-caylloma-noticia-670750, accessed 26 April 2017.

Sage, Colin. 2013. The interconnected challenges for food security from a food regimes perspective: energy, climate and malconsumption. *Journal of Rural Studies* 29: 71–80.

Salas, Guillermo. 2019. *Lugares parientes: comida, cohabitación y mundos andinos*. Lima: Fondo Editorial Pontificia Universidad Católica del Perú.

Salazar-Soler, Carmen. 1987. El Tayta Muki y la Ukupacha: prácticas y creencias religiosas de los mineros de Julcani, Huancavelica, Perú. *Journal de la Société des américanistes* 73: 193–217.

Salomon, Frank. 1998. How the *huacas* were. The language of substance and transformation in the Huarochirí Quechua manuscript. *RES: Anthropology and Aesthetics* 33: 7–17.

Salomon, Frank and Mercedes Niño-Murcia. 2011. *The Lettered Mountain: A Peruvian Village's Way with Writing*. Durham, NC: Duke University Press.

Schmidt, Jeremy. 2017. *Water: Abundance, Scarcity, and Security in the Age of Humanity*. New York: New York University Press.

Schreiber, K. and J. Lancho Rojas. 2003. *Irrigation and Society in the Peruvian Desert: The Puquios of Nasca*. New York: Lexington Books.

Schultz, Jim. 2008. The Cochabamba water revolt and its aftermath. In *Dignity and Defiance: Stories from Bolivia's Challenge to Globalization*, edited by Jim Schultz and Melissa Crane Draper. Pontypool: Merlin Press.

Scott, James C. 1998. *Seeing Like a State: How Certain Schemes to Improve the Human Condition Have Failed*. New Haven, CT: Yale University Press.

Seemann, Miriam. 2016. *The Formal Recognition of Local Water Rights in Yanque, Colca Valley, Peru*. Basingstoke: Palgrave Macmillan.

Seemann, Miriam and Rutgerd Boelens. 2014. Forced engagements: water security and local rights formalization in Yanque, Colca Valley, Peru. *Human Organization* 73(1): 1–12.

Seligmann, Linda J. 1995. *Between Reform and Revolution: Political Struggles in the Peruvian Andes, 1969–1991*. Stanford, CA: Stanford University Press.

Sherbondy, Jeanette. 1982. El regadío, los lagos y los mitos de origen. *Allpanchis* 17(20): 3–32.

Sherbondy, Jeanette. 1994. Water and power: the role of irrigation districts in the transition from Inca to Spanish Cuzco. In *Irrigation at High Altitudes: The Social Organization of Water Control Systems in the Andes*, edited by David Guillet and William Mitchell. Washington, DC: Society for Latin American Anthropology.

Sherbondy, Jeanette. 1998. Andean irrigation in history. In *Searching for Equity: Conceptions of Justice and Equity in Peasant Irrigation*, edited by Rutgerd Boelens and Gloria Dávila. Assen: Van Gorcum, pp. 210–214.

Shiva, Vandana. 2010. Resources. In *The Development Dictionary*, 2nd edn, edited by Wolfgang Sachs. Zed Books, pp. 228–42.

Smith, Gavin. 1989. *Livelihood and Resistance: Peasants and the Politics of Land in Peru*. Berkeley: University of California Press.

Solfrini, Giuseppe. 2001. The Peruvian labor movement under authoritarian neoliberalism: from decline to demise. *International Journal of Political Economy* 31(2): 44–77.

Statista. 2018. Quinoa market: statistics and facts, 19 Sept. 2017: https://www.statista.com/topics/2813/quinoa-market, accessed 19 November 2018.

Statista. 2020. Average price of quinoa worldwide from 2010 to 2019 (in U.S. dollars per kilogram), 25 June 2020: https://www.statista.com/statistics/520974/average-price-of-quinoa-worldwide/, accessed 1 July 2020.

Stengers, Isabelle. 2005a. Introductory notes on an ecology of practices. *Cultural Studies Review* 11(1): 183–196.

Stengers, Isabelle. 2005b. The cosmopolitical proposal. In *Making things public: atmospheres of democracy*, edited by Bruno Latour and Peter Weibel. Cambridge, MA: MIT Press.

Stensrud, Astrid B. 2015. Raining in the Andes: disrupted seasonal and hydrological cycles. In *Waterworlds: Anthropology in Fluid Environments*, edited by Kirsten Hastrup and Frida Hastrup. New York: Berghahn.

Stensrud, Astrid B. 2016a. Dreams of growth and fear of water crisis: the ambivalence of 'progress' in the Majes-Siguas irrigation project, Peru. *History and Anthropology Journal* 27(5): 569–584.

Stensrud, Astrid B. 2016b. Climate change, water practices and relational worlds in the Andes. *Ethnos: Journal of Anthropology* 81(1): 75–98.

Stensrud, Astrid B. 2016c. 'We are all strangers here': transforming land and making identity in a desert boomtown. In *Identity Destabilised: Living in an Overheated World*, edited by Thomas Hylland Eriksen and Elisabeth Schober. London: Pluto Press, pp. 59–76.

Stensrud, Astrid B. 2016d. 'It seems like a lie': the everyday politics of world-making in contemporary Peru. In *Critical Anthropological Engagements in Human Alterity and Difference*, edited by Synnøve Bendixsen and Bjørn E. Bertelsen. Basingstoke: Palgrave Macmillan, pp. 253–272.

Stensrud, Astrid B. 2016e. Harvesting water for the future: reciprocity and environmental justice in the politics of climate change in Peru. *Latin American Perspectives* 43(4): 56–72.

Stensrud, Astrid B. 2017. Precarious entrepreneurs: mobile phones, work and kinship in neoliberal Peru. *Social Anthropology* 25(2): 159–173.

Stensrud, Astrid B. 2018. Settlers and squatters: the production of social inequalities in the Peruvian desert. In *The Social Life of Economic Inequalities in Contemporary Latin America: Decades of Change*, edited by Iselin Strønen and Margit Ystanes. Basingtoke: Palgrave Macmillan, pp. 231–252.

Stensrud, Astrid B. 2019a. Safe milk and risky quinoa: the lottery and precarity of farming in Peru. *FOCAAL Journal of Global and Historical Anthropology* 83: 72–84.

Stensrud, Astrid B. 2019b. 'You cannot contradict the engineer': disencounters of modern technology, climate change and power in the Peruvian Andes. *Critique of Anthropology* 39(4): 420–438.

Stensrud, Astrid B. 2019c. The social embeddedness of hydraulic engineers in the regulation of water and infrastructure in Peru. *Environment and Planning C: Politics and Space* 37(7): 1235–1251.

Stensrud, Astrid B. 2019d. The formalisation of water use and conditional ownership in Colca Valley, Peru. *Water Alternatives* 12(2): 521–537.

Stensrud, Astrid B. 2019e. Water as resource and being: water extractivism and life projects in Peru. In *Indigenous life-making projects and politics of extractivism in South America: Ethnographic approaches*, edited by ed. Juan Javier Rivera Andía and Cecilie Vindal Ødegaard. Basingstoke: Palgrave Macmillan, pp. 143–164.

Stevenson, Lisa. 2014. *Life Beside Itself: Imagining Care in the Canadian Arctic*. Berkeley, CA: University of California Press.

Strang, Veronica. 2004. *The Meaning of Water*. Oxford, Berg.

Strang, Veronica. 2016. Infrastructural relations: water, political power and the rise of a new 'despotic regime'. *Water Alternatives* 9(2): 292–318.

Strathern, Marilyn. 2004 [1991]. *Partial Connections*. Walnut Creek, CA: AltaMira Press.

Strønen, Iselin Å. and Margit Ystanes. 2018. Introduction. In *The Social Life of Economic Inequalities in Contemporary Latin America: Decades of Change*, edited by Iselin Å. Strønen and Margit Ystanes. Cham: Palgrave Macmillan, pp. 3–34.

Swyngedouw, Eric. 2004. *Social Power and the Urbanization of Water: Flows of Power*. Oxford: Oxford University Press.

Swyngedouw, Eric. 2009. The political economy and political ecology of the hydro-social cycle. *Journal of Contemporary Water Research and Education* 142: 56–60.

Swyngedouw, Eric. 2015. *Liquid Power: Contested Hydro-modernities in Twentieth Century Spain*. London: MIT Press.

Taussig, Michael. 1980. *The Devil and Commodity Fetishism in South America*. Chapel Hill, NC: University of North Carolina Press.

Trawick, Paul B. 2003. *The Struggle for Water in Peru: Comedy and Tragedy in the Andean Commons*. Stanford, CA: Stanford University Press.

Treacy, John M. 1994. *Las chacras de Coporaque: Andenería y riego en el Valle del Colca*. Lima: Instituto de Estudios Peruanos.

Trouillot, Michel-Rolph. 2001. The anthropology of the state in the age of globalization. *Current Anthropology* 42(1): 125–138.

Tsing, Anna L. 2005. *Friction: An Ethnography of Global Connection*. Princeton, NJ: Princeton University Press.

Tsing, Anna L. 2015. *The Mushroom at the End of the World: On the Possibility of Life in Capitalist Ruins*. Princeton, NJ: Princeton University Press.

Ullberg, Susan Baez. 2019. Making the megaproject: water infrastructure and hydrocracy at the public–private interface in Peru. *Water Alternatives* 12(2): 503–520.

United Nations. 2014. Integrated water resources management (IWRM). *International Decade for Action 'Water for Life' 2005–2015*: https://www.un.org/waterforlifedecade/iwrm.shtml, accessed 6 February 2020.

Urteaga-Crovetto, Patricia. 2016. Between water abundance and scarcity: discourses, biofuels, and power in Piura, Peru. *Antipode* 48(4): 1059–1079.

Valderrama, R. and C. Escalante. 1988. *Del Tata Mallku a la Mama Pacha: riego, sociedad y ritos en los andes peruanos*. Lima: Desco.

Vera Delgado, Juana. 2011. *The Ethno-politics of Water Security: Contestations of Ethnicity and Gender in Strategies to Control Water in the Andes of Peru*. PhD thesis, Wageningen University, The Netherlands.

Vera Delgado, Juana and Margreet Zwarteveen. 2008. Modernity, exclusion and resistance: water and indigenous struggles in Peru. *Development* 51: 114–120.

Verdery, K. 1998. Property and power in Transylvania's decollectivization. In *Property Relations: Renewing the Anthropological Tradition*, edited by C.M. Hann (ed.). Cambridge: Cambridge University Press, pp. 160–180.

Verdery, K. 2003. *The Vanishing Hectare: Property and Value in Postsocialist Transylvania*. Ithaca, NY: Cornell University Press.

Verran, Helen. 2013. Engagements between disparate knowledge traditions: Toward doing difference generatively and in good faith. In *Contested Ecologies: Dialogues in the South on Nature and Knowledge*, edited by Lesley Green. Cape Town: HSRC Press.

Verzijl, Andres. 2020. *Water Movements: Fluidity and Visibility among Andean Worlds*. PhD thesis. Wageningen University, The Netherlands.

Vilca Begazo, Rolando. 2020. ¿Qué comprende la adenda 13 de Majes Siguas II?, *Encuentro* 7 September: http://encuentro.pe/actualidad/que-comprende-la-adenda-13-de-majes-siguas-ii/, accessed 18 October 2020.

Viveiros de Castro, E. 2004. Perspectival anthropology and the method of controlled equivocation. *Tipití: Journal of the Society for the Anthropology of Lowland South America* 2(1): 3–22.

Vuille, M., B. Francou, P. Wagnon, I. Juen, G. Kaser, B.G. Mark and R.S. Bradley. 2008. Climate change and tropical Andean glaciers: Past, present and future. *Earth-Science Reviews* 89:79–96.

Vuille, M. et al. 2018: Rapid decline of snow and ice in the tropical Andes – impacts, uncertainties and challenges ahead. *Earth Science Reviews* 176: 195–213.

Wagner, John R. (ed.). 2013. *The Social Life of Water*. New York: Berghahn.

Weber, Max. 1978. *Economy and Society*, vol. 2, edited by Guenther Roth and Claus Wittich. Berkeley: University of Berkeley Press.

Weiss, Linda. 2012. The myth of the neoliberal state. In *Developmental Politics in Transition: The Neoliberal Era and Beyond*, edited by Chang Kyung-Sup, Linda Weiss and Ben Fine. Basingstoke: Palgrave, pp. 27–42.

White, Richard. 1995 *The Organic Machine: The Remaking of the Columbia River*. New York: Hill and Wang.

Wittfogel, Karl A. 1957. *Oriental Despotism: A Comparative Study of Total Power*. New Haven, CT: Yale University Press.

Wolf, Eric. 1955. Types of Latin American peasantry: a preliminary discussion. *American Anthropologist* 57(3): 452–471.

World Bank. 2009. *Project Appraisal Document on a Proposed Loan in the Amount of US$ 10 million to the Republic of Peru for a Water Resources Management Modernization Project*. Report No: 47689-PE, 29 May. Sustainable Development, Ecuador, Peru, Bolivia and Venezuela Country Management Unit, Latin America and the Caribbean Region: http://documents1.worldbank.org/curated/en/506571468294326664/pdf/476890PAD0P107101Official0Use0Only1.pdf, accessed 29 July 2020.

Worster, Donald. 1985. *Rivers of Empire: Water, Aridity, and the Growth of the American West*. New York: Pantheon Books.

Yates-Doerr, Emily. 2014. Care: provocation. Fieldsights – Member Voices, Society for Cultural Anthropology, 17 March: https://culanth.org/fieldsights/497-care-provocation, accessed January 2020.

Zamalloa, Edgar Bravo. 2013. *Reseña histórica del distrito de Majes*. Lima: Corporación Grafical.

Zhan, Mei. 2009. *Other-worldly: Making Chinese Medicine through Transnational Frames*. Durham, NC: Duke University Press.

Index

note: *ill* refers to an illustration; *n* to a note

The Pluto Press Newsletter

Hello friend of Pluto!

Want to stay on top of the best radical books we publish?

Then sign up to be the first to hear about our new books, as well as special events, podcasts and videos.

You'll also get 50% off your first order with us when you sign up.

Come and join us!

Go to bit.ly/PlutoNewsletter